W9-BLI-451

# That's al

## The Art of Warner

# ll Folks!

## Bros. Animation

Steve Schneider

*Foreword by Ray Bradbury*

A Donald Hutter Book

HENRY HOLT AND COMPANY
NEW YORK

*Page 1: Cel of Bugs Bunny from* Slick Hare, *1947. Pages 2-3: Background painting by Philip DeGuard from the Road Runner series, c. 1953. These pages: Background painting by Paul Julian from* Tweet, Tweet, Tweety, *1951.*

Copyright © 1988 by Steve Schneider.
All rights reserved, including the right to reproduce this book or portions thereof in any form.
Published by Henry Holt and Company, Inc.,
115 West 18th Street, New York, New York 10011.
Published in Canada by Fitzhenry & Whiteside Limited,
195 Allstate Parkway, Marham, Ontario L3R 4T8.

Library of Congress Cataloging-in-Publication Data

Schneider, Steve.
  That's all folks!

  "A Donald Hutter book."
  1. Warner Bros. Cartoons. 2. Animated films—United States—History and criticism. I. Title.

NC1766.U52W3737n.1988     741.5′8′0979493     88-81823
ISBN 0-8050-0889-6

First Edition

Designer: Allan Mogel
Project Editor: Lori Stein
Prepared and Produced by Sammis Publishing, Inc. and Layla Productions, Inc.

Printed in Italy
10 9 8 7 6 5 4 3 2 1

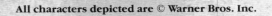

ISBN 0-8050-0889-6

To my mother and
my father

# Contents

# AUTHOR'S NOTE

Like the films that it describes, this book in fact represents a large collaborative effort. That one person receives the entirety of the credit for it is no more than a convenient shorthand, one that is seemingly necessary in our culture but by no means accurate. To resort to the encomium "without whom this book could not exist" about my collaborators is also false; the book could exist, but it would be drastically diminished in quality and content. My collaborators pitched in precisely because they wouldn't stand for the book being anything less than it might. And now that the truth is out, I can start naming names.

For twenty years, admirers of animation and comic art have owed an automatic debt of gratitude to Michael Barrier, the historian, writer, and publisher who has continually applied the most exacting standards of scholarship to a field once notorious for having none. This book only increases that debt. Mike's generous sharing of information, materials, and ideas has gone far beyond what reasonably could have been expected. And for once this claim is not empty words.

Major thanks also go to Jenice and Ken Rosen, of Citadel Granada Hills, for their very patient, very tolerant support over the many years of preparation that preceded the writing of this book. Their great courtesy, understanding, and stockpiles of Lysol have contributed much to the preservation of a cherishable American art form.

Similarly, a tip of the cap must go to Greg Ford, whose almost selfless promotion and championing of Warner cartoons over the last fifteen years, as well as his insightful criticism, has helped open many people's eyes to these films. In a real sense, Greg has been Warner animation's apostle.

Special thanks are also in order for the eternal Mark Kausler, whose unflagging devotion to the art and history of animation has made him the indispensable ally of all researchers into the field.

Further gratitude is due to the many people who have provided assistance with facts, materials, illustrations, films, and other necessities. Each one has made significant contri-

8

butions to this book. Thanks go to Shelly Bade, Jerry Beck, Dorothea Brown, John Canemaker, Sody and Ruth Clampett, Bill Exter, Will Friedwald, Lu Guarnier, Bruce Goldstein, Joe Grant, Steve Greene, Kathleen Helppie, Don Hutter, Linda Jones, Collin Kellogg, Dan Kletzky, Fred Lad, Carrie Makover, Leonard Maltin, Eric Marshall, Alan Mogel, Kim Murton, William Nadel, Mark Newgarden, Bill Owen, Barry Putterman, Beth Rousos, Lou Sabo, John Sammis, Adam Schneider, J.J. Sedelmaier, Red Skelton, Lori Stein, Karl Thiede, Christopher Walsh, Kevin Wollenweber, and Chani Yammer.

As much as possible, this book is illustrated with original artwork used in the production of the Warner Bros. cartoons, both to give a sense of the artistry and craftsmanship that underlie the finished films and to supplement what is already available on screen. However, as a small division of a large studio, Warner Cartoons never had a policy of saving its animation artwork—unlike the Disney Studio, which has maintained a tremendous morgue. In fact, as late as the 1970s, Warner's disposed of its last remaining pieces from the "Looney Tunes" for clerical reasons. What survives exists solely through serendipity or the foresightfulness of a few individuals.

Grateful mention is made of those people who have shared parts of their past, or of their collections: Lila Bakke, Robert Bentley, Jean Blanchard, Bob Bransford, John Carey, the Bob Clampett Collection, Mr. and Mrs. Herman R. Cohen, Mr. and Mrs. Maurice Fagin, Mr. and Mrs. Sid Farren, Friz Freleng, Mike Glad, Willie Ito, Chuck Jones, John Lange, Norm McCabe, Mel Millar, Fred S. Niemann, Maurice Noble, Hawley Pratt, Vivie Risto, Virgil Ross, Dea Shirley, Irv Spence, Richard H. Thomas, Richard Thompson, Tim Walker, Cornett Wood, Bill Wray, and several anonymous contributors.

Steve Schneider
June, 1988
New York

*Concept painting by Maurice Noble from* What's Opera, Doc?, *1957.*

## How Merry the Melodies, How Looney the Tunes: You Realize This Means War

If you should ever want to have dinner with me on Halloween, forget it. I'm out with the kids, tricking or treating. That is, when I'm not at home handing out goodies or showing friends around my junk-filled Halloween basement.

Forget Halloween. What about Saturday mornings when most decent hardworking folks are snuggling in bed? Would you dare call me on the phone? No! Why?

I'm watching the Bugs Bunny show. Which means I am watching Tweety and Daffy Duck and Yosemite Sam and Sylvester and all the other glorious twits and maniacs who first stormed across movie screens to fill our lives more than fifty years ago. And the best part of it is, they will continue to storm Saturday morning screens and video cassettes for the rest of the century or until Duck Dodgers really opens at Loew's Moon Crater cinema.

Thank God for the *deja vu* machine: TV. Otherwise my Saturday mornings would be sunk in that whipped candy fluff mush, that weekend drivel which depresses manic-depressives and causes the sick in hospitals, trapped in their TV viewing beds, to slug back the secret booze-stash and welcome death.

Is this merely gaseous nostalgia? Were "Merrie Melodies" and "Looney Tunes" really that fine? They were, they are, they will be. If, once upon a time, we dearly loved Mickey Mouse and Pluto,we were madness maddened for Bugs when he finally arrived, all calm logic and sanity, to teach behaviour to a world that, we knew, had gotten out of hand. If a gorilla grew bramblehair, Bugs knew how to comb its wig. If the Red Sea opened at the wrong time, Bugs put a zipper on it. If Yosemite Sam's fuse burned forever, Bugs shortened it to sweet explosion.

The list is long and glorious.

How many of us, coming out of a theatre, or seated in front of the set, have tried to remember, in all its crazed detail, the exact dialogue of "Duck Season, Rabbit Season, shoot 'em, shoot 'em!"

Have we not, at dinner, on ten dozen nights, regaled our friends with recitations of "Hello my baby, hello my honey, hello my Ragtime Gal" from *One Froggy Evening,*which the operatic frog performs only for his owner and never for the waiting mob?

Have we not run with the Road Runner and simultaneously failed (as we have often failed halfway through an issue of *Popular Mechanics)* with Wile E. Coyote?

Have we not failed again and again with Sylvester as he boxes with a tiny mouse somehow ballooned to monster kangaroo size?

Shut me up, before I run further. Enough of characters and situations. How about a litany of souls and names, the great pratfall roustabout writers and animators of the above? The names Tex Avery and Chuck Jones and Friz Freleng and Bob Clampett blink across the screen much too quickly. It is good to see them set in type and fixed on paper here.

I have, in another place, described Disney's animators as nice golfing gents, the sort of amiably macho chaps my father used to drag home from the eighteenth hole. If that's true, how do we describe the Warner Bros. alumni? As both gate-keepers and inmates of the grandest penal nuthouse in the world.

While Disney's cartoonists dreamed up and scribbled down a lovable Mickey and Minnie, plus a dear Horace Horsecollar and Clarabelle Cow, and a very dear Goofy, with only Donald Duck to explode in rages overall, the "Merrie Melodie" and "Looney Tune" folks banged off rubber walls, tore a real world into surreal shreds and put it all back together with Bugs Bunny, Yosemite Sam, and Daffy Duck. Only Wile E. Coyote and Sylvester verged on sweetness, but their daft plans to murder and devour always ended with self-given hotfoots and self-invented and instantly tripped-on landmines. Their animators tossed on the screen, as they often did in life, sketches ripped into confetti, to be reassembled in as yet undreamed-of shapes. Their cartoons often suggested those "Name the President" Contests of the Thirties where you had to guess, reshuffle and repaste Lincoln's brow with Washington's nose, with Grant's chin whiskers.

Above the Burbank Studio the motto should have read: You Realize, This Means War!?

For Bugs was always creating such warfares as riccocheted off him and gunshot the opposition, while Daffy Duck and Yosemite Sam, like Rumpelstiltskin, tore themselves up the seam in frustrated outrage. And what was the pursuit of the Road Runner but a neverending pursuit for battles lost even before the first joke grenade exploded.

These are all manic moral fables, of course. What better way to preach "the wages of greed are eternal frustration" than through *One Froggy Evening* where the opera entrepreneur's frog burps into silence when his profit-making aria looms?

Or, the wages of snobbism are Bugs destroying a piano, an orchestra and a whole symphonic evening by simply raising an eyebrow?

On a final personal note: I have known Chuck Jones for 22 years and he is Foghorn Leghorn, Yosemite Sam and the Tasmanian Devil stuffed in one enchilada. He has often called me mid-day, saying, "Guess what?"

"You've been at your Encyclopedia Britannica again!" I would cry.

"Yep," Chuck would say, "did you know that during the building of the North African transcontinental railway, when they ran out of fuel, the locomotive engineers ran in the handiest tomb, stole mummies, and shoved them in the firebox to restart the engines?"

Whereupon I would throw down the phone, leap to my typewriter, and write a poem and screenplay titled "THE NEFERTITI-TUT EXPRESS!"

As with Jones, so, I would guess, with the other crazed folks, real and unreal, who inhabit this book.

I'll shut up now. For this text says it all brightly, intelligently and with a proper intuition as to what it once was all about.

And, anyway, who can outshout Yosemite Sam?

I won't even try.

**Ray Bradbury**

# PART ONE:
# THE STUDIO

Leon Schlesinger
invites you to a
Christmas Luncheon
to be held on this lot
Tuesday, December 24
at 12 Noon
on stage 2

Kindly present this invitation
at the stage entrance

# INTRODUCTION

"**Y**ou never know where you're going till you get there," sings a street cat named Sylvester, while stomping up a ruckus in the night—after weary homeowner Elmer Fudd has heaved boots, pots, and books through a window at him to prevent such outbursts—in a typically rambunctious "Merrie Melodie" from 1948 entitled *Back Alley Oproar*. Merely one of a stream of "Let's keep Elmer from getting any sleep" gags that provide the premise for this cartoon, it's nevertheless a telling moment within the world of Warner Bros. animation—for its exuberance, its verbal facility, its evocation of memorable characters, and considerably more.

For over thirty years, the Warner cartoon shop specialized in this kind of animation, producing some 1,000 one-reel mixtures of character comedy, reckless irreverence, and split-second timing that, when in high form, were the funniest and most inventive animated shorts ever made. Along the way, Warner Cartoons won six Academy Awards and created more cartoon stars than any other studio: Bugs Bunny, the Road Runner,

Above: *Animation drawing of Sylvester by Virgil Ross, from* A Mouse Divided, *1953.* Below: *Publicity frame from* Rabbit Fire, *1951*.

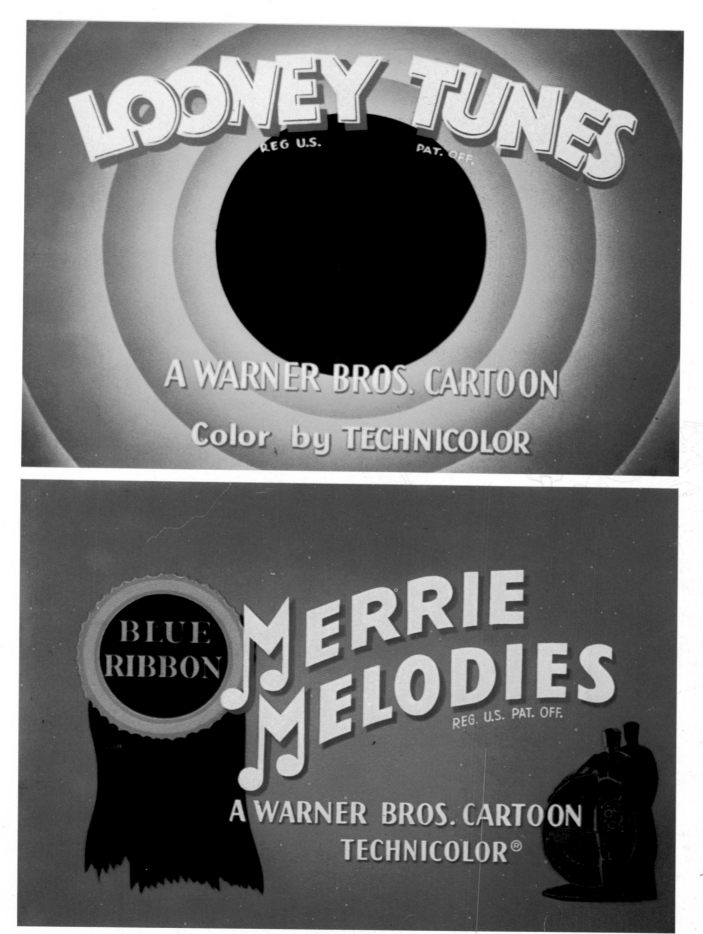

*Opening graphics.* Above: *From a "Blue Ribbon" re-release of a "Merrie Melodies"* Top: *From a "Looney Tune."*

No cartoon characters are born stars. Usually, they first appear as supporting players or as leads in one-shot films; if they work well with audiences, they are sent to center stage and progressively refined over several cartoons. Some, like Bugs Bunny, become part of America's heritage. Others, like Bosko, the first featured character in cartoons released by Warner Bros., become part of America's history. Below: *Promotional drawing of Bosko from* Yodeling Yokels, *1931.* Right: *Cel of Bugs from* Rabbit Hood, *1949.*

**Opposite**
*Publicity frame from* 'Zoom and Bored, *1957.*

16

Wile E. Coyote, Sylvester, Tweety, Daffy Duck, Porky Pig, Elmer Fudd, Yosemite Sam, Pepé Le Pew, Speedy Gonzales, and Foghorn Leghorn—to name only the most obvious. At once vintage and ageless Americana, the Warner characters are internationally known celebrities and smile-bringers, the cornerstones of what amounts to a library of modern folklore.

Moreover, in some cases nearly fifty years after their creation, they are still about the most popular players in their league. For example, in a 1985 readers' poll in *People* magazine—about as grassroots as it gets— the "Best puppet or cartoon character" category was won by Bugs Bunny.

And this was in a field awash with Garfield and Mickey and Kermit and the rest, most of them much more heavily promoted than the Warner gang. Notably, Bugs and the Road Runner were the only characters originated before the age of television even to place on the list of *People* finalists.

And in other, perhaps more significant ways, the antic inkblots known as "Looney Tunes" and "Merrie Melodies" have infiltrated the fabric of our lives. Such Warnerisms as "What's up, Doc?" and "That's all, folks!" are obvious parts of the national patois, but even such lesser turns as Sylvester's sibilant "Sufferin' succotash" or Bugs Bunny's jeered "*What a maroon!*" have entered the repertory—not to mention that mythical manufacturer of anything-a-coyote-ever-needs called "ACME."

The problem was, no one ever really paid much mind. In all the encyclopedias of film history, in all the vivisections of popular culture, non-Disney animation was either ignored, scorned, or given the shortest

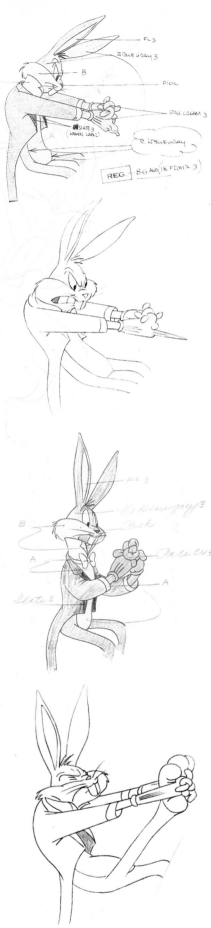

of shrift. Animated cartoons combined all the ingredients that virtually guaranteed their never being taken seriously: their pipsqueak length, their genre (comedy, forever ignoble), and their alleged target audience—children. Besides, there were so many of them—more than forty new ones a year from Warner Bros., in its prime. Rarely promoted and never showcased, cartoons were throwaways, distractions for the kids while their parents slipped to the lobby for a smoke.

Occasionally, however, someone spoke up. As early as 1943, critic Manny Farber wrote about the Warner cartoons in *The New Republic:* "The surprising facts about them are that the good ones are masterpieces and the bad ones aren't a total loss." And in 1946, none other than James Agee noted in *The Nation* about stumbling "without warning" on the Warner cartoon *Rhapsody Rabbit,* in which Bugs battles through a performance of Liszt's "Hungarian Rhapsody No. 2" at a grand piano, despite an upstart mouse dwelling within the instrument. "The funniest thing I have seen since the decline of sociological dancing is 'Rhapsody Rabbit,' " Agee wrote. "The best of it goes two ways: one, very observant parody of concert-pianistic affectation, elegantly thought out and synchronized; the other, brutality keyed into the spirit of the music to reach greater subtlety than I have ever seen brutality reach before. . . . It killed me." And that was about it as far as noteworthy critical attention during Warner's years of production.

All that had changed by the 1970s, with the help of an ally called television. As the children of the first television generation came of age, many of their cartoon-battered minds developed an awareness that the "Looney Tunes" once delightfully espied in the cartoon ghettos of afterschool and Saturday morning were often as wonderful as memory declared them to be. And as their cinematic literacy grew, many also saw that the Warner shorts were not only breathlessly funny cartoons, they were also masterful films, exhibiting remarkable control and manipulation of cinematic technique. Soon enough, the cartoons began to be screened at film festivals, museums, revival houses, film schools, and universities around the world; dissertations were written; substantial articles and interviews appeared in national magazines.

Above and right: *Animation drawings by Virgil Ross from* Rhapsody Rabbit, *1946.*

*Background painting by Philip De Guard from* Duck Dodgers in the 24½th Century; *layout by Maurice Noble.*

Indeed, an indebtedness to the Warner cartoons—references, quotations, stylistic borrowings—began cropping up all over the place, from Thomas Pynchon's *Gravity's Rainbow* to Steven Spielberg's *Sugarland Express* and *Close Encounters* to "Saturday Night Live" to graffiti art to Tobe Hooper's *Poltergeist* to Joe Dante's *Gremlins* to even "The Annotated *Lolita*." George Lucas requested that a 1953 Daffy Duck sci-fi spoof, *Duck Dodgers in the 24½th Century*, be shown with the San Francisco premiere of his *Star Wars*. Clearly, the anarchic brashness of Warner animation was speaking to a new generation.

But the culmination of this came in September 1985, when Warner's became the first animation studio to be given a full-scale retrospective by New York's Museum of Modern Art. For four-and-a-half months, the ultra-prestigious MoMA opened some of its august gallery space to drawings of stuttering pigs and libidinous skunks, and on weekends showed films with titles like *Wabbit Twouble*. Most of the time, the screenings drew turnaway crowds; often as not, the cartoons elicited—in addition to the predictable laughter—applause both after and *before* they emblazoned the screen. By now, even the cartoons' titles were known.

And this time, the press responded as if it had been waiting for the chance to pounce—over seventy feature articles nationwide, just for a local museum exhibition. *Time* magazine described the Warner cartoon-

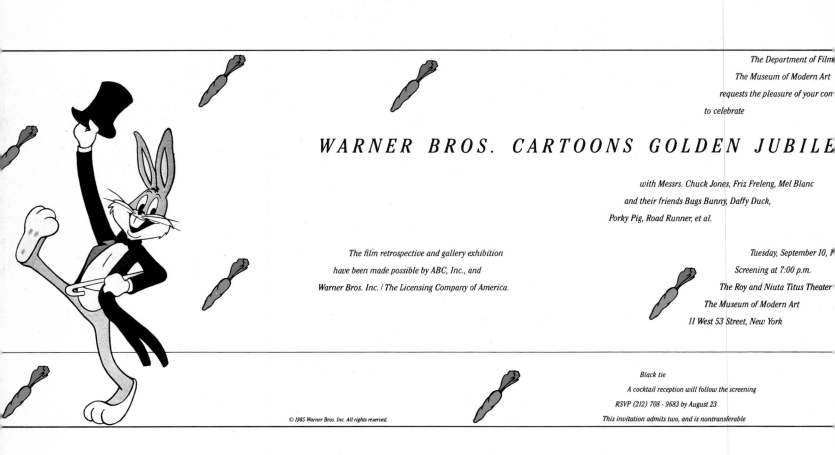

The Department of Film
The Museum of Modern Art
requests the pleasure of your com
to celebrate

## WARNER BROS. CARTOONS GOLDEN JUBILE

*with Messrs. Chuck Jones, Friz Freleng, Mel Blanc
and their friends Bugs Bunny, Daffy Duck,
Porky Pig, Road Runner, et al.*

*The film retrospective and gallery exhibition
have been made possible by ABC, Inc., and
Warner Bros. Inc. / The Licensing Company of America.*

*Tuesday, September 10, I
Screening at 7:00 p.m.
The Roy and Niuta Titus Theater
The Museum of Modern Art
11 West 53 Street, New York*

*Black tie
A cocktail reception will follow the screening
RSVP (212) 708 - 9683 by August 23
This invitation admits two, and is nontransferable*

Above: *The invitation to the opening-night gala at the Museum of Modern Art.*

*Model sheet from Friz Freleng's* Mouse Mazurka, *1949, a dialogueless cartoon that exhibits the director's keen ability to mix music and imagery in mutually enlivening ways.*

ists as "some of the top film artists and pleasure givers of the past half-century," while *Newsweek* spoke of "the geniuses who worked at Warner's." Critic Jay Cocks wrote in *TV Guide* that "The best of these cartoons are as funny, and as enduring, as the film comedy of Chaplin and Keaton, Capra and Sturges. They are classics." And in *The Washington Post*, Tom Shales called the Warner animators "men who well may qualify as among the century's great humorists, [who] made an invaluable contribution to the culture that only in recent years has begun to receive the outpourings of appreciation it deserves." *Film Comment*, the scholarly journal of the Film Society of Lincoln Center, deemed the studio "a masterpiece factory," while *The New York Times* described the MoMA exhibition as "a tribute richly deserved."

Even in an age of habitually over-inflated hoopla, these were weighty words. Yet they merely confirmed what many people had suspected for quite some time. Official sanction had finally arrived. Or, to update singing Sylvester, the Warner cartoon studio never had the foggiest where it was going, but it had certainly gotten there.

What all the hubbub was about, bubs, was cartoons that were unprecedented in their sophistication and their spirit. In animation's infancy, in the 1910s and 1920s, cartoons were replete with bizarre, surreal, free-associative images. Such healthy primitives as the Fleischer brothers and the "Felix the Cat" cartoonists filled their frames with impossible movements and fantastic visions—twisting staircases, talking apartment houses, detachable tails, metamorphoses (a dog turns into a window; a nose becomes a worm). These untutored penmen took a kind of perverse delight in the fact that the totality of their film world was under their control. But when Walt Disney began building his Magic Kingdom in the 1930s, such outré magic was progressively excluded from the premises. Disney preferred to make animation function as an extension of Hollywood live-action cinema, with increasingly "realistic" settings and character movement. Disney also led the way toward making animation very much a children's affair, trafficking in fairy tales and backwoods idylls, saccharine and sentimental and storybookish.

Warner cartoons pursued an altogether different set of values. With nowhere near the resources that were available at the Disney plant, the Warner artists were forced to use their wits to make cartoons that could compete with Disney's lavishness. And for inspiration, they looked close to home: elsewhere on the Warner lot, Humphrey Bogart and James Cagney were starring in the live-action films that were the studio's signature in the 1930s and 1940s. And the cartoon division, with deliberate intent, picked up on the snappy and street smart tough-guy attitudes cultivated on the sound stages right next door.

"We wrote cartoons for grownups, that was the secret," longtime Warner storyman Michael Maltese said in a 1971 interview. Yet that was not where the difference left off. For in addition to developing the first "adult" sensibility in Hollywood animation, the Warner cartoonists also embraced the kinds of freedoms that had marked their medium in its earlier, pre-classical-Disney days. In the Warner cartoons, mental maturity was coupled with a youthful ebullience which insisted that, come what may, anything goes.

The combination proved so successful that, by 1940, the Warner cartoons had transformed the tone and temperament of all American short-subject animation. Such rival houses as Walter Lantz (which featured Woody Woodpecker), MGM (Tom and Jerry), Columbia (Fox and Crow), and even Disney in his one-reel cartoons distinctly showed the Warner influence—albeit without matching its excellence. And the brand of humor hatched at Warner's is still repercussing in film, television, and other arts of today.

More specifically, the Warner cartoonists took the Disney style of personality animation—which is based on the creation of knowable, recognizable characters—to a different and eminently hipper level. The turnabout could not have been more extreme: where cartoons had been soft and frolicsome, Warner's made them hard and brassy and confrontational. An ideal of charm and gentle humor yielded to shameless slapstick

Above: *Such subjects as greed, self-doubt, the crass exploitation of art, and the capriciousness of fate were handled both ironically and cynically in Warner cartoons, as in Chuck Jones'* One Froggy Evening, *1955.*

Below: *In Friz Freleng's* The Three Little Bops, *1957, a woodsy fairy tale was given a jazzy, urban, up-to-the-moment spin.*

The THREE LITTLE BOPS

# Warner Animation and Warner Animators

A spectacularly labor-intensive form of filmmaking, the kind of animation produced by Warner Bros. was developed during the first decades of this century in the United States and Europe. Typical six- or seven-minute cartoons would be in production at Warner's for periods ranging from several months to over one year. Supervised in every phase by the director, the animation was created as follows:

After an idea was hatched, the studio's writers would develop it in the form of "story sketches," which were tacked in sequence onto a large "story board" so as to describe the film almost in the form of a comic strip. When the story was finalized, its dialogue was written down and recorded by the voice artists, who were usually professional actors. Then their performances were transcribed from the soundtrack on to "exposure sheets" so the animators could accurately fit mouth actions to the dialogue.

Elsewhere, a layout artist drew "background layouts," the preliminary designs for each scene that mapped out the visual field in which the activity occurred. Model sheets—studies of characters in various poses—were drawn, copied, and distributed to all artists working on the characters in question. The director meticulously timed each scene, and assigned it with its appropriate background layout sketch to an animator; in addition, most directors provided numerous "character layout" drawings for each scene—rough sketches that indicated the characters' movements through space.

For any action, the animator drew only the characters' key poses, called the "extremes," which exactingly captured the flavor of the action. He then gave these key poses to a series of assistants, who smoothed out the action by filling in the drawings that came between the extremes. This work was done in pencil on paper; after the scene was animated and checked, all of the animated drawings were traced in ink onto transparent sheets called "cels" (short for celluloids). With the characters' outlines thus in place, the cels were turned over and the outlines filled in with opaque paints, using a technique that leaves no brushstrokes visible on the front surface.

The cel(s) were placed on top of "background paintings," which were derived from the background layout sketches and usually executed in watercolors; the parts of the background painting that were not hidden behind the character(s) showed through the transparent cel(s). This composite image was photographed by a motion picture camera adapted to shoot one frame of film per exposure. After the cel(s)-and-background image was photographed, the cel(s) were replaced with successors from the scene, and the new image, only slightly different, was shot. The background could also move slightly, if desired, and would eventually be replaced when dictated by the action. Later, music, sound-effects, and dialogue tracks were added to complete the film.

Some of the many artists who contributed to the Warner cartoons were:

Writers: John Dunn, Warren Foster, Ernest Gee, J. B. Hardaway, Rich Hogan, Cal Howard, Lou Lilly, Michael Maltese, George Manuell, Sid Marcus, Mel Millar, Jack Miller, Dave Monahan, Fred S. Niemann, Tedd Pierce, Bill Scott, Lloyd Turner.

Background and layout: Peter Alvarado, Eugene Fleury, Robert Givens, Boris Gorelick, Robert Gribbroek, Phil De Guard, Griff Jay, Johnny Johnson, Paul Julian, Earl Klein, John McGrew, Tom McKimson, Maurice Noble, Ernest Nordli, Tom O'Laughlin, Hawley Pratt, Michael Sasanoff, Don Smith, Richard H. Thomas, Cornett Wood, Irv Wyner.

Animation: Lou Appet, Tom Baron, Warren Batchelder, Wes Bennett, Robert Bentley, Richard Bickenbach, Norm Blackburn, Jean Blanchard, Ted Bonnicksen, Jack Bradbury, Bob Bransford, Pete Burness, Robert Cannon, John Carey, Jack Carr, Ken Champin, Gerry Chiniquy, Ben Clopton, Herman Cohen, Shamus Culhane, Cal Dalton, Keith Darling, Basil Davidovitch, Arthur Davis, Phil De Lara, Nelson Demorest, Joe D'Igalo, Russ Dyson, Izzy Ellis, Maurice Fagin, Sid Farren, A. C. Gamer, Les Garcia, George Grandpre, Lu Guarnier, Emmanuel Gould, Rollin Hamilton, Ken Harris, Emery Hawkins, David Hoffman, Willie Ito, Rudy Larriva, Art Leonardi, Abe Levitow, Harry Love, Paul Marron, Larry Martin, Robert Matz, Carmen Maxwell, Norm McCabe, Charles McKimson, Robert McKimson, J. C. (Bill) Melendez, Phil Monroe, Robert North, Doris Ness, Al Pabian, Jim Pabian, Auril Pebley, Manuel Perez, Tom Ray, Vivie Risto, Virgil Ross, Rod Scribner, Paul Smith, Irv Spence, Cecil Surrey, Sid Sutherland, Richard Thompson, Riley Thompson, Frank Tipper, Gil Turner, Lloyd Vaughan, Elmer Wait, Sandy Walker, Ben Washam, Volney White, Bob Wickersham, Don Williams, Madilyn Wood, Marilyn Wood.

*Developmental stages, from preliminary sketch to finished background, from* What's Opera, Doc? *1957*

and mordant satire. The innocence of the forest was supplanted by the savvy of the city (it's quite a journey from Disney's cartoon *Lullaby Land* to Warner's *Bowery Bugs*). Fairy-tale timelessness gave way to constant visual and verbal reference to topical matters and "real life" concerns (from the Big Bad Wolf to the "wolves" hanging out on the corner of Hollywood and Vine). And the pacing of these gag-jamborees could become almost incomprehensibly fast.

The other key advance made by the Warner crew was in the realm of cartoon character. Whereas most cartoon personalities rarely go beyond being one-dimensional character types, the leading Warner players were endowed with complex, richly nuanced psyches—a fact that accounts mightily for their enduring appeal. Thus, Bugs Bunny was witty and self-assured and always in control, and a master of the one-liner, as well. Only he was capable of convincing a behemoth of a wrestler that his shorts are ripped, so that Bugs could impersonate a tailor, maneuver his opponent into a greatcoat, and then literally pin the big galoot's shoulders to the canvas (in *Bunny Hugged,* 1951). And the Warner characters could be deeply conflicted, too: how else to explain a desert coyote's unquenchable—yes, even neurotic—need to punish himself in the pursuit of a scrawny, oblivious bird that it has become unavoidably clear he will never be able to nab?

Perhaps one indication of the richness of the Warner characters can be found in an incident that occurred in the 1960s. In Hollywood, a man introduced his son to Warner cartoon director Chuck Jones, and explained that he was the artist who draws Bugs Bunny. "He doesn't draw Bugs Bunny," the boy corrected. "He draws pictures of Bugs Bunny."

Pictures of Bugs Bunny: for one cartoon watcher, at least, the

*From Chuck Jones' Bunny Hugged: Cel of Bugs as "Stychen Tyme—the Tailor," with background.*

23

character has so real an existence that he is not created through animation, but illustrated by it. What made this possible, of course, is that the filmmakers themselves felt much the same way: "People talk about our characters as though they were alive. Well, we thought they were alive too," says Jones. "I mean, Bugs Bunny, the Road Runner, the Coyote, and Pepé Le Pew are more alive to me than a lot of people, until I get to know them."

Ultimately, the richness of the characters' inner lives derives from the gifts of their creators. "The characters were multiplications of our own foibles," says Jones. "Otherwise, they wouldn't communicate at all, and they wouldn't be funny. Bugs and Pepé, for example, represent my aspirations—what I would like to be. But Daffy and the Coyote are my realizations—what I fear I am."

Yet the relationship between creators and cartoons extends still deeper. If the Warner cartoons are chockablock with gags and good-natured mayhem, it's because, according to all parties concerned, the studio itself was much the same way. What ended up in the films was a direct reflection of the nonstop prankishness that animated the shop, and that helped keep its young artists returning to work for what could be painfully meager pay. Constantly, it's been said, the cartoonists were scribbling caricatures of one another or playing practical jokes—tossing dud firecrackers into a peopled room, then following them with a live one; replacing the soda in a machine-dispensed bottle with hard alcohol (or worse); setting fire to the studio's walls to see if they would burn. One studio employee rigged a system whereby little lights would go on at the cartoonists' desks to signal when the boss came in; but the artists used this cue to *stop* working and *start* shining their shoes, reading newspapers, whatever—leaving the bollixed boss to wonder how all the work

Above: *Gag idea by Mel Millar from the late 1930s.* Right: *1936 Christmas card drawn by T. Hee, containing caricatures of the principal members of the Leon Schlesinger Studio staff. An example of the studio's in-house humor came when some of the drawings on this sheet were used as models for the destructive gremlins in the 1944 cartoon* Russian Rhapsody.

**Opposite**
*Gag background paintings by Richard H. Thomas.* Top: *A birthday cake with a bang; from* Oily Hare, *1952.* Bottom: *A flea circus on a dog's coat; from* A Horsefly Fleas, *1947.*

was getting done. Or there was another animator, dexterous with his hands, who would glue tiny paper wings to flies he had caught, so that visitors to the studio would be treated to the sight of itsy paper airplanes flitting by.

Yet there was a purpose to this communal jesting. As Michael Maltese later told Joe Adamson: "We knew, writing these cartoon stories, that the kidding around that we all did sort of broke down the barrier and enabled us to go unashamedly, almost like children, into making absolute idiots of ourselves. An outsider would see us and say, 'Well, for heaven's sake! Grown Men!' But we understood."

Although competition existed among the Warner cartoonists to come up with the strongest films, the studio was favored with a generous spirit of camaraderie—everyone was invited to contribute what they would. There were usually three or four units working separately on cartoons at the Warner studio, with an entire workforce that numbered up to around two hundred during the years of heaviest production. Each unit was

*Cel of Porky and Daffy from* Boobs in the Woods, *1950.*

Above: *Rough "background layout" drawing by Maurice Noble, indicating how a piece of action moves through a scene; from* Rabbit Seasoning, *1952.*
Left: *Early Porky Pig model sheet, 1936.*

headed by a director, who guided the efforts of all the artists working with him. These would include four or five animators; as many assistant animators; a "layout" artist, who conceived each cartoon's overall design, drew in pencil the elaborate settings in which the animated action took place, and planned camera movements; and a "background" artist, who rendered the layout artist's scenic sketches in paint. All of the units shared a common pool of actors, musicians, and other artists who completed the more mechanical aspects of animation production. And this involved a vast amount of work, for the Warner cartoons were made in "full animation"—using many thousands of drawings for each short, to endow their characters' movements with grace and subtlety and flowing expressiveness.

LT BL

29

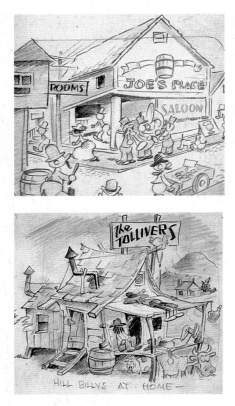

*Story sketches by Mel Millar. Above: From Tex Avery's* A Feud There Was, *1938. Top: From a late 1930s "Merrie Melodie."*

**Opposite**
*Concept painting by Maurice Noble from* What's Opera, Doc? *1957.*

After its first few years of operations, Warner Cartoons also had a "story department," artists who were hired with the express purpose of developing gags and story lines. By the mid-thirties, Warner's had teams of writers who would work together with whichever director was ready to move on to his next cartoon. But by the early 1940s, individual writers were mostly paired with individual directors—although, again, everyone was welcome to chip in on any film.

Yet without question, the principal responsibility for the finished film lay with the director. Animation is probably the ultimate "auteurist" cinema, as its directors can control every element of their films' content with a precision that extends down to the individual frame. And this was certainly the case at Warner's, where the directors were given virtually absolute control of their material (beyond meeting the requirements of Warner's distribution organization, such as a certain number of Bugs Bunny or Tweety cartoons per year). If the cartoons were ignored by critics and other would-be arbiters of culture, at the least the Warner directors had the compensation of being left alone by studio management—and they reveled in this full freedom. With their pencils and their stopwatches, the Warner directors ultimately determined such ingredients as choice of story, pacing, character design, composition of the film frame, character expression, color values, character movement, background feel, actors' line-readings, and other variables. By and large, the directors acted out each gesture and inflection made by their characters, and often put them down again in sketches, conveying to their animators the precise flavor of the actions and reactions that they were seeking to bring to the screen.

And if it's true that in comedy, "it's all in the timing," then here was where the Warner directors excelled above all others. For the Warner cartoons are often little miracles of crispness and concision. Director Tex Avery once spoke of learning that he needed only five frames—about one-fifth of a second—for a gag to register, while Chuck Jones remembers planning his actions down to the individual frame. "When the Coyote fell off a precipice, I knew that he had to go exactly three or four feet and then disappear for eighteen frames before he hit," he told Greg Ford. "When I put down a twelve-frame hold, that didn't mean thirteen frames or eleven frames—it meant twelve frames exactly." Rarely, if ever, do live-action directors control their actions with such precision.

Moreover, this precision had to be applied to films that were, in effect, pre-edited. Most scenes in commercial live-action films are shot several times, and/or from several angles; all this footage is then combined afterward, by editors who splice together the various pieces—long shots, close-ups, etc.—in the ways they desire. But the Warner cartoon directors had to determine all of their, "editing" before anything was photographed, charting the way the final film would look—shot by shot, frame by frame—without having any raw footage in front of them. "It was really mental editing," says Chuck Jones, "and I've never met a live-action director, or editor, who understood how this could be done. It's just like shooting these little clips of film in live action, at exactly their proper length, and putting them all together."

But these were not the only constraints imposed on the Warner directors. The assembly-line setup of the shop required the directors to finish a new cartoon about every five weeks (although time could be slightly redistributed to accommodate some favorite projects, such as Chuck Jones did with *What's Opera, Doc?* in 1957). Moreover, budgets were minuscule. For example, by the middle 1930s, Disney was routinely

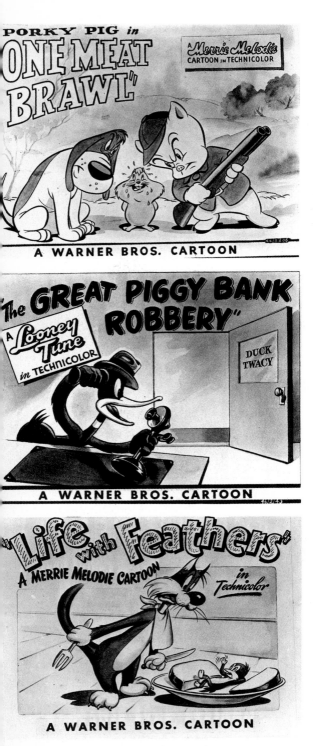

Above: *Three directors, three promotional drawings.* Top: *From Robert McKimson's* One Meat Brawl, *1947.* Center: *From Bob Clampett's* The Great Piggy Bank Robbery, *1946.* Bottom: *From Friz Freleng's* Life With Feathers, *1945.*

spending up to $60,000 for each of his "Silly Symphonies" cartoons, and several later shorts went as high as nearly $100,000; in contrast, in 1937, Warner Bros. was paying Leon Schlesinger only $9,000 for each of his cartoons—and after Schlesinger had subtracted his profit, what actually went into making the films was considerably less. (Of course, budgets did rise over the years.) Because of this, retakes of scenes were never possible; once a piece of action had been photographed, it *had* to be used—unlike at Disney's, where scenes were routinely reworked or discarded, as necessary. Further, the cartoons' length was eventually fixed at as close to six minutes as possible; earlier cartoons had run as long as seven or eight minutes, but Warner's money people progressively whittled it down to the absolute minimum that the exhibitors would accept.

Given these conditions, the ability of the Warner directors to create full and intricate animated worlds each time out seems all the more masterful. Working within the various constraints built into their system of production, as well as within the traditional frameworks of the Hollywood "genre" cartoon, the Warner directors could still be strongly individualistic artists—artists who consciously cultivated chosen aspects of their craft. The stronger directors imposed their visions and personalities on their films to a degree that makes them unmistakably the product of an individual sensibility. Clearly, the achievements of the Warner cartoons are the achievements of their directors. And, appropriately, the principal Warner cartoon directors—Chuck Jones, Bob Clampett, Friz Freleng, Tex Avery, Frank Tashlin, Robert McKimson—are the unrivaled titans of their field.

Although animated shorts were designed to be seen individually, as a kind of piquant palate cleanser during the many-course menu of old film programs, the output of the Warner studio, when considered as a whole, falls into distinct phases. Again and again, throughout the studio's diversity, themes and stylistic consonances emerge. Like a healthy organism, the studio traversed clear periods of growth, rowdy adolescence, maturity, and decline; and each of these periods directly corresponds with the strongest work of a particular director, whose dominant temperament seems to have influenced the entire shop.

Thus, after a few years of infancy—which saw the rise of Warner's foremost craftsman of classically styled animation, Friz Freling—the studio discovered its identity through the work of Tex Avery, a prodigious innovator and experimenter. With these gains in place, Bob Clampett unleashed the cartoon tumult of the 1940s, a time of excess and explosiveness and careening energy. Thereafter, beginning in the late 1940s, Chuck Jones led the studio through its maturity, when a kind of distillation and refinement brought films of brilliant acuity. And then there were the last years, a period of diminishing powers.

It is a measure of the Warner studio's achievement that so many of these cartoons, thirty or forty or fifty years old, have retained their luster and their ability to entertain. Are there any other films from 1946 that seem so essentially undated as Bob Clampett's *The Great Piggy Bank Robbery?* The Warner cartoons, to a remarkable extent, have anticipated the humor and filmmaking spirit of our age—and, clearly, contributed to its development. Indeed, when the Warner cartoons are now screened, the laughter is often so loud that hearing the soundtrack becomes a real chore. "That's the nice thing, for me," says Chuck Jones. "When I go to these festivals and universities, the cartoons are treated as if they were just done. I'm treated as an artifact, but my films are not. And boy, that is nice."

And this is a situation that seems likely to continue. More and more, it is evident that the Warner cartoons are an important and joyous corner of American cultural history, as rich and rewarding in their way as any part of cinema. In particular, the Warner cartoons produced from the early 1940s through the early 1950s, as well as Chuck Jones' films for many years thereafter, are so good, so often, as to be almost an astonishment. And that's not all, folks.

*A* Chaplinesque *conclusion from* The Unruly Hare, *1945. Background painting by Richard H. Thomas.*

# Building A Studio: 1930–35

Above: *An early model sheet of Bosko.*
Top: *Promotional drawing for* Sinkin'
in the Bathtub, *1930.*

**Opposite**
Top: *Layout drawing from* Bosko's Holiday, *1931.* Bottom: *The first and last pages of the contract between Leon Schlesinger and Hugh Harman and Rudolph Ising, setting into motion what would become Warner Bros. cartoons.*

**Overleaf**
*Cels and background from a later labels-come-to-life cartoon, Bob Clampett's* Goofy Groceries, *1941. Spoofing Billy Rose's "Aquacade," the scene is populated by Mr. Peanut, a Gold Dust Twin, and other figures from advertising.*

Like most everything in Hollywood animation, the Warner Bros. cartoon studio had its origins in the work of Walt Disney. The shop that was to become Warner Cartoons was founded in 1929 by Hugh Harman and Rudolph Ising, friends of Disney's from his early years in Kansas City. Harman (1903–82) and Ising (born 1903) had joined Disney's small Kansas City staff in 1922, during one of Disney's first independent ventures, producing silent cartoons called "Laugh-o-Grams" for a local theater. The cartoons were extremely primitive, although humorous, retellings of such fairy tales as "Little Red Riding Hood" and "Jack and the Beanstalk." When the "Laugh-o-Grams" folded in 1923, Disney relocated to Los Angeles and persuaded Harman and Ising to join him in June 1925.

After animating for Disney's two subsequent series, the "Alice in Cartoonland" and "Oswald the Lucky Rabbit" cartoons, Harman and Ising broke with Disney in 1928 to join forces with George and Margaret Winkler, the brother-and-sister financiers of the Oswald the Rabbit shorts. The Winklers were setting up their own studio to produce further Oswald cartoons, and lured away several other former Disney staffers to assist. But after about a year of work at the Winkler studio, Universal Pictures, the owner of the Oswald character and the cartoons' distributor, discontinued relations with the Winklers, and thereby put Harman, Ising, and their colleagues among the unemployed.

Soon, Harman-Ising (a name-coupling as felicitous as any) were trying to establish themselves as independent producers, and in the summer of 1929 completed a three-minute "pilot" film to show to prospective distributors. Called *Bosko the Talkink Kid,* the plotless cartoon—which was never released to the public—features Rudy Ising sitting at an animator's drawing board and interacting with Bosko, a character of no known genus and species, but who resembled a kind of humanized Mickey Mouse and who favored a derby hat. "Hugh Harman first drew the Bosko character," recalled Ising. "It was supposed to be an inkspot sort of thing. We never thought of him as human, or as an animal. But we had him behave like a little boy."

As its title indicates, the pilot reel was intended to make the most of filmdom's new infatuation with talking pictures; indeed, this is probably the first cartoon in which actual speech (rather than squawks or squeals or other noises) was synchronized with animated drawings. "Sound had just come in," Ising said, "and that was what we were selling—synchronized lip motion." And the film also contains the seedling of another cartoon tradition: it ends with Bosko squiggling back into his inkwell and calling, "So long, folks!"

After shopping the short around, but getting no results, Harman and Ising linked up with Leon Schlesinger, then head of Pacific Art and

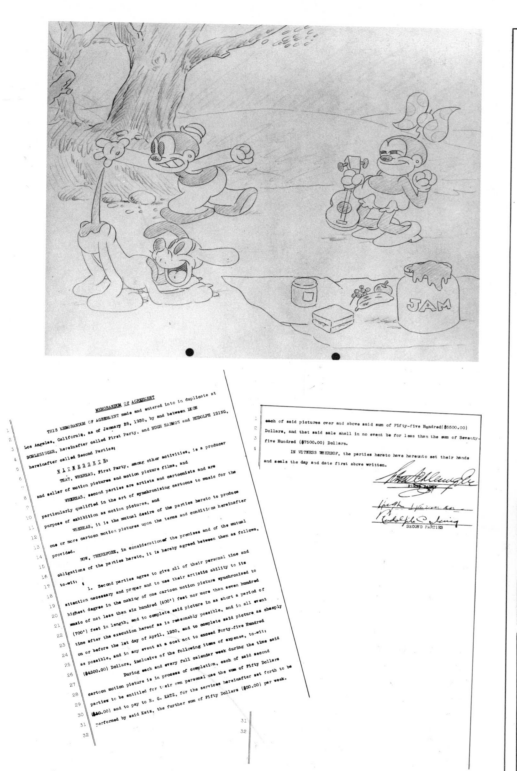

Hugh Harman and Rudolph Ising originated the Warner Bros. and MGM cartoon studios, and the cat and mouse characters Tom and Jerry first appeared in a 1940 short produced by Ising for MGM. Their own partnership began auspiciously, as well, as indicated by this excerpt from *Variety*'s May 14, 1930, review of the first Harman-Ising cartoon, *Sinkin' in the Bathtub:*

"Very amusing short comedy cartoon. . . : [T]his short may be especially placed on a program where a laugh is called for as it guarantees that laugh.

"As the first of a series contemplated by Warners' Vitaphone Varieties, WB has something worth a lot here if the series can commence to hold up to its start. . . .

"Regardless of the song itself or the other values it may contain, 'Looney Tunes' has made a flying comedy start."

Above: *Promotional drawing from* Sinkin' in the Bathtub, *1930.* Top: *A photograph taken in Hollywood, c. 1927, when Walt Disney was making his "Alice in Cartoonland" shorts. Left to right:* Friz Freleng, Walker Harman *(Hugh's brother),* Walt Disney, *the girl who played "Alice,"* Rudolph Ising, Ub Iwerks, Hugh Harman, Roy Disney.

Title, a leading maker of movie title-cards and artwork that is still at the top of its field. Schlesinger (1884–1949) was closely acquainted with the Warner brothers and, according to legend, had helped finance the Warners' risky, first-ever talkie, *The Jazz Singer.* Jack Warner had suggested that Schlesinger go into cartoon production, so Schlesinger approached the Warners with the idea of distributing a series of Bosko shorts; his principal selling point was that the Warners could use the cartoons to promote songs from their feature films and their several music-publishing concerns. "Schlesinger wanted to get into something new because he thought that with the advent of sound, he would be out of business," said

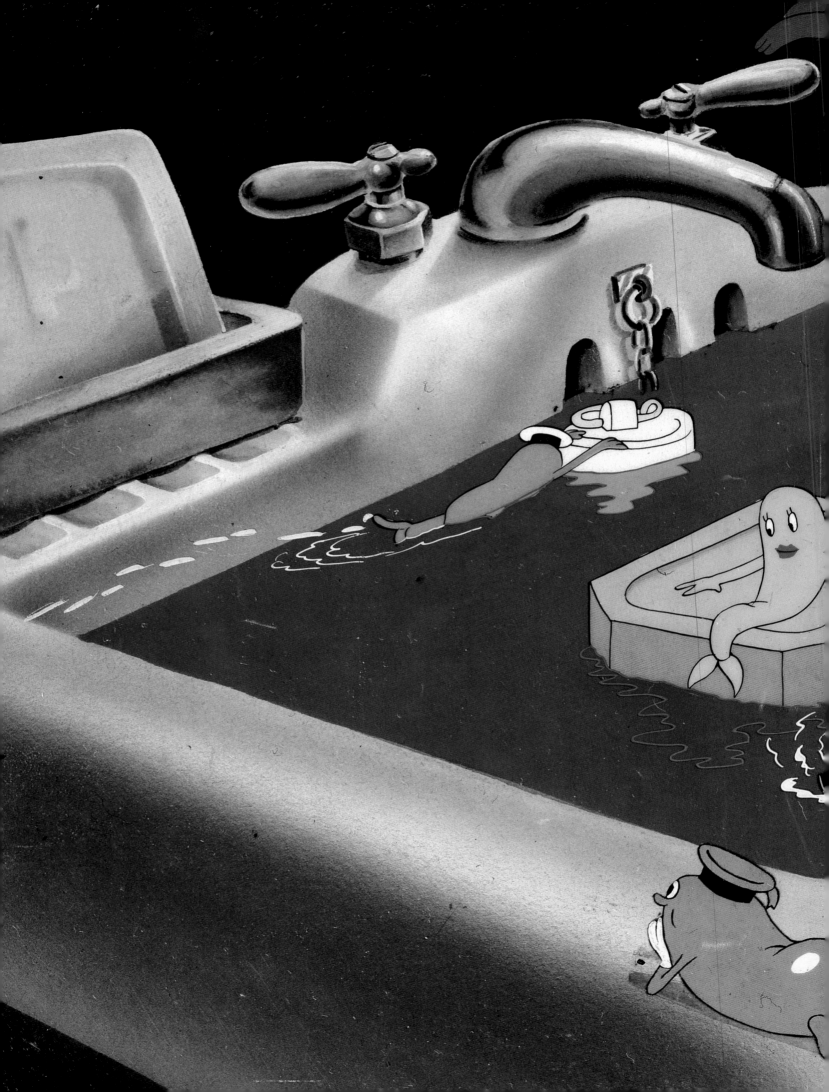

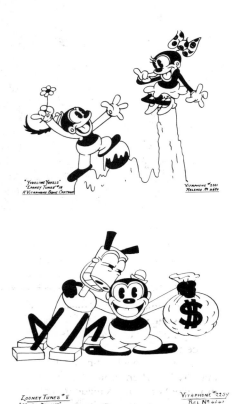

Above: *Promotional drawing for the eighth "Looney Tune,"* Ups'N Downs.
Top: *Promotional drawing for the tenth "Looney Tune"* Yodeling Yokels.

**Opposite**
*Layout drawing of Foxy from the first "Merrie Melodie"* Lady Play Your Mandolin, *1931.*

Ising. "Eighty percent of Pacific Art and Title's business was the dialogue cards in the silent pictures, and those were about to end."

Schlesinger signed a contract with Harman and Ising—who are described on the document as "particularly qualified in the art of synchronizing cartoons to music"—on January 28, 1930. The contract provided for Harman and Ising to deliver a single cartoon by April 1, 1930, and for Schlesinger then to have three successive options to commission yearly series of cartoons, to be delivered by Harman-Ising on a monthly basis. After the Warners approved the first cartoon, Schlesinger exercised his first option "almost immediately," Ising said.

Schlesinger positioned himself as middleman between the Warners and the cartoonists: he handled the flow of money, while Harman and Ising were responsible for producing and directing the shorts. A quintessential capitalist, Schlesinger even installed his brother-in-law, Ray Katz, as business manager of Harman and Ising's studio. "Schlesinger was absolutely out for money and he didn't care how he got it," Chuck Jones has said. "He was a dandy," remarked Ising. "He used to wear a flower in his lapel and carry a cane, and he used an awful lot of cologne all the time."

But Jones has also had less harsh words for the pudgy, lisping Schlesinger, whose favorite pastimes were gambling and going to the races. "He was a very vulgar, peculiar, nice, lovely man," Jones said. "He once bought a yacht from Richard Arlen and called it the 'Merrie Melodie,' with a little dinghy on the back that he called 'Looney Tunes.' One day I said, 'Mr. Schlesinger, when are you going to take us out on your yacht?' And he replied, 'I don't want any poor people on my boat.' But, of course, he was the reason we were poor."

Nevertheless, the lazy Schlesinger fostered an atmosphere in which his directors could develop individual approaches to cartoonmaking. "I will say this for Leon, when he finally found a director he had confidence in, he left him alone," Bob Clampett told Mike Barrier in 1969. "And he let us try new ideas."

The "Looney Tunes" were the studio's first series, and its name's obvious derivation from Disney's "Silly Symphonies" gives a clear indication of the predominance that Disney had already achieved since the birth of Mickey Mouse, in 1928. The first "Looney Tune," called *Sinkin' in the Bathtub,* opened in New York on May 6, 1930, at the Warner Bros. theater on Broadway, playing with the Warner feature *Song of the Flame*; and it immediately reveals Harman and Ising's belief that the only way to compete—or even to survive—in the cartoon trade was to cleave to the Disney vision. (Also contributing to the Disney mimicking was that artists whom Harman and Ising hired—including animators Friz Freleng, Rollin Hamilton, Carmen Maxwell, and Paul Smith—had done indoctrinating toil with Disney in the 1920s.)

*Sinkin' in the Bathtub* finds the Mickey-knockoff Bosko (his Mickey-like falsetto supplied by Carmen Maxwell) paired with a most Minnie Mouse-ish girlfriend called Honey (whose voice was Rochelle Hudson's). Forever moving in time to the film's music, the characters cavort through Disneyesque gags (a bathtub dances, a car prances, Honey steps from her window down to the ground on a series of bubbles) in a benign, carefree world that is rendered in the simplest graphic shorthand. Warner songs flood the soundtrack—the still-thrilling novelty of sound made all these early cartoons mini-musicals—while the finale finds Bosko performing impossible stunts to save Honey in their runaway jalopy. Finally, they land in a lake, their car becomes a bathtub, and all is merriment.

The "Looney Tunes" series continued in much the same vein, with Bosko branching out to such roles as hot-dog vendor and World War I aviator by the end of his first year. Eventually, he picked up a Pluto stand-in dog called Bruno. If these cartoons seem formula-bound and rudimentary today, they are nevertheless chipper and amusing, and on a par with Disney's productions of the era. Time and budget requirements permitted little else.

Yet the "Looney Tunes" were popular—so much so that Warner Bros. commissioned a second series from Schlesinger; these were the "Merrie Melodies," and their release began in August 1931. Largely marketed as a series of musical short-subjects—most of the cartoons' titles were taken from Warner songs—the "Merrie Melodies" were obligated to include a performance of at least one complete chorus of a Warner-owned tune. But this requirement—which continued until late in the 1930s—frequently arrested the cartoons' momentum. As Bob Clampett said in 1969, "We'd have a great story going along, but then we'd have to stop and have the singing chorus." According to Ising, the music for the "Merrie Melodies" was supposed to be performed by "name bands," not the Warner Bros. orchestra. Apparently, this idea was abandoned after Abe Lyman's Brunswick Record Orchestra played on a few of the first releases.

At first, these black-and white cartoons featured characters named Piggy and Foxy—the most flagrant of the Mickey clones, except that the round ears tapered to a point and the tail was bushy—but they were soon dropped. For many years thereafter, the "Merrie Melodies" were a series of "one shot" cartoons, with no continuing characters. Until the early 1940s, the "Looney Tunes" remained the showcase for Warner's cartoon stars—Bosko, Honey, and those that followed. Also, whereas Harman and Ising had previously collaborated on direction, they now decided to work with separate units; for the most part, Harman directed the "Looney Tunes" and Ising handled the "Merrie Melodies," although Friz Freleng did some directing on both series.

## Leon Schlesinger

When Harman and Ising broke with him, Leon Schlesinger was no abandoned victim. An eager entrepreneur, he was glad to be free of his obligations to other parties. "He definitely wanted his own studio—Leon Schlesinger Productions. He wanted that title," said Rudolph Ising. "He was a little conceited."

He was also a hard-nosed businessman. Twice when some of his newly unionized employees made demands that would bring them higher pay, Schlesinger briefly shut his shop down—in May 1941 and in October 1942. In 1938, he withdrew his cartoons from competition for the Academy Award, to protest what he contended was "preferential treatment" being accorded Walt Disney. And from 1937 through the early 1940s, he established a separate company under his brother-in-law, Ray Katz, to produce some of the "Looney Tunes." The arrangement brought some tax benefits to Schlesinger and threw a little business to a family member.

Schlesinger also produced a considerable body of work outside his run of Warner-released cartoons. His studio provided animated segments for such films as RKO's 1937 Joe E. Brown comedy *When's Your Birthday?* (the sequence was Bob Clampett's first direction for Schlesinger); Paramount's *The Big Broadcast of 1938*; Republic's 1939 *She Married a Cop*; and Paramount's 1940 *Love Thy Neighbor.* And in the 1930s, Schlesinger produced a number of live-action B-Westerns—including, in 1932 and 1933, some of the first screen appearances of a young actor named John Wayne.

When he died, on Christmas Day, 1949, Schlesinger left an estate worth $904,700.

Above: *Animation drawing of Buddy and Cookie from* Buddy's Adventures, *1934.* Top: *Layout drawing of Buddy and Cookie from* Buddy Steps Out, *1935.*

Despite the series' differences, however, they were similar in their flat-out appropriation of ideas, gags, and conventions originated at Disney's, and the fact that production seemed stuck at a bare-bones elementary level. Occasional sparks came in such films as *Ride Him, Bosko* (1932), a tale of the Wild West (where "men are men, nine times out of ten"): in the middle of Bosko's dashing horseback sprint to save Honey, who is caught in a runaway stagecoach, the camera pulls back to reveal Rudy Ising and two other young men watching the cartoon on a small screen. They discuss how best to end the story ("Say, how's Bosko gonna save the girl?," "I don't know," "Well, we gotta do *something*," "Let's go home," "Good idea") before they simply pack it in for the night—and perhaps provide a comment on their own commitment to ingenuity.

Among the "Merrie Melodies," the early *Freddie the Freshman* exhibits some verve in telling of a raccoon-coated college football star who leads his team to victory. And "Merrie Melodie" number two, *Smile, Darn Ya, Smile,* inaugurated what quickly became a Warner Cartoon mainstay, from an idea by Bob Clampett; as Foxy and his girlfriend ride in a trolley car, characters from the trolley's advertising cards—a dog hawking "Narrow" collars, the cough-suppressing Sniff Brothers—come to life and perform small bits of business. The studio quickly became obsessed with this device, repeating it in subsequent cartoons with magazine covers, grocery labels, billboards, and the rest. 1932's *Three's a Crowd* finds dozens of characters from books—including The Three Musketeers, Robinson Crusoe, and Omar Khayyam—coming to life and helping to save Alice, sprung from Wonderland, from the clutches of Mr. Hyde. And a follow-up film from 1933, *I Like Mountain Music,* combined the device with the longtime cartoon ploy of using celebrity caricatures, as Eddie Cantor, Will Rogers, and others rise from popular magazines and foil a gang's attempted heist.

Almost from the beginning, the aggressive Hugh Harman had been pushing Leon Schlesinger for more money to better the quality of the studio's releases, then, later to move into color. But Schlesinger steadfastly refused to cut into his profits. Tensions on this issue grew to the point where, in mid-1933, Harman and Ising split from Schlesinger, taking Bosko, their star of thirty-nine cartoons, with them. (In 1934, Harman–Ising began releasing their cartoons through MGM; they continued to feature Bosko, who eventually became a recognizable black boy, until 1938.)

The move left Schlesinger virtually empty-handed, owning the rights to the phrases "Looney Tunes," "Merrie Melodies," and "That's all, folks!" but with no staff and no known characters. Quickly, Schlesinger set about establishing his own studio, and took over a building on the old Warner Bros. lot, on Sunset Boulevard. He hired cartoonists away from Disney and other shops, and also lured back such former Harman-Ising personnel as Friz Freleng and animator Bob Clampett. Gag cartoonist Melvin "Tubby" Millar and comic-strip artist Ben Hardaway came from Kansas City, upon Freleng's recommendation. Among Schlesinger's first directors were former Disney hands Tom Palmer, Jack King, and Earl Duvall.

Once in operation, the studio first pinned its hopes on a character created by Duvall. Named Buddy, this new star of the "Looney Tunes" series was a wide-eyed humanoid whom Bob Clampett once described as "Bosko in whiteface"—testament to the animators' continuing impulse to stick to the tried and true. Through twenty-three cartoons released from 1933 to 1935, Buddy proved himself to be a creature of limitless

blandness, even when paired with a Betty Boop-ish flapper girlfriend called Cookie and a trusty surrogate-Pluto dog, Towser. His debut film, *Buddy's Day Out*, is a nondescript adventure spree, while the later cartoon *Buddy's Showboat* finds him defending Cookie from some loutish Mississippi deckhands. Probably the best of the run is his farewell film, *Buddy the Gee Man*, in which he is cast as a federal agent who infiltrates "Sing Song" Prison and converts its harsh conditions into something resembling a day camp. But about the most that can be said for Buddy (whose voice was provided by animator Jack Carr) is that he is distinctly forgettable.

Somewhat more endearing and enduring from this time are the "Merrie Melodies," which used the lyrics of Warner songs to inspire stories—usually pretty flimsy ones—that benefit from flows of continuous movement. Dancing and frolicking mermaids (in *Mr. and Mrs. Is the Name*), forest animals (*Pop Goes Your Heart*), even clothing (*The Girl at the Ironing Board*) populate these cartoons, which are capable of provoking smiles and occasional admiration for their choreography.

For the 1934 all-insect extravaganza *Honeymoon Hotel*—a story of frustrated bug amour—Schlesinger responded to competitive pressures and made Warner's first cartoon in color. But until its 1935–1936 release season, the studio was limited to using two-tone processes—first by Cinecolor then by Technicolor—which employed only the red and the green segments of the spectrum. (Crafty Disney was then in the middle of an exclusive contract with Technicolor for use of its richer, three-color technique in cartoons.) Eight more black-and-white "Merrie Melodies" were made, but beginning with 1934's *Those Beautiful Dames*, all of the "Merrie Melodies" were made in color, while the "Looney

Above: *Cel of the chicken hopefuls waiting for an audition; from* A Star is Hatched, *1938.* Below: *a layout drawing from* Freddie the Freshman, *1932.*

# Friz Freleng

For longevity, flexibility, and excellence of accomplishment, Friz Freleng has few peers in the history of American animation. Beginning as the lead artist for Harman and Ising—originally, he says, he was supposed to have been an equal creative partner—Freleng made crucial contributions to every phase of Warner Bros.' development. Effortlessly, he adapted to the stylistic changes that swept through the studio, embellishing them with personal touches that resulted in dozens of outstanding cartoons. As a director, his impeccable timing and ability to fashion fully rounded, credible characters gave his cartoons a kind of classicism—a wholeness and balance through which humor and beauty became one. While his showman's sense generally favored the pratfalls and pain gags of slapstick, he often found room for moments of tenderness. Working off this unique contrast, Freleng was alone in animation in his ability to make cartoons that were both charming and rowdily funny. As Chuck Jones has written: "No student of animation can safely ignore the wizardry of [Freleng's] cartoons—if he can stop laughing long enough to seriously study their beauty."

Top right: *A 1959 publicity photograph of Friz Freleng with layout artist Hawley Pratt (standing), taken upon Freleng's winning his fourth Academy Award for* Knighty-Knight Bugs. Above: *Animation drawings by Virgil Ross from 1953 Freleng films,* Hare Trimmed *(left) and* A Mouse Divided *(right). Right:* Promotional drawing for Birds Anonymous, *1957, the third of Freleng's four Oscar winners at Warner Bros.*

Tunes" continued in black and white as far forward as 1943.

For several years, starting in early 1934, many of the "Merrie Melodies" were assigned for direction to Friz Freleng. If there is any person who can be said to *be* Warner Bros. cartoons, it is Isadore Freleng, whose oft-misspelled nickname was derived from that of a fictional congressman called Frizby who was featured in a column in the *Los Angeles Examiner*. One of the group that migrated from Kansas City to work with Walt Disney in the 1920s, Freleng, who was born in 1906, received screen credit for animation on the first-ever "Looney Tune," went on to direct more Warner cartoons than anyone (about 266), and was a key player within the studio's operations into the mid-1980s. When in form, his work was solidly funny and well crafted, and his presence seemed to be the pivot around which the studio spun. "The spark plug to that studio was Friz Freleng," said Warner animator and director Arthur Davis.

From the outset, Freleng's two passions were music and show business. Drawing on his real gifts for close synchronization, he built dozens of cartoons around music, such as his droves of early "Merrie Melodies." Probably his greatest musicals, however, were his several masterly visualizations of Liszt's "Hungarian Rhapsody No. 2" (such as James Agee's favorite, *Rhapsody Rabbit*). Even more often, Freleng gloried in the world of show biz, filling his cartoons with Hollywood lore and caricatures of radio and film stars. For example, 1937's *She Was an Acrobat's Daughter* is a six-minute abbreviation of an entire evening's film program, complete with an introductory double feature (advertised on the marquee as "'Thirty-Six Hours to Kill' with 'His Brother's Wife'"), a rather risqué sing-along, a "Goofy Tone Newsreel," and another film, called "The Petrified Florist," featuring caricatures of Bette Davis and Leslie Howard. *Clean Pastures* (1937) brings many of the black entertainers of the time—Louis Armstrong, Cab Calloway, Bill "Bojangles" Robinson—to heaven's "Pair O' Dice" for a rousing jam session. And *Malibu Beach Party* (1940) finds much of the Hollywood community at Jack Benny's Pacific Coast home for a sandy shindig.

Interestingly, many of Freleng's show-biz spoofs involve attempts to break in to the big time, such as through arduous auditions for callous studio chiefs, or disappointment at the failure of being accepted or acknowledged. In *A Star Is Hatched* (1938), a star-struck chicken who speaks with Katharine Hepburn's voice dreams of Hollywood triumph, but can't even get a listen from bigwig rooster director J. Megga Phone. Or, in *Curtain Razor* (1949), a zealous fox literally has to blow himself into the hereafter to impress talent scout Porky Pig (of the "Goode and Korny Talent Agency").

Something of this also informs an important scene in Freleng's 1935 *I Haven't Got a Hat*. Set in a small-town schoolroom, the film features a kiddie show put on by a group of new Warner characters; according to Bob Clampett, the characters had been created for this cartoon upon Leon Schlesinger's directive for the studio to come up with a cartoon equivalent of Hal Roach's "Our Gang." The new kids on the block included two puppies, called Ham and Ex, Little Kitty, Oliver Owl, Tommy Turtle and another duo linked solely by name, Porky and Beans. Beans was a no-nonsense cat, and Porky a timid pig.

At one point, Porky is called to the front of the class to recite "The Midnight Ride of Paul Revere." The porker becomes so distraught in his nervous stuttering—sweating and suffering in horrific embarrassment—that he somehow switches his recital to "The Charge of the Light Brigade." It was a moment that adroitly mixed comedy and pathos, and one that would be remembered later. This was one pig that we would be hearing from—albeit in altered form—again.

*Model sheet from* I Haven't Got a Hat, *with all of the new featured players. The pose of Porky comes from his recitation scene, in which he struggles with his words; the character's comic/trenchant flaw made him the first Warner creation with real star potential. Somehow, Freleng had found a bit of Chaplin in small pink pig.*

# Breaking Away: 1936–40

By the mid-1930s, Disney's dominance in the world of animation was complete. His was an overpowering presence, one that exerted a tremendous influence on the decisions of the other cartoonists in the Hollywood community. At Warner's, for example, Disney was looked upon "with absolute awe," Chuck Jones has said. "We didn't really believe we were doing the same thing."

But by then, Disney had also begun to restrict the range of what he found acceptable. As the flagship in film's family entertainment, Disney felt an ever-greater need to keep his work within the bounds of straightforward storytelling, creating fantasies that would envelop viewers through traditional narrative means. For Disney, this meant developing ever-greater realism in his films, as well as suppressing many of the signals that would remind audiences that what they were watching was, in fact, a cartoon.

With neither the time, the money, the expertise, nor—at bottom—the inclination to compete with Disney in this arena, the Warner animators led the movement away from the restrictions that had begun to caramelize cartooning. In part, they accomplished this by spearheading advances in the art of animation that, in a sense, were deliberate retrogressions: in force, they returned to the impossible gags, visual tricks, and playful outrageousness—in short, the flagrant cartooniness—that had been animation's specialty until Disney's ascendancy. At Warner's, cartoons once again became aware that they were cartoons, and the directors began to make the most of the boundless freedoms available to the medium. Rather than creating "the illusion of life," the Warner animators began asking audiences to recognize that theirs was an art of pure illusion—but even so, go with it, folks; jump on for the rip-roaring ride. Yet it was not only a matter of retreating into past practices. For in the hands of four tremendously talented artists who began directing at Warner's in the second half of the 1930s, the ancient freedoms of animation were wedded to a new, cheeky sophistication.

The principal architect of this change was a venturesome perfectionist from Taylor, Texas. In 1935, after a few years at the Walter Lantz studio, Fred "Tex" Avery (1908–80) applied for a director's position at Schlesinger Productions, after having heard that Schlesinger was looking to start up a third unit. Yet the ambitious applicant seems to have faked his way in: Avery told Schlesinger that he had directed two cartoons for Lantz, although no screen credits exist to that effect.

"I don't know why or how Schlesinger gambled on me," Avery told Joe Adamson some thirty-five years later. "Evidently he was quite desperate. . . . He said 'I'll try you on one picture. I've got some boys here—they're not renegades, but they don't get along with the other two crews. They're not satisfied working with the people they're working with.' Evidently there was some rub. And he gave me Chuck Jones, Bob Clampett, and Bob Cannon. Chuck was creative; so was Bob Clampett. Bob Cannon was a terrific draftsman.

Left: *Rudeness, effrontery, and lunacy, as Bob Clampett makes one of his characters jut his face into the screen, as if attempting to break out past two dimensions. Animation drawing of Flat Foot Flookey from* Porky's Tire Trouble, *1939.* Below: *Model sheet from Tex Avery's* The Sneezing Weasel, *1938. When this title character wants to change costume, he momentarily pulls a tattered curtain down to cover the entire screen and emerges a new man. Derivations of this shifty weasel were featured in the 1988 mixed live action-animation feature* Who Framed Roger Rabbit.

**Opposite**
*Story sketches by Mel Millar from Tex Avery's* A Day at the Zoo, *1939.*

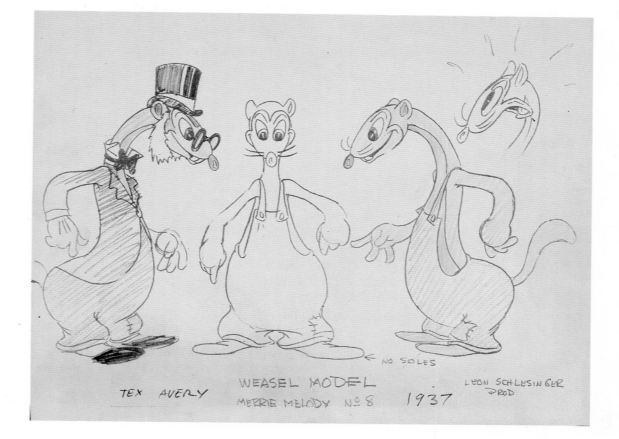

TEX AVERY    WEASEL MODEL    1937    LEON SCHLESINGER PROD

MERRIE MELODY Nº 8

NO SOLES

Above: *The crew at Termite Terrace, as captured in a frame of film from Bob Clampett's home movies. Left to right: Virgil Ross, Sid Sutherland, Tex Avery, Chuck Jones, Bob Clampett.* Below: *"Eh-beh-thee, Eh-beh-thee, Eh-beh-that's all, folks!" Animation drawing of Porky saying farewell, used at the end of the "Looney Tunes."*

"And they were tickled to death," Avery went on; "they wanted to get a 'new group' going, and 'we could do it,' and 'let's make some funny pictures.' It was very encouraging. . . . We worked every night—Jones, Clampett, and I were all young and full of ambition. My gosh, nothing stopped us!"

Indeed, nothing did: to give his new unit isolation in which to freely create, Schlesinger temporarily installed the Avery crew—which also included two animators Avery had brought from Lantz, Virgil Ross and Sid Sutherland—in a separate cottage-like building on the Warner Sunset lot. "It was just a white, one-story bungalow, with a few rooms," recalled Ross. But within moments of their arrival it became clear that they were not alone. The building, it seems, was also home to a thriving population of termites. Nevertheless, the infested shack—quickly dubbed Termite Terrace—is now renowned as the unstoppable seedbed for the radical renovation of short-subject animation.

Avery began his assignment by reviewing some of the studio's recent cartoons to search for workable characters, and hit upon Porky and Beans from *I Haven't Got a Hat*. For his first film, called *Golddiggers of '49*, Avery changed the duo into adult animals, and also, in a sense, set the studio on the track to making adult cartoons. The cartoon's story line is nothing new: Beans rescues a valuable package for Porky during the gold rush of the 1840s, in an attempt to win Porky's daughter's hand in marriage. Yet *Golddiggers of '49*, which was released late in 1935, is unmistakably supported by a new vision. It is, to be sure, hobbled by the primitiveness of Warner's mid-thirties work: slowly paced and crudely drawn, the film features a foully fat Porky who has a piggy-bank slit on his back. But the cartoon plays with absurdity and slapstick in ways that hadn't been seen in years: when Beans calls "I found gold in the gulch" to a man taking a bath, the man stands and hustles away, pulling the tub up around his waist like a barrel. And the film ends with a nifty chase that makes excellent use of novel speed effects, when Beans and his car dissolve into a haze of coruscating lines. Absurdity, exaggeration, slapstick, speed: the ingredients were being assembled.

Avery directed several more Porky shorts in 1936 and 1937, helping to make the character Schlesinger's first cartoon star. (And Porky's place in world history was assured at this time, as he was given the privilege of bursting from a bass drum and delivering the squealy-stammery "That's all, folks!" at the end of the "Looney Tunes." In the years previous, many characters had called out the cartoons' farewell.) Along the way, Avery piloted other films filled with innovative ideas, including 1936's *Page Miss Glory*, which uses Art Deco backgrounds and character designs to tell of a dreamy bellhop transported to a chic New York hotel.

But throughout these efforts, Avery began inserting moments that helped create the cartoon territory that was Warner's alone. Not only were the characters on screen growing more irreverent, the cartoon makers themselves began showing a gaggy irreverence to the very conventions of cinematic storytelling in which they were participating. In many films, little signs or placards would suddenly appear on screen, ironically commenting on the cartoon's events while they are taking place ("This is an electric eel, folks," clarifies a hand-held sign in 1937's *Porky's Duck Hunt*, just before the wiggly thing flashes into becoming an underwater lightning bolt). In other spots, characters would step out of their parts to directly address the audience ("We do this kinda stuff to him all through the picture," says Cecil Turtle in 1941's *Tortoise Beats Hare*, after his latest flummoxing of Bugs Bunny). Or they would shoot a little flick of

## Tex Avery

More so than any other person, Tex Avery was the father of
Warner Bros. cartoons. He developed the studio's first lasting
star, Porky Pig, created the character that signaled the studio's break from ingrained Hollywood conventions, Daffy
Duck, and perfected the player that best defined the studio's
particular temperament, Bugs Bunny. Further, his gag-filled
anti-authoritarianism and his purposeful demolishing of sentimental expectations put the studio on the course that
would earn it a niche in American culture.

Above left: *A June 1936 photograph. Left to right: Frank Tashlin, Tex Avery, Henry
Binder (Leon Schlesinger's assistant), Leon Schlesinger, Ray Katz, Friz Freleng.* Above
right: *Layout drawing of Porky Pig from* Golddiggers of '49. Top left: *Layout drawing
of the "pickled herring" from* Fresh Fish, *1939.* Top right: *Avery's wolf reacts to an
intrusion by Egghead; animation drawing from* Little Red Walking Hood, *1937.*

the eyes audienceward, establishing a sneaky conspiracy between character and viewers before the character would unload his next antic.

Other devices were more elaborate: in Avery's 1940 *The Bear's Tale*, which stages a collision between the "Goldilocks" and "Red Riding Hood" fables, Red telephones Goldie and the screen is divided by a diagonal line to show them both chatting; but at the end of the call, Red reaches over the line to hand Goldie a note she wants her to read—violating the "special effect" of the split screen. And in several cartoons, what appears to be the silhouette of a man in the audience stands up and interacts with the cartoon characters on screen. In *Thugs With Dirty Mugs*, a civic-minded moviegoer, after saying that he's "sat through this picture twice," squeals to the cartoon cops and lets them know where the film's gangsters are holed up. And in *Daffy Duck and Egghead*, one poor slob in the sixth row is gunned down by a rifle-toting cartoon hunter. That's entertainment.

When combined with other Avery madness—abrupt changes in the pace of action, from slow-and-easy to ultra-quick and back, or affronts to logic—the effect of all this business is to disrupt the audience's absorption in the story line, and thereby lay bare the artifices that sustain the film's fabricated world. By violating the illusions being created on screen, Avery reminds his cartoon's viewers that what they're viewing is not real—a stance directly opposite from Disney's, whose goal was to enfold his spectators ever more thoroughly in his opulent spectacle. Rather, Avery's self-reflexive shenanigans deliberately call attention to the fact that what's on screen is an animated cartoon. (Or, as a hick opines in 1938's *A Feud There Was*: "In one of these here cartoon pictures, a body can get away with anything.") A postmodernist to the core, Avery sought

*Model sheet of Owl Jolson from I Love to Singa.*

48

to challenge the manipulations that are at the center of his art, not to conceal them.

In doing this, Avery also aligned himself—and, ultimately, the entire studio—with the tradition of satire, which declares that all received pieties must be relentlessly razzed. Low blows must be dealt to the pretenses of high culture. An early and very fetching illustration of this is 1936's *I Love to Singa*, a cartoon reply to *The Jazz Singer*. In this snappy short, pompous old Professor Owl goes into a rage when his son denounces classical music and won't sing the syrupy "Drink to Me Only with Thine Eyes"; Junior prefers to pipe the hep title song in the manner of his namesake, "Owl Jolson." (Yet the stuffy professor changes his tune when Junior wins a radio talent contest.) And soon after this reel, Avery embarked on a series of films that spoofed what had come to be the typical fare of animated cartoons—fairy tales and nursery rhymes. The titles include *Little Red Walking Hood*, *Cinderella Meets Fella*, and *A Gander at Mother Goose*. Why, it's almost as if Avery were thumbing his nose at Disney directly.

Yet perhaps even more significant than Avery's experiments with film forms were his innovations in cartoon character. The turning point here, quite clearly, was 1937's *Porky's Duck Hunt*, in which hunter Porky has the misfortune of crossing paths with a duck that was making his first appearance, and who would soon be christened Daffy. For Daffy was a character who outdid, in terms of unfettered and unmotivated craziness, even the knockabout cartoon imps of the silent years. From his first scene, madly hopping and skittering and bouncing on his head across a lake, crossing his eyes, imitating Stan Laurel, and yipping "Woo-hoo! Woo-hoo!," Daffy declared that there were no rules of decorum in the cartoon universe. Like the films they appeared in, cartoon characters could do anything, no matter how nutty. How radical a break was this? An answer comes in trying to imagine any of Disney's stars comporting themselves with such indecorous dementia. It's easier to picture Ronald Colman doubling for Fatty Arbuckle. The looniness had been let loose in the "Looney Tunes."

If Tex Avery brought cartooniness back to cartoons, Frank Tashlin, the next to become a director at Schlesinger's, brought a richer awareness of live-action filmmaking to Warner animation. Tashlin (1913–72), who replaced Jack King when he returned to Disney in 1936, had earlier worked as a newspaper and magazine cartoonist, but he had always been, as he described it, "a nut movie fan." And as a director (he had previously worked as an animator for Schlesinger) Tashlin introduced many simulated live-action techniques to his cartoons. Montage, dissolves, oblique camera angles, up-shots, down-shots, and other borrowings from live-action vocabulary gave Tashlin's cartoons a visual variety and fineness of timing that was new to the studio, and that made a strong impression throughout it. Such titles as *Wholly Smoke*, with its hallucinatory anti-smoking montage, and *Now That Summer Is Gone,* with its forestful of squirrels processing nuts for the winter, provide ample evidence of the richness of Tashlin's visual thinking.

But Tashlin's love of film was expressed in other ways. He made a run of scintillating cartoons that burst with celebrity caricatures, casting his stand-in stars as, among others, speed demons (*Porky's Road Race*), magazine covers rising to life (*Speaking of the Weather*), and forest animals participating in a community sing (*The Woods Are Full of Cuckoos*). And *Porky's Romance*, from 1937, introduces the character of Petunia Pig in a little prologue that holds enough Hollywood ballyhoo to fluster any first-time starlet: a bombastic announcer booms, "Ladies and Gentlemen, introducing Leon Schlesinger's new 'Looney Tune' star, Petunia Pig!" before a curtain parts and the rouged sow attempts to welcome "her public." But Petunia gets so jittery from all the attention that

The Crazy-
Darnfool
Duck

COMPARATIVE SIZES
OF
CHARACTERS

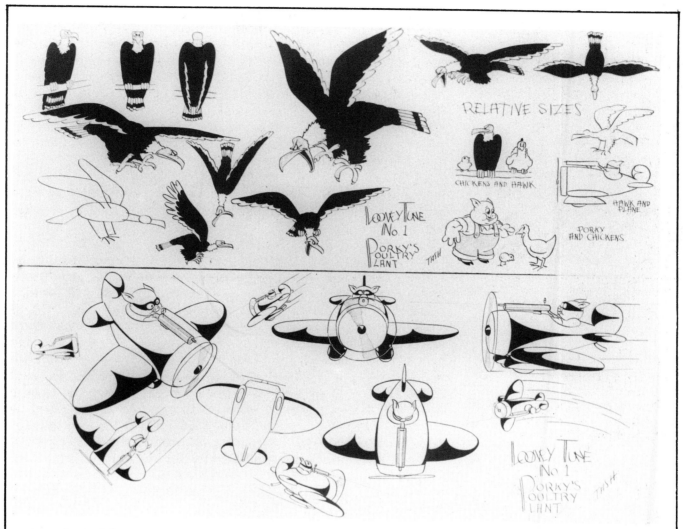

## Frank Tashlin

Frequently referred to in screen credits by one of his nicknames, "Frank Tash" or "Tish Tash," Frank Tashlin was the most versatile humorist to work in animation. Beginning his career in New York, Tashlin came to Hollywood in 1933 to work for Leon Schlesinger; but Schlesinger soon fired him when he refused to give the producer part of the revenues he was earning from a syndicated comic strip he was drawing after hours. Nevertheless, Schlesinger twice hired Tashlin back to direct cartoons. Tashlin also worked for the Iwerks, Disney, and Columbia animation studios; was a cartoonists' union activist; published cartoons in magazines; was a gag writer for the Hal Roach Studio, the Marx Brothers, Lucille Ball, and many others; and, beginning with his uncredited work on 1950's *The Lemon Drop Kid,* wrote and directed a score of comedy features. From 1946 to 1952, while working extensively in film and television, he wrote and illustrated the contemporary fables *The Bear That Wasn't, The Possum That Didn't, The World That Isn't,* and *The Turtle That Couldn't.*

Right: *Tashlin on the set of* Marry Me Again, *1953.* Above: *Model sheet drawn by Tashlin, from* Porky's Poultry Plant *(1936), the first cartoon that he directed. Tashlin's interest in working with unusual and dramatic camera angles is apparent in the poses he assembled for this model.*

*From Frank Tashlin's films:*
Above: *Cel of automobilist Edna Mae Oliver from* Porky's Road Race, *1937.*
Below: *Animation drawing of Greta Garbo rocking on her legendary feet; from* Speaking of the Weather, *1937.*

**Opposite**
*Model sheet from* The Woods Are Full of Cuckoos, *1937.*

she explodes into a ranting breakdown right in the middle of her big moment.

Years later, Tashlin would realize his dream by becoming the only major animation director to develop a successful career directing live action. Beginning in the 1950s, Tashlin made over twenty popular screwball comedies, including, in Peter Bogdanovich's words, "the funniest and only enduring Martin-and-Lewis films," as well as such titles as *The Girl Can't Help It*, and *Will Success Spoil Rock Hunter?* Later on, these films were widely praised—Jean-Luc Godard, for one, championed them—for their, of course, cartoony qualities.

But it was not only the directors who, around this time, began raising the Warner cartoons to levels of unmatched excellence. In 1936, composer Carl W. Stalling joined the Schlesinger shop, coming from the Ub Iwerks studio. Before then, Warner's cartoon scores had been written by Frank Marsales, from 1930 to 1933, and Norman Spencer and Bernard Brown, working in tandem from 1933 to 1936. But with Stalling, the cartoons' music attained a marvelous wittiness, inventiveness, and vigor—unquestionably the finest in the cartoon trade.

The composer had mastered this touch while working in Kansas City as an accompanist to silent movies, playing the organ or conducting a pit orchestra; one impressed listener was the young Walt Disney, who invited Stalling to join his staff in Hollywood in the late 1920s. As an accompanist, Stalling's job was to complement the images on screen, using original music, popular songs, or classical snatches to add vitality and atmosphere. And he continued this with remarkable consistency and deftness at Warner's, where he composed scores for some six hundred cartoons over some twenty-two years—a rate that averaged about one a week. Stalling also conducted the fifty-piece Warner orchestra—the same ensemble that played for Warner's feature films—when it recorded the cartoons' music tracks.

ALEXANDER OWLCOTT –

– BEN BIRDIE –

– WALTER FINCHELL

– MILTON SQUIRREL –

BILLY GOAT AND ERNIE BEAR

– WENDALL HOWL –
"THE RED HEADED MUSIC MAKER"

– POLLY –
THE SPONSER'S DAUGHTER

– EDDIE GANDER –

SOPHIE TURKEY
"THE LAST OF THE RED
HOT GOBBLERS"

W. C. FIELDMOUSE
Jimmy Mack

PORTLAND

DEANNA TERRAPIN –

– IRVIN S. FROG –

AL GOATSON
"THE SINGING KID"

DICK FOWL –

RUBY SQUEALER –

– GRACE MOOSE –

– LILY SWANS –

LENNY HISS

M.M.#5
SHEET #2

FRED McFURRY – BING CROWSBY –

FRED ALLEN

53

## The Music of Raymond Scott

*Carl Stalling*

*Raymond Scott*

Among the wide-ranging inventory of popular music that Carl Stalling used to spice his scores, he seems to have had a particular affection for the novelty tunes of Raymond Scott. The quirky rhythms, untraditional textures, and, perhaps most of all, exotic titles that Scott gave his compositions proved irresistible to Stalling. Although Scott's music is very seldom revived nowadays, it is instantly familiar to watchers of Warner cartoons, through the dozens of times that Stalling employed colorful Scott excerpts.

After he rose to prominence with a radio broadcast in January 1937, Scott was principally known as the composer and ensemble-leader who gave his pieces unusual names: "Reckless Night on Board an Ocean Liner," "Bumpy Weather over Newark," "In a Subway Far from Ireland," and others. Indeed, the sound of names seems to have been a concern of Scott's throughout his life. Born in Brooklyn in September 1908 as Harry Warnow, Scott picked his stage moniker from a telephone book. And although his first significant group contained six musicians, the pianist called it The Raymond Scott Quintet—because " 'Quintet' has a crisp sound."

In 1937 and 1938, Scott appeared in such films as *Happy Landing,* with Sonja Henie; *Sally, Irene and Mary,* with Fred Allen; *Rebecca of Sunnybrook Farm,* with Shirley Temple; and *Ali Baba Goes to Town,* with Eddie Cantor. A gifted engineer and inventor, he later had his own recording studio and record label, Audivox, and conducted the orchestra on "Your Hit Parade" and other network radio and television shows.

Stalling got access to the Scott catalogue around 1941, and soon began littering his scores with Scott tunes. In 1943's *Wackiki Wabbit,* for example, a snippet of Scott's "The Penguin" accompanies the two castaways as they set up their dining table and kettle, and when Bugs Bunny manipulates their dinner bird like a marionette. The same year's *Jack-Wabbit and the Beanstalk* features Scott's syncopated "Twilight in Turkey" as the giant repeatedly whooses his hand down to grab the fleeing and jumping Bugs Bunny. Scott's "The Toy Trumpet" inspires the marching mother goose and her goslings near the beginning of *Booby Hatched* (1944) and is heard under the titles of *Daffy the Commando* (1943) and *Rebel Rabbit* (1949). "In an Eighteenth Century Drawing Room," Scott's jazzy transcription of Mozart's first Piano Sonata, helps introduce the bears in *Bugs Bunny and the Three Bears* (1944), and "Dinner Music for a Pack of Hungry Cannibals" is sounded while Gruesome Gorilla chases Bugs Bunny through the jungle in *Gorilla My Dreams* (1948) and during some of the chases in 1943's *Greetings Bait.*

Without question, however, the Scott piece employed most memorably was "Powerhouse," his 1937 tune whose several harried or chugging sections were intended to evoke the Machine Age. Stalling used "Powerhouse" with the assembly-line sequences in *The Swooner Crooner* (1944) and *Baby Bottleneck* (1946); while the cat is demonically stamping dog paw-prints throughout the living room in *Hiss and Make Up* (1943); during the introductory swooping descent from the cosmos to the United States to "Mousa-chewsetts" to a mouse hole in Fluger's Delicatessen in *The Mouse-merized Cat* (1946); and in several spots in *The Great Piggy Bank Robbery* (1946): as Daffy paces behind his mail box; when he speaks on the phones in his detective's office; and while he follows Mouseman's footprints up a wall, across the ceiling, and even over a hanging light-fixture. "Nothing's impothible to Duck Twacy!"

In addition to his own greatly humorous and evocative original music, Stalling used a vast number of popular tunes—some hoary, some fresh from the hit parade—in ways that provided a kind of unconscious commentary on the cartoon's events. When the Coyote, a napkin tied around his neck and clutching fork and knife, charged after the Road Runner, Stalling broke into a ditty called "A Cup of Coffee, a Sandwich, and You." Or in 1944's *Booby Hatched,* a chicken coop suffers the worst of

After model sheets are drawn, they are printed and distributed to the artists who are working on subject characters to insure uniformity of construction and conception. Although made exclusively for production purposes, they were often composed to be appealing and inspiring. Above: *From* Porky's Romance, *1937, directed by Frank Tashlin.* Left: *One of Chuck Jones' "Curious Puppies" used in the late 1930s and early 1940s. The penciled-in skeletal structure is an indication of the director's desire to simulate naturalistic movement in the character's animation by basing his actions on correct anatomy.* Below left: *From* Little Blabbermouse *and* Shop, Look and Listen, *both 1940; directed by Friz Freleng.*

Above: *Animation drawing from* Booby Hatched, *1944; directed by Frank Tashlin.* Below: *Cel from Chuck Jones' first cartoon as a director,* The Night Watchman, *atop a background painting from Hardaway and Dalton's* Katnip Kollege; *both cartoons were released in 1938. In the late 1930s and early 1940s, Leon Schlesinger marketed a modest selection of artwork from his cartoons. Often, however, individual pieces brought together a cel and a background from different films.*

a winter frost—hens shivering, eggs shivering, everything shivering—to the sound of "Am I Blue?" When heard in conjunction with the boisterous sound effects supplied by Treg Brown, who joined the studio in 1934, Stalling's music gave the Warner cartoons an aural identity as rich and distinct as their visual one. And this extended from the moment the films lit the screen until their end. Stalling also chose what became the theme songs for Warner's two series: for the "Merrie Melodies," a tune called "Merrily We Roll Along," and "The Merry-Go-Round Broke Down" for the "Looney Tunes."

The soundtracks of the Warner cartoons next came to profit from an artist whose extravagant gifts have earned him greater renown than anyone to work in animation, with the exception of Walt Disney. In 1936, one man named Mel Blanc brought 1,000 voices to Schlesinger's studio, and stayed to use them all with hilarious virtuosity. Born in San Francisco in 1908 and raised in Portland, Oregon, Blanc "tried for a year and a half to get an audition" at Schlesinger's, before he could get Treg Brown to hear him. His audition consisted of simulating the speech of "a drunken bull, crocked on sour mash," Blanc said.

Previously Blanc had performed in radio, where he had developed the immense variety of his voices and their prodigious flexibility. Blanc created the voices for all of Warner's major characters (with the exception of Elmer Fudd), and performed them with a diversity and verve that was truly wondrous. From Bugs Bunny's sassy rasp to Sylvester's sloppy drawl to Yosemite Sam's hellfire fury, Blanc was a brilliant comic actor, and he made an immeasurable contribution to the cartoons' quality and popularity. He also provided most of the voices for the

innumerable other characters that enlivened Warner's shorts over the decades, although Blanc was for many years the only performer to receive screen credit for "voice characterizations" in Warner cartoons!

Early in 1941, Blanc signed an exclusive contract with Schlesinger for cartoons—previously he had worked for Lantz, MGM, Columbia, and even once for Disney—but he continued to perform in radio, functioning as a kind of one-man repertory company for Jack Benny, Burns and Allen, Abbott and Costello, Judy Canova, and others. Yet Blanc's uniqueness can be indicated in other ways. Once, Blanc recalls, he was examined by a leading throat specialist. And the specialist came back to him and said that he had seen throat muscles like Blanc's in only one other man: Enrico Caruso.

Blanc's first lasting contribution to the studio was to create a new voice for Porky Pig, who, as Schlesinger's fledgling star, had become the featured player in the "Looney Tunes" series. In his first films, Porky had passed through many forms, most of them altogether grotesque. But the character was attractively redesigned by Bob Clampett and his unit when Clampett was elevated to direction in 1937. Early in 1937, Leon Schlesinger assigned Clampett, Chuck Jones, and such other staffers as Jack Carey and Lu Guarnier to work at the Beverly Hills Studio of Ub Iwerks, who, as an early Disney animator, had done the first drawings of Mickey Mouse. Schlesinger had subcontracted with the financially ailing Iwerks to produce Porky cartoons, but after completing two of these films, Iwerks temporarily went out of business. Clampett then took over much of this crew when it came back to the Warner Bros. lot.

Assisted by Blanc's appealing new voice, Clampett directed a string

Above: *Publicity photograph of Mel Blanc, c. 1945. Ironically, Blanc, the voice of Bugs Bunny, had adverse reactions to carrots when he had to crunch them for the cartoons' dialogue. "They make my throat tighten up to the point where I don't sound like the character,"* he says. *Celery, apples, and other produce were tried as replacements, but nothing sounds quite like a carrot. So Blanc saved his carrot-crunchings to be recorded last, and had them spliced in where necessary.* Below: *Promotional drawing by Mel Millar from* Porky's Super Service, *1937, the second of two cartoons produced by Ub Iwerks for Leon Schlesinger.*

Publicit Porky Super Service

## The Early Chuck Jones

*One of Chuck Jones' "Curious Puppies."*

In ironic contrast to his later work with the Road Runner and other characters, Chuck Jones' first cartoons were the most Disneyesque that Warner Bros. released after the departure of Harman and Ising. Two films from 1940 explicitly attempted to engage identification from children. The first, *Mighty Hunters,* animated characters from James Swinnerton's popular "Canyon Kiddies" newspaper strip; intended to be the first of a series, the Canyon Kiddies never returned at Warner's. Swinnerton himself painted some 50 backgrounds of desert vistas for this cartoon, perhaps the first time that oil painting was used in animation. And *Tom Thumb in Trouble* was the most Disney-like of all Warner cartoons; virtually humorless, this sentimental tale even boasts an original song.

*Model sheets by Robert Givens.* Right: *From* Tom Thumb in Trouble. Below: *From* Mighty Hunters.

of black-and-white "Looney Tunes" that lifted Porky to significantly greater popularity. The reason was simple: From the outset, Clampett's cartoons were terrifically funny and imaginative. Clampett was the studio's foremost devotee of post-Averyan all-out zaniness, but his touch was lighter than his mentor's, his sense of the absurd freer, his humor more highly spirited and unrestrained. If physician Daffy Duck wants to call a conference in a hospital run by Clampett (in 1938's *The Daffy Doc*), Daffy need only conk himself on the head with a mallet and consult with the three ghost images of himself that soon appear. Or if trainer Porky sees that his prize-fighter Daffy is in trouble in the Clampett ring (in *Porky and Daffy*), then Porky need only call out, "Get on your bicycle, Daffy!" for the duck to hop upon an imaginary bike and pedal wildly around the ring while clobbering his opponent. "I'm so crazy, I don't know it's impossible!" Daffy yowls.

But it was in 1938's *Porky in Wackyland* that Clampett officially mapped out his own mind-set. In this cartoon, aviator Porky penetrates "Darkest Africa" in search of the coveted dodo bird, and lands at the border of the mysterious, uncharted Wackyland. There, a sign warns, "It

RAY KATZ prod   L.T. #13 — The DO-DO BIRD

From Bob Clampett's black-and-white "Looney Tunes." Top: *Model sheet from* Porky in Wackyland, *1938.* Far left and left: *Layout drawings from* Porky in Wackyland. Bottom left: *Model drawing from* Kristopher Kolumbus, Jr., *1939. Clampett has cited this character as a forerunner of his Cecil the Seasick Sea Serpent.* Bottom right: *Layout drawing by John Carey from* We, the Animals, Squeak, *1941.*

Can Happen Here"—and forever declares the Clampett manifesto. Porky then enters a wildly surreal world, where the skewed Dali-like landscape turns out to be a stage prop and the sun only rises with help from a team of acrobats. An elevator car drops in from the heavens and lifts off again, while the Warner Bros. "W-B" shield, supporting the reclining dodo, zooms in from a vanishing point before dwindling back to a speck. Further, the place abounds in flora and fauna rather unlikely to be seen elsewhere, including a broad-billed duck who Jolsons across the screen yapping "Mammy! Mammy!" a creature whirling about in perpetual self-struggle (because one end of its sausagelike body is a dog and the other is a cat), a goggle-eyed rabbitoid swinging on a swing that is suspended from his own ears, a drummer who crashes away atop a tulip, and many other denizens even more difficult to describe. The lord of cartoon misrule, Clampett established conclusively that in animation, realism is irrelevant.

Quite the opposite sense, however, informs the early work of Chuck Jones, the last of the four great directors to rise at Schlesinger's in the second half of the 1930s (all of whom were under thirty years old when they received their appointments). In 1938, Jones took over Frank Tashlin's unit after Tashlin left the studio to work elsewhere in Hollywood.

For several years, Jones' cartoons stayed heavily under the Disney influence; the director favored slower and atmospheric pacing, more deliberate character movement, realistic backgrounds, and a striving for "cuteness" throughout. "It was a learning time for me," said Jones. "I wasn't quite satisfied with the quality of the animation then. That's why so many of my early pictures are so damn slow—I was trying to find out how to do it." Sometimes charming, sometimes cloying, these cartoons became a bit brighter when they featured Jones' first star, a talkative little mouse called Sniffles. (Sniffles' squeaky voice was provided by Bernice Hansen, who also spoke for many of the other small, cuddly characters of the 1930s and early '40s.)

*Sniffles, Chuck Jones' first star, was introduced in 1939's* Naughty But Mice, *in which he has a "code in da nose"— thus his name. His last appearance came in 1946's* Hush My Mouse. *By that time, Sniffles was thoroughly Clampett-tized, a satirization of the cuteness that he was originally intended to embody.* Above: *Animation drawing from* The Unbearable Bear, *1943.* Right: *Model sheet, 1940.*

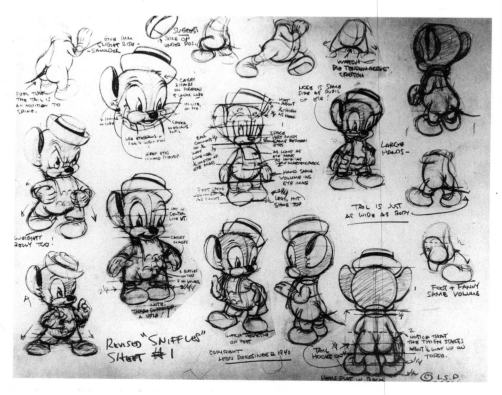

## Hardaway and Dalton

Veteran Schlesinger Studio personnel, Joseph Benson "Bugs" Hardaway and Cal Dalton directed as a team during Friz Freleng's interval at MGM, from 1937–1939. Previously, Hardaway had been a gag writer and solo director, and Dalton a ranking animator. Relatively unsophisticated in their approach to cartoon-making, Hardaway and Dalton's most significant contribution to the studio was their introduction and development of the formative Bugs Bunny, and the bequeathing of Hardaway's nickname to the hare. Around 1940, Hardaway left Schlesinger's to write for Walter Lantz and other studios; he died in 1957 at the age of 62. Cal Dalton for many years returned to the rank of animator.

Above: *Layout drawing from* Katnip Kollege, *1938, the first cartoon that Hardaway and Dalton directed together.* Below: *Cel of the early Bugs Bunny joy-buzzing his hunter, from* Hare-um Scare-um, *1939.* Left: *Drawings by Mel Millar.* Top: *Character study for* Hobo Gadget Band *1939; in the finished film, these derelict cats became derelict dogs.* Bottom: *Early story sketch for* Fagin's Freshmen, *1939.*

Above: *Animation drawing of Porky Pig from* Old Glory, *1939. Below: Model sheet by Robert Givens of the Bookworm from* Sniffles and the Bookworm, *1939.*

Years later, Jones spoke of being "pretty scared" of directing his first cartoon, and traces of this appear in much of his early work. A remarkable number of his initial films deal with characters, usually small or infantile, who end up in an environment that terrifies them, or who have to go through some manner of harrowing initiation. Jones' opus one, for example, *The Night Watchman*, tells of a kitten substituting for his father in guarding a kitchen, and of the gang of ruffian mice who bullyrag him. *Ghost Wanted*, from 1940, concerns itself with a naive and gentle boy ghost who, after reading the "Haunt Ads," applies for a job to spook a mysterious mansion; but he ends up the spooked party when a jolly adult-ghost "personnel director" tests his mettle. (The adult ghost's resonant, chuckling voice—also used in several other cartoons of this period—was provided by Tex Avery.) An unknown house is again the fearful setting in *Dog Gone Modern* (1939), when two small dogs—who played in several early Jones efforts—wander into a model "home of the future" and are assailed by appliances, gadgets, and robotlike servants that seem to have minds of their own. Later that same year, *Curious Puppy* brought the same doggie duo to an amusement park after hours— whereupon the master switch is thrown and the park springs to frightening, incomprehensible life.

Several other early Jones works involve characters who are struggling to achieve some sort of mastery—again, perhaps a reflection of Jones' initial insecurities. One winning example is 1939's *Old Glory*, which was commissioned by Warner Bros. as a counterpart to a series of live-action shorts dealing with American history and patriotism. Here,

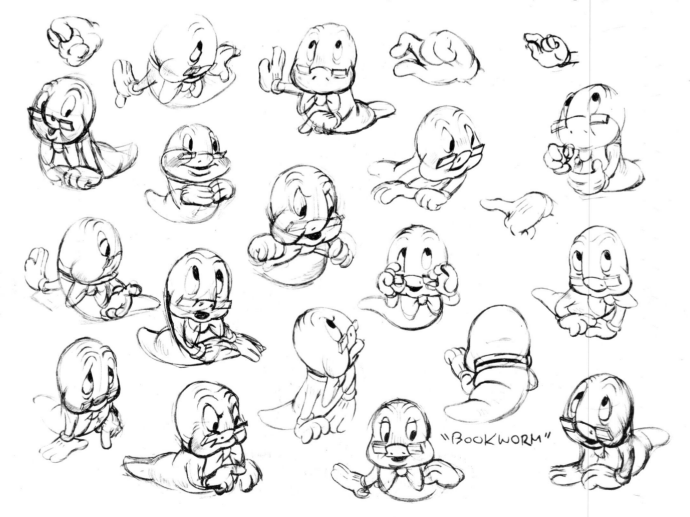

"BOOKWORM"

Left: *Model sheet of Daffy Duck from* You Ought to Be in Pictures, *1940.* Top: *Model sheet by Robert Givens of the adult ghost from* Ghost Wanted, *1940. Givens has said that this character is a caricature of director Chuck Jones.* Above and below: *Model poses by Charles Thorson from* Little Lion Hunter, *1939.* Above: *Inki.* Below: *The Minah Bird.*

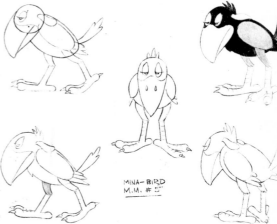

Porky has difficulty learning to recite the Pledge of Allegiance and, in his tongue-tied vexation, prefers simply to drop off to sleep; when he stretches out upon the ground, a towering Uncle Sam materializes, takes Porky by the hand, and recounts the story of America for him. The film makes good use of montage, rotoscoping, and dramatic frame compositions. One of the few wholly gagless Warner shorts, *Old Glory* also enjoys another distinction: It later became a favorite at New York's Fillmore East rock-concert house, where it would be screened between acts. The late sixties audiences, it seems, enjoyed a film that ends with a pig saluting the flag.

But the early Jones was not, of course, entirely outside Warner's nascent tradition of smart-assed irreverence. Even so innocuous a barnyard fable as his 1939 *The Good Egg* makes room for the house style: when a desperate, childless hen decides to take her own life, she leaves a sign on her nest that reads "Goodbye, cruel world"—before returning to add another advertising "Space to Let." And with the same year's *Little Lion Hunter*, Jones launched a series of five cartoons starring an African

*Cels from Tex Avery's* Hollywood Steps Out, *1941.* Above: *Edward G. Robinson.* Right: *Peter Lorre.* Opposite: *Clark Gable.*

boy named Inki, who in later outings returned to hunt the enigmatic Minah Bird (a beaky thing that hops around in time to Mendelssohn's "Fingal's Cave Overture"). Eerily, inexplicably funny, the dialogueless Inki and Minah Bird cartoons foreshadow Jones' great pantomime series, the Road Runner.

In October 1937, Friz Freleng left Schlesinger's to direct cartoons for MGM, who had offered him $375 in weekly salary versus Schlesinger's $250. Freleng's chores were taken over by Ben Hardaway and Cal Dalton, and they directed several funny, scampish cartoons. But in 1939, Freleng was back—MGM had discontinued the "Captain and the Kids" series he had been hired for—and he soon made one of the very best of his shorts. *You Ought to Be in Pictures* is typically Frelengian in story line, as Daffy goads Porky into trying to enter the more illustrious world of feature films (so that Daffy can move up to being Schlesinger's big star). But it is unique for Warner's in that the characters play out this scenario in a live-action setting. To wonderful effect, the cartoon combines live-action footage with the animated characters, so that Porky walks into Leon

Above: *Model sheet from* The Crackpot Quail, *1941.* Below: *Title cel from* Porky's Preview, *1941.* Below right: *Model sheet from* Of Fox and Hounds, *1940.*

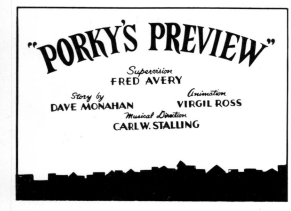

Schlesinger's office and asks the man himself to release him from his cartoon contract. ("He'll be back," Schlesinger confidently asides.) Porky then takes his putt-putt roadster through the traffic-clotted streets of Hollywood, and uses ploy after ploy to get into a live-action sound stage—before being given the quick heave by a burly crew member. It's a delightful example of the believability of the Warner characters—the sense that they are real beings capable of interacting with the real world—and a tribute to the technical abilities of their creators.

Elsewhere, Tex Avery's satirical eye was taking aim at just about everything. With 1938's *The Isle of Pingo Pongo*, Avery inaugurated an extensive series of sham travelogues and documentaries in which an off-screen narrator (usually Robert C. Bruce) spouts platitudes about people, places, or events before the animated world plays havoc with his clichés. Thus, in *Detouring America*, a mighty geyser has the courtesy to use a spittoon, while in *Screwball Football* a player "fading back" dissolves into invisibility. And in *Cross Country Detours*, a placid marshland frog "croaks" with help from the gun he brings to his head. *Pingo Pongo* was also Warner's first "spot gag" cartoon, in which related bits of humor are separated by brief blackouts—a precursor to the structures of obsession in the Road Runner series.

And so it went on. After spoofing amateur performers (in *Hamateur Night*), celebrity affectations (*Hollywood Steps Out*), Mayflower mythology (*Johnny Smith and Poker-Huntas*), gangster movies (the brilliant *Thugs With Dirty Mugs*), and much more, Avery provided the natural conclusion to his satirizing and self-reflexive tendencies by lampooning himself. In 1941's *Porky's Preview*, a prideful Porky holds a screening for a barnful of animals of an animated cartoon that he has drawn. ("It wasn't hard," the porcine *auteur* tells his audience, "because, shucks, I'm an artist.") Yet when finally unveiled, Porky's magnum opus

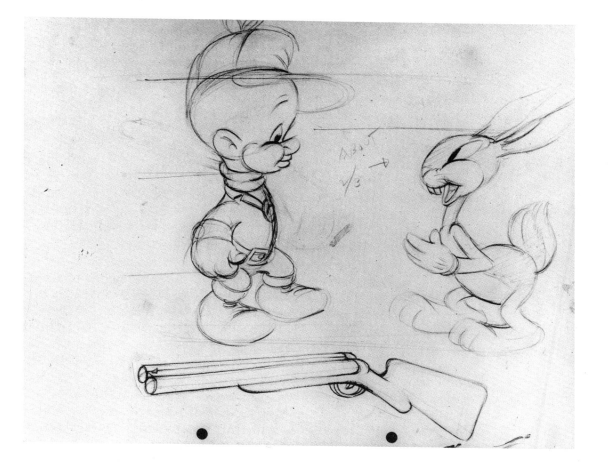

*The arrival: model sheet by Robert Givens from* A Wild Hare, *1940.*

leaves something to be desired: startlingly primitive, it consists solely of infantile stick figures moving erratically over bare white backgrounds, in short sequences of songs, dances, and marches. And it has its share of misfires, to boot: at a few points, the rickety music stops and a scrawly Mexican dancer is crossed out on screen; then the music and the corrected animation begin anew. Well, it probably wasn't only the Disney employees in the audience who were shocked to see this gleeful trashing of all cartoon conventions.

In 1940, Avery came up with something else that left audiences talking. During the two previous years, the studio had released four cartoons featuring a rapscallion rabbit, a character much reminiscent of the early Daffy Duck in his boundering flightiness. But for a fifth rabbit film, *A Wild Hare*, Avery redesigned the character both outwardly and inwardly, and made history. Avery replaced the rabbit's craziness with a measure of unflappable cool; he also endowed him with a mental savvy that had never been seen before in cartoons. Within one year, the immediately popular Bugs Bunny would help transform the Warner studio, indeed the whole of animation. Such is the magic of star power.

Bugs, in fact, was so evidently a winner that Avery tried to re-create the rabbit's essence in two other characters, hoping to repeat his powerful success. In 1940's *Of Fox and Hounds* and 1941's *The Crackpot Quail*, a fox and a quail respectively speak with a most Bugsian voice and act in a most Bugsian manner. They even redo some of the rabbit's very own routines. Yet they didn't catch on like their model. Such is the inscrutable magic of star power.

*The Warner artists' new sureness of line and expression were present in their model sheets.* Below and bottom: *Drawings by Tom McKimson from the model sheet for Bob Clampett's* The Old Grey Hare, *1944.* Below right: *Sketches from Chuck Jones'* From Hand to Mouse, *1944. The mouse in this cartoon shares the design of Jones' Hubie and Bertie.*

From *A Wild Hare*'s first "What's up, Doc?" the Warner animators knew they had something. The earlier rabbit cartoons had, as well, been extremely well received, but there was something in the formulation of the new Bugs Bunny that was unprecedented. Audiences *adored* the rabbit's brashness and wit. For the first time, here was a cartoon character that was hip and on top of things, rather than being childlike or simpletonish. Avery had created a funny cartoon animal who, unlike all others, was an adult, and had an adult's mental wherewithal. (Ironically, Bugs was the very antithesis of Daffy, the Warner sensation that had preceded him. Whereas Daffy would fly into dithers of derangement for no reason at all, Bugs maintained perfect control even with a hunter's shotgun parting his hair. Throughout the forties, this was the polarity off of which Warner's played: elements of craziness clashing with elements of full control.) And the audiences' more fervent responses to the new rabbit character reinforced the Warner artists—giving them the confidence to pursue their own paths, which in turn helped consolidate the many advances that had been developing throughout the studio since 1936.

Baby Buggsy Bunny

**Opposite**
*Cel of Bugs Bunny from Friz Freleng's* Slick Hare, *1947.*

By 1945, Bugs Bunny's stature was such that The New York Times—*not a newspaper to jump on passing fads*—published a feature profile of the rabbit in its Sunday "Arts" section. "There would appear to be enough evidence on hand to substantiate the opinion of Edward Selzer, chief of the Warner's cartoon studio, that 'Bugs is the most popular cartoon character on the screen today,' The Times *said on July 22, 1945. "Mr. Selzer and the others also are proud of the service record supplied by the United States Marine Corps for Bugs. His impertinent likeness serves as the insignia for many branches of the armed services, including the hospital ship U.S.S. Comfort. Bugs and his uneaten carrot were painted on the lead Liberator bomber that made the first attack on Davao, which started this country's march back to the Philippines."*

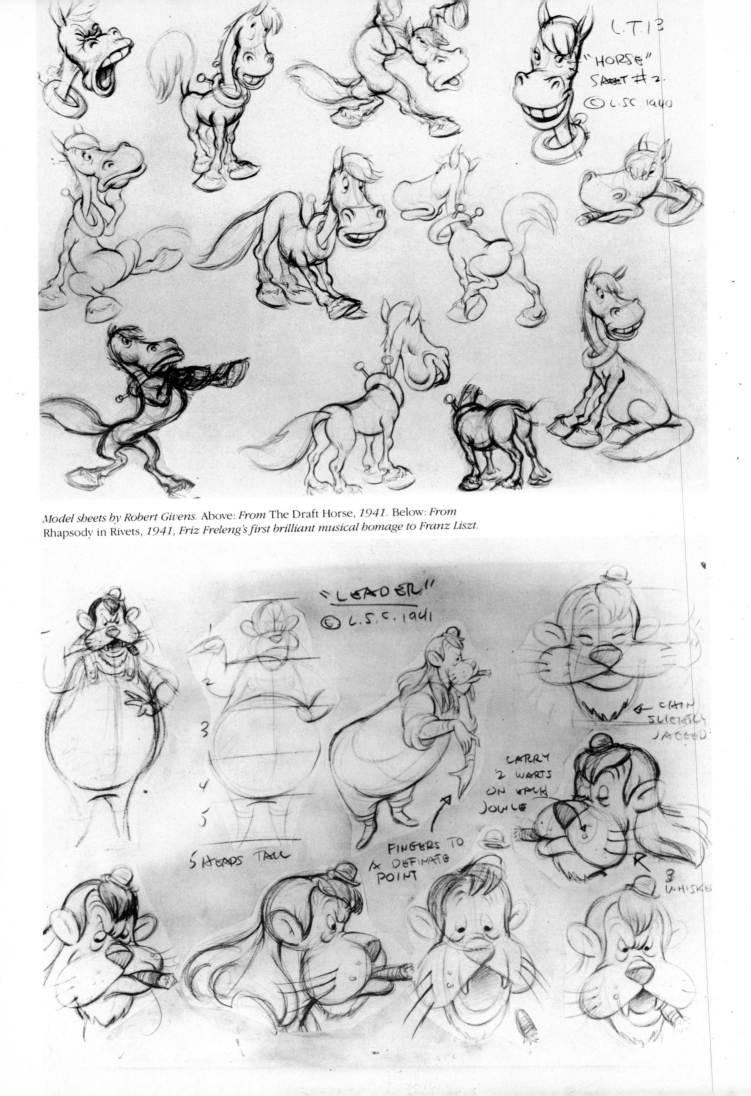

*Model sheets by Robert Givens.* Above: *From* The Draft Horse, *1941.* Below: *From*
Rhapsody in Rivets, *1941, Friz Freleng's first brilliant musical homage to Franz Liszt.*

Moreover, now that the spirit was willing, finally the flesh was able. By 1941, the Warner artists had mastered the drawing and movement skills that were needed to support their expanding visions. This had been a stumbling block for years: many gags in Avery's cartoons, for example, seem better in conception than in execution, and studio employees were known to say that Avery's often hilarious ideas frequently shed much of their humor when put through the process of animation. But this was no longer the case. The Warner cartoonists had achieved an easy facility with the kind of caricature (for all cartoon animals are caricatures of their models) that served as the foundation of American theatrical animation.

And Warner's had very many brilliant animators. It is perhaps unfair to single out individual artists among the dozens who worked at Warner's, many of them for two or three decades, but the directors did acknowledge their heavy hitters, and earmarked key scenes for them in each cartoon. Rod Scribner, for instance, handled most of the frenzied, hyperactive movement—all those thrashing limbs and gnashing teeth and knotting brows—in Bob Clampett's cartoons of the 1940s. Animating for Avery, Clampett, then many years for Freleng, Virgil Ross brought great elegance and expressivity to his solidly drawn work. And Ken Harris animated many marvelous speed scenes and dances for Chuck Jones over the course of some twenty years.

The best evidence of the Schlesinger animators' new mastery can be found in two of the studio's last releases of 1941. In *Rhapsody in Rivets*, Friz Freleng based an entire cartoon on Liszt's "Hungarian Rhapsody No. 2" for the first time, using it as accompaniment to a group of animals building a skyscraper. Standing at the front of the construction site, the foreman "conducts" from his blueprints, directing his workers to piece together the tower in a high-rise brick-and-girder ballet. And *Wabbit Twouble* was Bob Clampett's first turn with the Bugs and Elmer pairing: Elmer visits "Jellostone" National Park for some "west and wewaxation at wast!"— but encounters a wabbit intent on vexing that vacation urge.

Both cartoons are greatly inventive and funny. But beyond that, they have a precision and ease of execution that give their humor much greater punch. The cartoons' timing has become sharper, and a bit swifter; there is no sense of gags fighting technical shortcomings. And, as important, the drawing itself has improved. Rather than being simplistic, all-purpose caricatures, the characters in these cartoons each seem to be individual creations, with distinct attitudes and personalities that are reflected in their every aspect—movement, design, facial expression. One feels as if the characters existed before they were drawn, not that they were created by drawing: they have that kind of independent reality. And this new fineness of design and movement was the precondition for the radical breaks from the past that would set fire to the Schlesinger studio in 1942.

For this was indeed the watershed year for Warner cartoons. By 1942, ripeness was all: in addition to the cartoonists' newly matured abilities, both Mel Blanc's voices and Carl Stalling's music had grown crisper and more vigorous. In all corners of their production, the Warner cartoons achieved the brassiness and funniness that became their franchise. And movie audiences quickly picked up on this: In 1945, Bugs Bunny cartoons won the leading popularity index in their field, when they were named the number one short-subject (which included animation and live action) by the *Motion Picture Herald*'s poll of exhibitors in the United States and Canada. It was an honor that the rabbit would go on to repeat for sixteen consecutive years.

*Balletic grace captured in hasty sketches: Animator's roughs of Bugs Bunny as a ballerina, from Bob Clampett's* A Corny Concerto, *1943.*

## Beaky Buzzard

Juvenile and rube-like, Beaky Buzzard was introduced in Bob Clampett's 1942 *Bugs Bunny Gets the Boid*. At first, Clampett called him "The Snerd Bird" because his voice and manner were direct imitations of Edgar Bergen's "Mortimer Snerd" character. Thereafter, Clampett cast him in 1945's *The Bashful Buzzard*. On the whole, Beaky's career was distinctly stop-and-go: Although he appeared only in those two cartoons in the 1940s, he was treated in promotional materials, comic books, and merchandising as one of the studio's leading lights. Nevertheless, he disappeared from the screen after Clampett left Warner's, then was suddenly revived for a pair of cartoons released less than two months from each other in 1950, Friz Freleng's *The Lion's Busy* and Robert McKimson's *Strife with Father*. Thereafter, the character never again returned in a theatrical short. At first, Kent Rogers provided Beaky's voice, but the character was later taken over by Mel Blanc.

Above: *Model sheet by Tom McKimson of Beaky Buzzard and kin, from* The Bashful Buzzard. Below: *Background painting by Richard H. Thomas from* Strife with Father.

Two distinct strains fueled Warner Cartoons' coming of age around the Summer of '42. The first was the "liberation" of Chuck Jones from his early devotion to Disneyism. In May, the studio released Jones' *The Draft Horse*, the story of a farmer's plow horse who becomes inflamed with the idea of enlisting for the wartime draft. In demonstrating his patriotism for the draft board, the horse goes through some heavy histrionics about the glories of battle; and later, when he is mistakenly caught in a war exercise, the horse's terrified reactions are more exaggerated still. According to Jones, in this cartoon, "I discovered that I could make people laugh—and not just be amused. And that's a heady thing. You get so you *want* to make them laugh."

Indeed, the "heady" intoxication of making people laugh seemed to break Jones from his preoccupation with cuteness and sentimentality. It also emboldened him to try further experiments. Around this time, for example, Jones began using highly stylized backgrounds in his cartoons—background paintings that did not literally depict every fern frond or castle stone, as was required by the Disney school of realism, but which created a setting that could be as caricatured as the cartoon characters that inhabited it. Layout artist John McGrew was instrumental in suggesting and developing this approach, along with Eugene Fleury and Bernyce Polifka. Trees, then, could be jagged washes of color, while other features in the landscape need only be suggested by various abstract forms. For example, in Jones' 1943 *The Aristo-Cat*, a rich and pampered pussycat becomes terrified after his abused butler off and quits. And as the cat bolts fearfully around the house, howling his butler's name—"Meadows! Meadows!"—the backgrounds register his emotional turmoil with flat fields of bright red, or angular, slashing colors. In nearly expressionistic ways, the backgrounds embody the character's emotions in vibrant visual terms; they do not only establish a setting for them. "We began to realize that color and backgrounds could have an enormous effect on the film," Jones said.

But perhaps the pivotal cartoon in Jones' early breakthrough is 1942's *The Dover Boys*, for here the director coupled his stylized backgrounds with equally stylized movement. The cartoon is a quite hilarious spoof of Gay Nineties melodramas, telling of three dashing blades at Pimento University ("Good old P.U.") who struggle to keep innocent Dora Standpipe from the clutches of that "coward, bully, cad, and thief," Dan Backslide. In trying to capture the spirit of the 1890s, Jones devised an equivalent in animation of the daguerreotypes of that time: his characters move highly unnaturally, often in jumps from sharp pose to sharp pose; in no way do they attempt to imitate realistic motion.

It's a funny effect—but more important, it provided the finishing touch for the first cartoon since the rise of Disney in which the demands of realism were almost entirely banished. Movement and setting were all of a non-Disney piece. And people noticed: "New York was shocked," Jones has said, referring to Warner's distribution office in the East. "I don't think they would have released it at all, except that they had to have a picture." Later in the 1940s, some of the founders of the UPA studio (which produced the first, highly stylized Gerald McBoing Boing and Mister Magoo cartoons) cited the film as an inspiration for their innovations.

In short, an alternative had been expressed.

The second revelation of 1942 was the quantum leap made in the work of Bob Clampett. In 1941, Clampett had taken over much of Tex Avery's crew

*Cel of Bugs Bunny and Elmer Fudd from Friz Freleng's* Slick Hare, *1947.*

*Publicity drawing for* The Dover Boys.

when the latter accepted a more lucrative offer to direct at MGM. Clampett then began making higher-budgeted color cartoons, with stronger animators than had been his for his previous black-and-white films. (In fact, Clampett directed the first color "Looney Tune," 1942's *The Hep Cat*. A few more black-and-white "Looney Tunes" were made, but in 1943 the series went all color; thereafter, there was no difference between "Looney Tunes" and "Merrie Melodies" except for the series' titles and theme music.)

Now, graced with these new resources, Clampett quite literally exploded. He began pushing his cartoons to the limits of cartooniness—picking up their pace, energizing their characters, exaggerating their existing exaggerations, replacing any trace of gentleness with slapstick and clamor. Absurdity and aggressiveness were raised to preposterous levels; understatement and overstatement became the only statements; gags detonated like bomb blasts. If animation is an extension of live-action cinema, then Clampett was intent on extending it almost to the breaking point, to places where human bodies and emotions could not possibly go.

To support his increasingly high-pitched and boisterous work, Clampett developed drawing techniques that enabled his artists to intensify their depiction of vigorous action and violent emotion. As in Tex Avery's MGM cartoons, Clampett's characters' bodies are often pulled drastically out of shape, giving physical expression to states of mind that are as overblown and cartoony as the film world in which they exist. This is most clearly visible in what are known as cartoon "takes"—those split-second moments of violent reaction in which Clampett converts his characters' bodies into anatomical exclamation points. (This device, however, was later corrupted elsewhere, such as in dozens of Paramount Studio "Casper the Friendly Ghost" cartoons.) Elsewhere, Clampett's characters move with immense elasticity, their bodies stretching and squashing in ways that make them seem to throb with barely controllable life. This kind of violent distortion would never have been permissible at Disney's; it virtually forces viewers to acknowledge that what's on screen is a drawn image.

Clampett also pursued a similar no-holds-barred approach to his development of stories. "After I had decided what my story was, I used to conduct what I called a 'no-no' session," the director told Mike Barrier. "I would encourage each of us to think up the wildest, most impossible ideas imaginable, and no matter how wild the gags got, no, but no one was allowed to say, 'Oh, no!' Thus the name, a 'no-no.' "

The one cartoon that best sums up the Clampett sensibility—and, for that matter, the new brazenness of the entire studio—is Warner's first release of 1943, *Coal Black and de Sebben Dwarfs*. Notorious now, the cartoon is virtually a scene-by-scene, character-for-character send-up of the fabled Disney feature, as enacted by an all-black cast. (The film's regrettable ethnic element, it must be added, is indicative of some of the conventions of that time. Ethnic humor was commonplace in radio, vaudeville, theater, and movies, and all groups took their turn. In animation, where caricature is the name of the game, this was particularly true. But in the case of *Coal Black*, it does say something about the satiric streak running through the Warner studio.)

Often frenetically paced, *Coal Black* transposes the familiar fairy tale to a contemporary wartime setting, where gravel-voiced "Queenie" calls Murder Inc. to "black out So White" and so keep her from snaring Prince Chawmin'—a zoot-suited, ever-bopping jivester with dice for

# "COAL BLACK
## AND DE
## SEBBEN DWARFS"
### — BOB CLAMPETT — DIRECTOR —
*gh*

QUEENIE          COAL BLACK          DE PRINCE

Coal Black and de Sebben Dwarfs *is in many ways a shocking film—most conspicuously for its racist content. Yet it was the product of another time, when such objectionable caricature was done innocently and unthinkingly. Although its stereotypes are appalling now, the cartoon was made without an iota of mean-spiritedness and its brilliance of execution makes it essential for any consideration of the Schlesinger Studio's history. Above: Model sheet by Gene Hazelton. Left: Layout drawing of the castle.*

Right and below: *Background paintings by Eugene Fleury from* The Dover Boys, *1942; direction by Chuck Jones, layout by John McGrew.*

teeth. Raunchy and rude and unforgettable, the cartoon abounds with outlandish gags and slangy patter, and is almost a summation of early 1940s street culture. In fact, according to animator Virgil Ross, Clampett took his crew to "four or five" nightclubs in Los Angeles' black district to become better acquainted with the dancing and the atmosphere there. "He wanted to get ideas for the picture," said Ross. "It was the only time we ever did anything like that."

And ideas there are, in a rush: the cartoon contains references to, among others, the supply shortages of the war years, the popular music of the time, and the black entertainers of the age, and it takes an out-of-

*Clampettian distortion appears in a cartoon directed by one of his colleagues. From Friz Freleng's* A Hare Grows in Manhattan, *1947; animation drawings by Virgil Ross.*

nowhere snipe at Orson Welles' *Citizen Kane*. In 1943, this is a Warner Cartoon fairy tale: a jazz-stepping, modern-day mock-melodrama of un-alloyed lust and vengeance. And a film masterpiece in miniature.

For some time, a rumor has circulated that the gag-crammed *Coal Black* was intended to be a two-reeler, but was cut back. Clampett later said that this was not the case, and that Schlesinger had no designs to go beyond his one-reel shorts. Indeed, whenever Schlesinger was asked about doing a feature-length cartoon, he generally replied with a rude remark.

Through the advances of Jones and Clampett—Jones' willingness to strip away Disney conventions, Clampett's desire to drive them to feverish extremes—the Warner studio finalized its coming of age. Whereas before, the studio had been twitting the styles and traditions of Disney, it was still operating within the Disney universe; now the Warner directors had moved on to worlds of their own. While still using the same alphabet, they were speaking entirely different languages: Disney sought to warm viewers' hearts; Warner wanted to kick them in the funny bone.

At Warner's, the key was the directors' newly developed faith in what Chuck Jones has called "believability." The Warner directors realized that their films need not be realistic, in the Disney sense, but believable—capable of sustaining their artifices. Once that had been achieved, the directors could go literally anywhere. And by 1942, the studio had the technical abilities to go there seamlessly.

The result was the beginning of a remarkable period of cartoon making for Warner Bros. A Golden Age had been born. But from 1941 to 1948, this new Gold was largely tempered by the spirit of Bob Clampett; all of Warner's very individualistic directors came under the sway of Clampett's sense of fast and urgent and unrestrained. It's easy to see why: beginning in 1942, Clampett had a burst of brilliance that was the equal of any in American film history. By late 1942, his cartoons were consistently wonderful. And they just got better: by 1945, they could be astound-

## Bob Clampett

For many viewers, the films of Robert Clampett define what is exemplary in Warner Bros. cartoons. Stylistically predominant during Warner's first period of maturity, Clampett's commingling of newborn's innocence and ultraviolence brought cartoons that were howlingly funny and, seemingly, unselfconscious. But Clampett was a rigorous and disciplined artist; his overriding discipline, however, called for rupturing the disciplines that hemmed in mainstream animation. The way his characters virtually break out of their own bodies—through Clampett's surging, stretching animation—is a perfect correlate to the ways in which his stories attempt to break out of conventional trappings.

A playful, idiosyncratic man, Clampett also liked to contribute songs and sound effects to his films. One of his proudest vocal effects was the sliding "Bayoowhuup!" used at the end, and elsewhere, of many cartoons.

Above: *Clampett (center) with storymen Melvin "Tubby" Millar and Warren Foster, c. 1940, in front of the story board for* Prehistoric Porky. *Below: Cels and background from* Porky's Hero Agency, *1937. Set in ancient Greece, the cartoon tells of Porky Karkus fighting a Gorgon whose glance turns people into* stone. *Among her victims apparently, were members of Clampett's unit at the time, here caricatured as forming the picket fence. From left to right: Lu Guarnier, Robert "Bobo" Cannon, John Carey, Ernest Gee, Bob Clampett, and Chuck Jones.*

### Opposite
*A typically energetic sequence from Clampett's* The Hep Cat, *1942, the first "Looney Tune" made in color; animation drawings by Vivie Risto.*

PICKET FENCE

ing. His varied and hilarious cartoons could not help influencing his peers.

Robert Clampett (1913–84) joined the Harman–Ising studio in 1931 and was proud of having worked on the first year of "Merrie Melodies" ever made. A lover of cartoons, comics, and puppetry since his boyhood in Los Angeles, he brought a sort of childlike, bright-eyed eagerness to his work as a director years later. In fact, many of Clampett's characters are childlike: they behave with an infantile lack of inhibition, and are often drawn with infantlike proportions—large heads (with large crania), large eyes, large rumps. (One of Clampett's favorite bits is to have a character stop and chirp, "I'm only three- and-a-half years old.")

The clearest example of Clampett's infantilism is the character of Tweety, the bite-size, baby-talking bird who first appeared in Clampett's 1942 *A Tale of Two Kitties*. But the characters needn't all be Tweety-tiny: for the same year's *Horton Hatches the Egg*, the infantile character is made more humorous by being humongous. For this memorable short, Clampett persuaded Schlesinger to buy the film rights to the popular Dr. Seuss tale, resulting in the only Warner cartoon to be adapted from a book. And here, large elephant Horton is as innocent and trusting as a babe ("I meant what I said and I said what I meant, an elephant faithful 100 percent") when he takes a bored bird's place sitting in her nest, or sings the nonsensical "The Hut-Sut Song."

**Overleaf:**
*Cels and background from* Horton Hatches the Egg.

Like many precocious children, one thing that Clampett particularly enjoyed was tastelessness. As Greg Ford has noted, Clampett's affection for sick or black humor had no rivals in animation until Ralph Bakshi and *Fritz the Cat*. And his enthusiasm for off-color gags is still talked about within the industry. In 1943's *A Corny Concerto*, for example, Clampett lampoons Disney's *Fantasia*, with Elmer Fudd standing in for both Stokowski on the podium and narrator Deems Tayor ("Gweetings, music wovers!" Elmer beams, before his ultra-formal black-tie attire rebels on him). But rather than animating graceful Disneyesque frolics, Clampett has Bugs, Porky, and hound stumble about in death throes to Strauss' "Tales of the Vienna Woods." Or in the early *Rover's Rival* (1937), an ancient, emaciated dog is commanded to roll over, but his tortured and creaky back-and-forth rocking becomes a drawn-out arthritic ordeal. And *An Itch in Time* (1943) finds Elmer's house dog sent into conniptions by a hungry flea, who uses a jackhammer, a drill, a pickax, dynamite, nitro, and other assaulters to prepare his fleshly meal. The cartoon also contains a gag that Clampett said had been put in for the studio's amusement, was supposed to have been cut out, but somehow wasn't: At one point, the dog caroms around the room with his derriere dragging on the ground, to relieve the exploding fireworks that the flea has set off on his rump; he then stops dead and says, "Hey, I better cut this out. I might get to like it," before panting happily and scooting off again. Fun with friction.

But Clampett's favorite ploy was to lead his stories to fugue states—hallucinations, dreams, or, better, nightmares. Here he could unleash his passion for surreal imagery and racing tempos, and justify his credo that animation should ignite the screen in ways that live action can't. In 1943's *Tin Pan Alley Cats*, a Fats Waller caricature of a cat passes up the spiritual calm of Uncle Tomcat's Mission and struts into the Kit Kat Club right next door, where he exhorts a smoky-hot jazz trumpeter to "Send me outta dis world!" And the bellowing musician does: after lofting little Fats way into the air with peals from his straining horn, the world bursts, and Fats is flung into a wackier version of Porky's Wackyland, where a pair of spooky lips fill the horizon—and boom like God's

*From* An Itch in Time. Above: *The dog strikes back.* Top: *"Hey, I better cut this out. I might get to like it."*

Right: *Animation drawing of Porky Pig, who thinks he has been shot; from* A Corny Concerto.

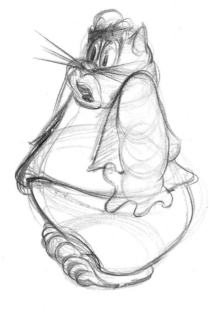

judgment—and Stalin pummels Hitler while doing a Russian dance. In *The Big Snooze* (1946), Elmer has had enough of his never-ending grief chasing Bugs Bunny, so he tears up his contract with Warner Bros. and goes off to sleep—whereupon Bugs invades his slumber (after singing a tune called "Someone's Rocking My Dreamboat") and splashes it with "Nightmare Paint." Inspired by reading a book entitled *A Thousand and One Arabian Nightmares*, Bugs conjures such traumas as having Elmer tied to a railroad track and run over by a chugging stream of baby bunnies, then being dressed in drag and hurled into a pack of Hollywood-and-Vine wolves ("Have any of you girls had an experience like this?" the bewigged and lipsticked Fudd appeals to the audience). Sufficiently affrighted, Elmer wakes, pieces together his contract, and gladly gets back to work being humiliated in rabbit-pursuit.

But the pinnacle of Clampett's phantasmagorias was reached in the astonishing *The Great Piggy Bank Robbery*, from 1946. Here, Daffy Duck, in an excess of joy over receiving a comic book of Chester Gould's Dick Tracy, inadvertently conks himself on the head and dreams himself to be that fearless de-tec-i-tive, "Duck Twacy." Taking up a magnifying glass—which doesn't prevent him from walking smack into Sherlock Holmes—he sets out to discover who's been stealing everyone's beloved piggy banks. Transported to the gangsters' lair, he encounters a host of hallucinatory, Chester Gould–inspired baddies—"Juke-Box Jaw," "Pickle Puss," "Eighty-Eight Teeth," "Hammerhead," and, gulp, "Neon Noodle"—in blistering scenes that perfectly capture a nightmare feel.

In a murky and uncertain underground setting, Clampett makes time and space contract and distend as Daffy squares off against the roaring, frightful villains, who sic their private airforce on him (the

*What all the roaring's about: model drawing of Daffy's depository from* The Great Piggy Bank Robbery.

planes are launched off a vast head of Gould's "Flattop" character) and continue their one-on-one assault. "Eraserhead" literally "rubs out" Daffy's body, after "Mouseman" turns out to be no squeak. And Clampett's rubbery, pulsing animation further destabilizes the film: at one point, after the massed monsters have all lunged at Twacy, Daffy's body shatters into tiny, writhing squiggles before he magically recombines and ma-chine-guns the goons topplingly down—a stunning piece of animation by Rod Scribner. With brilliant invention, Clampett expresses in ways that only animation can a kind of exhilarating, hilarious terror. And all this—and then some—is achieved in under seven minutes.

Yet Clampett's output during this period was sufficiently diverse as to defy any easy categorization. Other titles, all of them marvelously done, draw interest from their uniqueness or for the way they utilize studio traditions. All by itself, for example, is 1946's *Kitty Kornered*, a winter's tale that begins with Porky fighting to get his four cats out for the night. But when he finally succeeds, the quartet gains its revenge by staging an enactment of Orson Welles' "War of the Worlds" radio broad-cast—complete with bizarre little men from Mars who slip into bed with Porky, and four charging, sword-brandishing Teddy Roosevelts—that scares the stammering homeowner into the cold.

The same year's splendiferous *Book Revue*, in contrast, revives the studio's convention of bringing magazine and book covers to life. This time, Clampett weaves together celebrity-caricature illustrations—Benny Goodman is *The Pied Piper*, Frank Sinatra is *The Voice in the Wilderness*, Jimmy Durante's nose is *So Big*—along with the "Little Red Riding Hood" story *and* Daffy Duck doing a bravura turn as Danny Kaye (featuring a wild and delicious scat-sung warning to Red about the menace of the Wolf, courtesy of Mel Blanc). Dizzyingly skillful, the film was the last of its kind. Following years of things-coming-to-life Warner cartoons, after *Book Revue*, there was no reason to do more.

*Preliminary sketches from* Book Revue.

In many ways, Clampett was the right man for his time. His aggressiveness and lack of restraint fit the mood of the World War II years, when spirits were high and the entire country was in gear to strike out at an oppressor. At the Schlesinger studio, nearly half of the cartoons of the time in some way address the war, and often with a fierceness that reflects the tenor of the age. Friz Freleng's 1944 *Bugs Bunny Nips the Nips*, for

*War's savage fury: animation drawings by Virgil Ross from* Bugs Bunny Nips the Nips, *1944.*

**"RUSSIAN RHAPSODY"**

A MERRIE MELODIE CARTOON IN TECHNICOLOR

DISTRIBUTED BY *Warner Bros.*

A **LEON SCHLESINGER** PRODUCTION

*From* Russian Rhapsody. Top: *Promotional drawing.* Center: *Warner storyman Melvin "Tubby" Millar is caricatured as a gremlin in this animation drawing.* Above: *Animation drawing of one of "the little men who aren't there."*

example, takes the rabbit to an island for some squaring off with the Japanese (for instance, by driving a "Good Rumor" truck and selling Japanese soldiers ice-cream bars that conceal hand grenades); its battles can now be seen as vicarious morale-boosting propaganda. And in *The Ducktators* (1942), Hitler, Hirohito, and Mussolini are caricatured as barnyard fowl brutally vying for conquest (although the cartoon does contain a proper apology "to the nice ducks and geese who may be in the audience"). It was directed by Norm McCabe, a former Clampett animator who stepped up in 1941 when Clampett took over Avery's artists, and who went on to direct some fine, funny cartoons.

Predictably, the most explosive of the wartime cartoons are Clampett's. In 1943's *Falling Hare*, Bugs Bunny—first seen reading a tome entitled *Victory Through Hare Power*—encounters a nasty little gremlin, who gets the rabbit into an airplane and, with the help of banana peels, hairpin turns, and an endless free fall, gives Bugs about the worst case of motion sickness on record. In *Russian Rhapsody* (1944), a swarming mass of gremlins (many of whom are caricatures of Schlesinger staff members) sabotage Hitler's plane when Der Führer decides to personally pilot a bombing mission to Moscow; the teeming gremlins' zigzag approach to the flying aircraft, and their musical dismantling of it—while singing "We're the gremlins from the Kremlin" to the tune of "Orchechornya"—is a virtuoso piece of work. The frantic *Draftee Daffy* (1945) finds the duck rocketing right to hell to escape a bulb-headed little man from the draft board, carrying a letter with Daffy's name on it. And the uproarious *Baby Bottleneck* (1946), perhaps an anticipation of the postwar baby boom, features Porky and Daffy toiling on an assembly line that readies infant animals to be received by their parents; when an egg comes along that has no address, the shop systematically goes haywire in a hilarious mechanized nightmare.

Other extremely strong Wartoons were directed by Frank Tashlin, who returned to Schlesinger's after working for Disney and Columbia and replaced Norm McCabe. His comeback film, *Scrap Happy Daffy* (1943), contains a marvelously energetic, quickly cut sequence in which patriotic Daffy, defending some scrap metal from a hungry German goat, invokes the great ducks of American history and becomes transformed into a "Super American" duck. And *The Swooner Crooner* (1944) parodies work efforts on the American home front; at Porky Pig's "Flockheed Eggcraft" egg-laying plant, the chickens are inspired to mountainous productivity when Frank Sinatra and Bing Crosby (or chicken incarnations thereof) take to the farmyard stage. The moaning and shrieking bobby-soxer hens even raise their coops from the ground on top of their floods of eggs.

In addition to its customary cartoons, Schlesinger's also produced a number of special projects for the war. In 1942, Schlesinger released a three-minute fund-raiser directed by Bob Clampett in which Bugs dances and sings an Irving Berlin song called "Any Bonds Today?" After dressing as Uncle Sam and doing a blackface Al Jolson, Bugs is joined for the finale by Porky and Elmer. From 1943 to 1945, all of the Warner directors contributed to a series of more than twenty-five cartoons starring Private Snafu, a serviceman who lived up to his name (an acronym for "Situation Normal: All Fouled Up"). Commissioned by the United States Army, the black-and-white Snafu cartoons were included in wartime editions of "The Army-Navy Screen Magazine," a film program shown exclusively to American soldiers. The three- or four-minute cartoons consisted of instructional tales in which Snafu would commit a blunder or infraction,

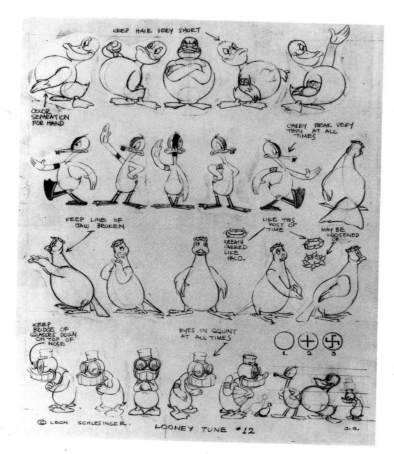

Above: *Animation drawing of Private Snafu from Bob Clampett's* Fighting Tools. *Left:* Model sheet by John Carey for The Ducktators. *Below:* Model sheet of the gremlin from Falling Hare.

## "BUGS BUNNY"

LEON SCHLESINGER

then learn the consequences of such errors. Topics included the importance of not leaking information and the value of caring for one's equipment. Because of their desire to develop a rapport with their military audience, these films tended to be a bit more risqué than typical theatrical cartoons—there were frequent "cheesecake" shots and an occasional "hell" would be heard—even though their storyboards had to be approved by the Pentagon. And Schlesinger produced a few similar "Hook" cartoons for the Navy.

These were to be among the last works produced by Leon Schlesinger. In July 1944, Schlesinger sold out to Warner's and headed for his yacht and retirement—although he continued to oversee the licensing of the characters until 1948—making what had informally been known as Warner Bros. Cartoons legally that. *Variety* reported that the selling price was "between $200,000 and $300,000." "Each of the directors got a gold pen and a gold pencil for all their years of working for Leon," Chuck Jones recalled. "And he had us to dinner at his house for the first time."

But if Schlesinger had been nettlesome, his replacement, Eddie Selzer, only served to make the Warner cartoonists nostalgic for their old boss. Edward Selzer (1893–1970) had been Warner's West Coast director of publicity from 1933 to 1937, and head of the studio's trailer and title department from then until his appointment as cartoon chieftain. According to many studio sources, his one qualification for the job was that

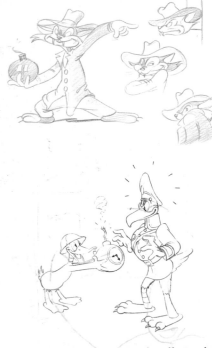

Above: *Layout drawing of Daffy Duck giving Uberkomt von Vultur "a little going-away present," from Friz Freleng's* Daffy the Commando, *1943.* Center: *Model sheet by Mel Millar from Norm McCabe's* Confusions of a Nutzy Spy, *1943.* Top: *Wartime promotion with Bugs Bunny.* Right: *Background painting by Richard H. Thomas from Frank Tashlin's* I Got Plenty of Mutton, *1944. During World War II, one hung a flag over one's door if someone in the household had been drafted.*

**WARNER BROS. PICTURES**

"Gate-Crashers Nothin', Doc—We're part of the Family now!"

he was born devoid of a sense of humor. "Jack Warner wanted to get him off the main lot because he fouled up on everything," said longtime background artist Richard H. Thomas.

In terms of physical description, Chuck Jones has noted that Selzer bore a distinct resemblance to Mister Magoo. And as regards character, Jones tells of an incident that took place on one unexceptional day. "A bunch of us were just sitting around laughing it up, when we looked over and saw Selzer standing and glowering in the doorway," Jones recalls. "And then he said, 'And just what the hell has all this laughter got to do with making animated cartoons?'" This is what is called inspired leadership.

Yet at this point, even Eddie Selzer couldn't staunch his crew's overflowing fertility. In the first five months of 1945, Warner's introduced three characters that would each become major stars in the cartoon galaxy: Pepé Le Pew, who first appeared in Chuck Jones' *Odor-Able Kitty*; Sylvester, in Friz Freleng's *Life With Feathers*; and Yosemite Sam, in Freleng's *Hare Trigger*. The depth of the filmmakers' creativity at the time applied not only to their stories and situations; their characters, as well, were richly conceived, ingenious, and greatly appealing—both the emerging stars and the continuing stream of bit players.

Yet a fourth future celebrity was created in 1946, with the debut of Foghorn Leghorn in *Walky Talky Hawky*. This was the fourth cartoon directed by Robert McKimson, who took over Frank Tashlin's unit after Tashlin departed the studio to pursue a career in live action. McKimson (1911–77) had joined Harman–Ising in 1930; his ability to endow characters with both suppleness and solidity led him to become a top animator for Jones, Avery, and lastly Clampett, for whom he animated many gorgeous and deeply expressive Bugs Bunny scenes. In fact, McKimson's feel for the character was so strong that in 1943 Clampett had him draw a model sheet of Bugs that is still considered the rabbit's finest realization.

As a director, McKimson's first films bring a Clampett-like exuberance to staging that accentuates flourishes of animation; his characters often ham it up, with broad gestures that recall the grandstanding of vaudevillians. And his stories, then being written by witty Warren Foster, have a rakish sassiness: in McKimson's first cartoon, *Daffy Doodles* (1946), the duck ushers in the age of graffiti by painting mustaches on every available Manhattan surface (and some that are not so available: at one point, Daffy brushes a mustache in midair, so that when pursuing

Above: *Painting by Richard H. Thomas from* Daffy Doodles. *Below: Animation drawing from* Acrobatty Bunny.

policeman Porky Pig runs by it gets plastered on his lip). *Acrobatty Bunny* (1946) pits Bugs against a lion on the day the circus comes to town (and features the rabbit singing a smashing version of "Laugh, Clown, Laugh" while wearing the operatic attire of *Pagliacci*). 1947's *The Birth of a Notion* begins with Daffy conning a doltish dog into letting him stay in his house for the winter, only to find that the home's owner is mad scientist Peter Lorre—heavy breathing and all—then looking for a duck's wishbone for an experiment. And *A Lad in His Lamp* (1948) finds Bugs doing business with a testy genie who, when the rabbit rubs his lamp, at one point springs out in the middle of a bath, then sitting at table with his dinner. ("Oh sweet spirits of camphor!" he objects, slapping his head. "Can't a man get any nourishment around here?").

The last Warner cartoon director of consequence, Arthur Davis, received his appointment in 1946, when the ambitious Bob Clampett left the studio to venture out on his own. After working on a few abortive projects, Clampett returned to his early interest in puppetry and brought the "Time for Beany" puppet show to daily television in 1949. The popular program ran for about eight years, picking up three Emmys and such fans as Groucho Marx and Albert Einstein along the way, before Clampett came back to cartoons with the animated "Beany and Cecil" show, which had its debut in January 1962.

Left: *Model sheet of the Hick mouse from*
A Hick, A Slick and a Chick, *1948.*
Below: *Background painting by Richard
H. Thomas of Peter Lorre's hidden
domestic laboratory; from* The Birth of
a Notion.

*From Robert McKimson's* Gorilla My Dreams, *1948, one of the most popular of all Warner Bros. Cartoons. Above:* Animation drawings of Mrs. Gorilla. Right: *Cel of Bugs Bunny with background.*

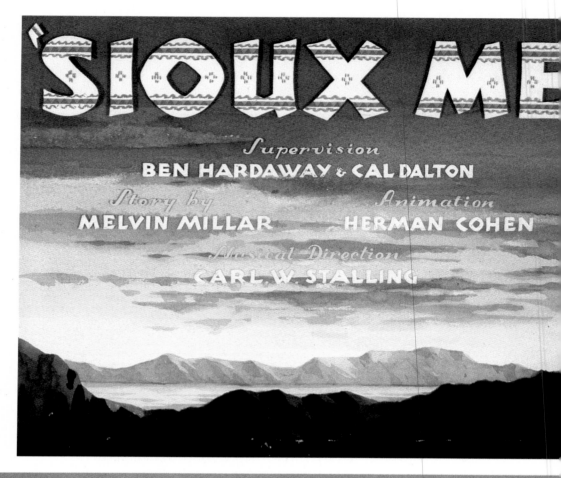

'SIOUX ME

*Supervision*
**BEN HARDAWAY** & **CAL DALTON**

*Story by* *Animation*
**MELVIN MILLAR** **HERMAN COHEN**

*Musical Direction*
**CARL W. STALLING**

Right: *The original title cels and background from Hardaway and Dalton's* Sioux Me, 1939. *When this cartoon was re-released in 1951 as a "Blue Ribbon" special, this image was cut and replaced by lettering only of the cartoon's title.* Below: *The initial establishing shot of* Bowery Bugs; *background painting by Philip De Guard.*

Left: *Model sheet by Tom McKimson from Arthur Davis'* The Foxy Duckling, *1947.*

**Overleaf**
*Background painting by Richard H. Thomas from* A Lad in His Lamp, *1948.*

Working with Clampett's crew, Davis proved adept at maintaining some of Clampett's fitful energy, if not his visionary genius. Nevertheless, there is a lovely stream-of-consciousness looseness to such Davis cartoons as *What Makes Daffy Duck* and *A Hick, a Slick and a Chick* (both 1948). And Davis' sole Bugs Bunny film, *Bowery Bugs* (1949), is a very funny retelling of the story of the mythical Steve Brody and his desperate leap from the Brooklyn Bridge.

But all this was coming toward the end of the period that saw the flowering of the Warner cartoon studio. Nearly all of its major characters were in place, and it had risen to become the unquestioned leader in short-subject animation. It was producing more cartoons than any other studio, and the other shops rarely approached Warner's quality and consistency. By any measure, Warner's cartoons were the most popular. In fact, so great was the demand for Warner cartoons that, in September 1943, the studio began a program of re-releasing some of its older titles, at a rate of 13 per yearly season. Identified on screen by an introductory panel showing a small trophy and a "Blue Ribbon" award, these releases are still commonly available. (Unfortunately, for many years the "Blue Ribbon" cartoons were released shorn of all their opening credits, except for the films' titles. Such masterpieces as Bob Clampett's *Book Revue* are now in general distribution without any acknowledgment of the director, or any of the other artists, who created them—to those artists' deep chagrin. Happily, Warner Bros. later changed this policy.)

In 1947, the studio received its first nod from the Motion Picture Academy when Friz Freleng's *Tweetie Pie* won the cartoon Oscar. And there was expansion into other fields. In the summer of 1941, the first "Looney Tunes and Merrie Melodies" comic book was published; its strong sales spawned separate comic-book series featuring Bugs Bunny, Porky Pig, and many other characters, imprints, and combinations. The Warner troops also did their bit in the war. "During World War Two, I personally drew over 150 Bugs Bunny insignias for different branches of the armed services," Robert McKimson said in 1972. "Another time, during a Bond Ralley, I drew a picture of Bugs for a lady for five thousand dollars." And in 1950, the studio provided the inspiration for a novelty recording that became a nationwide hit, when Tweety (AKA Mel Blanc) sung a Warren Foster lyric entitled "I Taut I Taw a Puddy-Tat." "I got a platinum record for it," crowed Blanc.

In short, a Golden Age was in full glow.

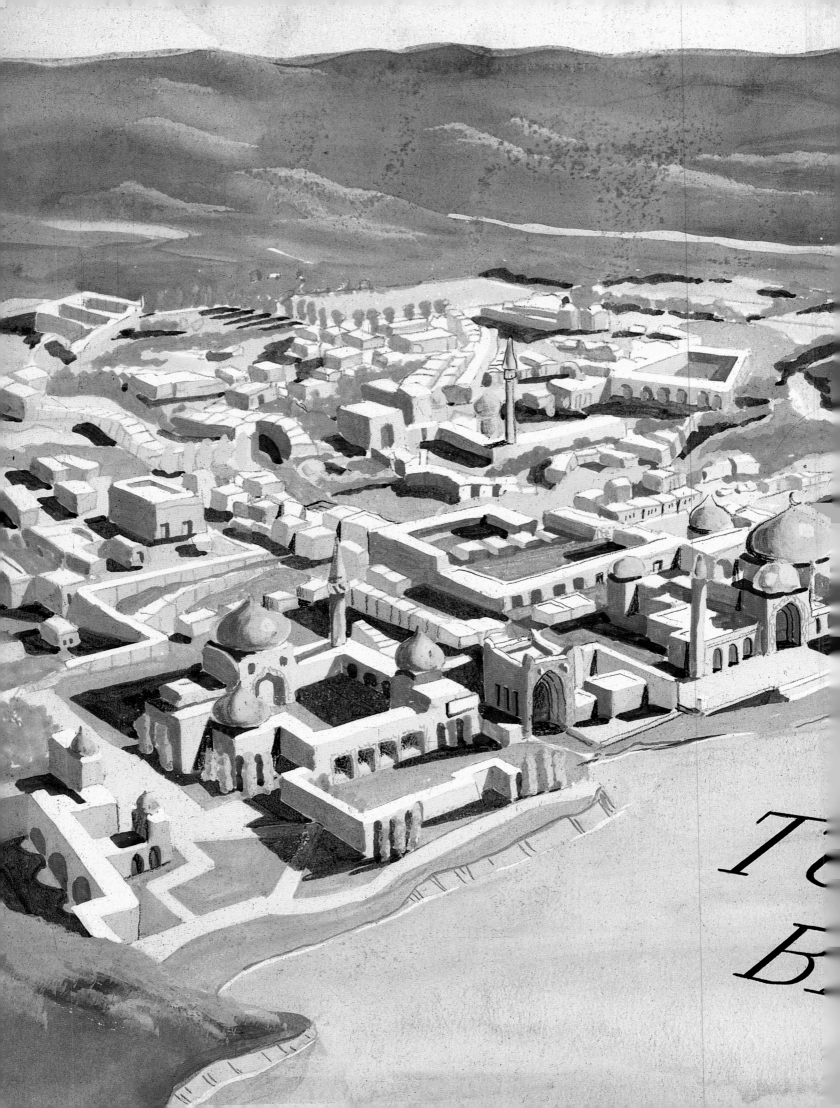

То
б

# Refining and Redefining: 1949–58

*Publicity photograph of Jack Carson from* My Dream Is Yours.

*Comics from the late 1940s.*

For the Warner studio, popularity and preeminence brought the opportunity to work on some unusual outside projects. For instance, in 1949 the United States Public Health Service commissioned Warner Cartoons to produce a short documentary on the advantage of having publicly financed health centers. Called *So Much for So Little*, the eleven-minute film was written by Freleng and Jones, who met with government representatives in Washington to plan the cartoon, and directed by Jones. And in 1950, it won the Academy Award for best documentary—the only time an animated film has taken the honor in that category.

Also around this time, Freleng directed animated sequences that brought Bugs Bunny into two Warner Bros. feature films. In 1948's *Two Guys From Texas*, Bugs gives a forlorn Jack Carson advice on love and dreams, while in 1949's *My Dream Is Yours*, he sings and dances with Carson (again) and Doris Day. Both segments are greatly charming.

In 1953, the Sloan Foundation, a New York-based philanthropic organization, commissioned three cartoons from Warner's containing informational segments about economics, as part of the Foundation's "popular education" program. Directed by Freleng, the theatrically released cartoons feature Sylvester in stories that break in the middle for a brief lesson. 1954's *By Word of Mouse* talks about the basic virtues of the American economic system; 1955's *Heir Conditioned* preaches the value of investment; and 1956's *Yankee Dood It* argues for modern production methods.

But perhaps the most unusual of the outside efforts is *Orange Blossoms for Violet*. Released to theaters in May 1952, this ten-minute "Vitaphone Novelties" presentation carries the screen credit "Written by I. Freleng and Charles M. Jones." Made in live action, the black-and-white film is a melodrama of a boy, a girl, and a predatory villain—as enacted entirely by a cast of monkeys. "Warner Bros. had maybe half an hour or 45 minutes of this footage, and they asked Friz and me if we could make a short subject out of it," said Jones. "So all we did is recut it and put it together."

But all these were only sidelines, with no real impact on the studio or its operations. Yet by 1949, other forces from outside the studio were beginning to have significant consequence for Warner Cartoons. The first was the growing influence of UPA, the iconoclastic cartoonists who wholly jettisoned Disney-style rounded realism and brought an awareness of modern art and contemporary graphics to animated films. Progressively, Warner's began incorporating UPA-inspired backgrounds—simplified, flattened out, willfully abstract—into its cartoons. And the second outside force affected the quality of movement that ranged over these backgrounds. In 1946, the Hollywood Cartoonists' Union demanded and received a 25 percent pay increase for all its artists, helping to rectify what had been some pretty abominable wage scales. As a result, all of Hollywood's cartoon studios had less money available for the costly process of animation, and the change can be seen in films released after

1947 or 1948. Fewer characters could be on screen, and their movement became more spare. (Presumably, the skimpier budgets also accounted for Warner's producing several cartoons in the cheaper Cinecolor process around this time.)

In a way, however, both of these developments played into the burgeoning of Chuck Jones' work in the late forties. Jones, of course, had begun utilizing stylized backgrounds for emotional or spatial effects in the early 1940s; in addition, he had also come to be interested in animated movement not for its abundance but for its precision—a preference that coordinated well with the cut-back budgets of the day.

In 1949, Arthur Davis' fourth unit at Warner's was discontinued, leaving Jones, Freleng, and McKimson to create virtually all of the studio's cartoons through the early 1960s. But the story of the studio in this period is largely that of Jones, whose work sharpened into consistent brilliance around 1948, and whose thinking came to deeply color the methods of his colleagues. Moreover, Jones' redefinition of the studio's shared players—Bugs, Daffy, Elmer, and Porky—was in great measure adopted throughout the shop, and has persisted in the common conception of these characters until today. Jones' influence cannot be overstated—even though the director is quick to point out that his accomplishments are not his alone. Through much of the fifties, Jones worked with a team of immensely talented and creative collaborators. These included background painter Philip DeGuard and animators Ken Harris, Lloyd Vaughan, Phil Monroe, Richard Thompson, Ben Washam, and Abe Levitow. (Background and layout artists Peter Alvarado and Robert Grib-

Above: *The stylizations of UPI were spoofed by Chuck Jones in his cartoons featuring Witch Hazel. This background painting by Philip De Guard from 1954's* Bewitched Bunny *depicts a typically slippery Hazel home; layout by Ernest Nordi.* Top: *Full realism: background painting by Paul Julian from Friz Freleng's* Mutiny on the Bunny, *1950.*

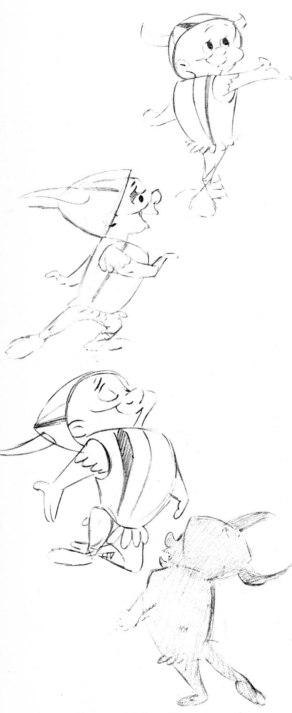

broek brought bright elegance to many of Jones' earlier films of this period.) But perhaps the greatest contributions to the excellence of Jones' cartoons came from two others: the writer Michael Maltese, whose words could pack as much compressed meaning as a haiku, and be smashingly funny besides; and designer/layout artist Maurice Noble, whose scenic sense was simply stunning—whether working in a down-to-earth snow forest or in a futuristic floating space-city.

Probably the most famous and acclaimed animation director of all time, Charles Martin Jones was born in Spokane, Washington, in 1912, and grew up in southern California. As a child, he worked as an extra in some of the silent movies that were being shot near his home, and he went on to study at the Chouinard Art Institute (now the California Institute of the Arts); for some ten years while he was directing, he also attended night classes with Don Graham, the drawing teacher known for his instruction at the Disney studio. Jones began in animation at the Ub Iwerks studio, then knocked around a few other cartoon houses before joining Schlesinger's as an assistant animator in 1933, when Schlesinger was starting up his own outfit.

Jones was perhaps the most intellectual and analytic of Warner's cartoon makers—he has spoken, for example, of basing the staging of his 1942 short *Conrad the Sailor* on the writings of Eisenstein, and is given to quoting G. K. Chesterton, George Santayana, and others. As early as 1946, Jones began publishing articles about animation and, for many years, he conducted art classes for his crew. And when he fully bloomed as a director, in the mid-to-late 1940s, Jones' analytic sense was put into the service of refining and distilling the possibilities of animation, to achieving the kind of exquisite precision that is only available to movie makers who craft their films individual frame by individual frame. But where Clampett used animation's potential to achieve a kind of overblown overstatement, Jones turned in the opposite direction—to bringing out the subtlest of shadings and nuances within his characters' personalities.

"I'm principally concerned with character," Jones says. "Not with what Bugs Bunny is, but *who* he is. I want to get inside him, and feel him from my viewpoint."

What made this possible for Jones is the expressiveness of drawing. Typically, Jones would make as many as 300 or 400 rough drawings for each of his cartoons—much more than most other directors—creating a stream of "poses" that would precisely capture, in visual terms, what his characters were thinking and feeling. Like the clowns from the silent era to whom he had been exposed as a boy, Jones saw that screen personality was expressed through the way a character stands, and carries his weight, and moves, and how he connects with other characters—and the audience—with his eyes. Thus Jones delved ever deeper into personality as the basis for his comedy, as communicated by drawings made to convey worlds of emotion—from the flick of a rabbit's lash to the bending of a duck's bill to the contortions of a coyote's face. And by the late 1940s, when Jones' more expressive poses mated with a superfine sense of timing, his cartoons gained a psychological penetration and depth of humor that were unparalleled.

As Jones moved more rigorously toward basing his films on the personalities of his players, he began removing other elements that did not directly arise from these personalities. For example, Jones saw Bugs Bunny as "a counter-revolutionary"—someone who gets riled when his world has been invaded (leading to the rankled snap, "Of course you

Above and below: *"An actor with a pencil": Chuck Jones' layout sketches from* What's Opera, Doc? *capture moods and manners through facial expressions and body positions.*

know this means war!"). Likewise, the director saw Daffy Duck as "a self-preservationist," albeit a greedy, egotistical, show-offy one. And whenever Jones would use these characters, he would make their every act and gesture cleave unto these frameworks. In such fashion, Jones applied what he called "disciplines" to much else in his work—establishing rules that defined the limits of the game. "Everyone I've ever respected always used restricted tools," he says. "The greatest comedians were the ones who wore the simplest costumes and worked in prescribed areas—like Chaplin." For Jones, the films needed nothing beyond their fundamental premises—anything else would only clutter up the interaction of the characters.

When all of these proclivities are put together, it almost adds up to a commandment for what arrived in 1949: a cartoon called *Fast and*

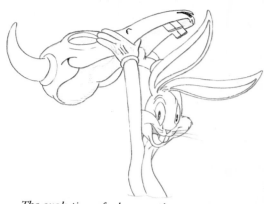

*The evolution of a bunny.* Above: *Animation drawing by Rod Scribner from Bob Clampett's* The Wacky Wabbit, *1942.* Below: *Cel from Chuck Jones'* Rabbit Hood, *1949.*

## Chuck Jones

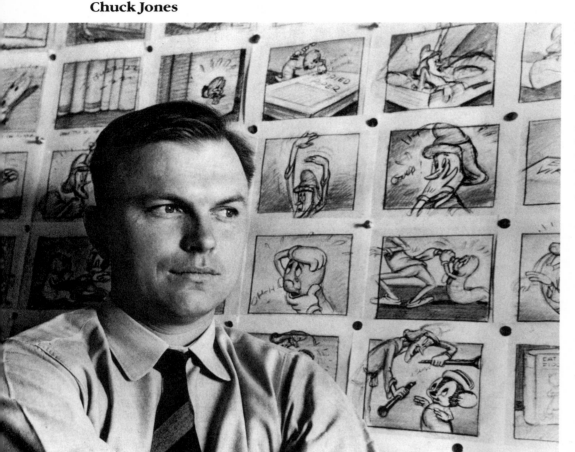

Left: *1939 photograph of Chuck Jones in front of the storyboard of* Sniffles and the Bookworm. *Below right:* Layout drawing by Jones from *Duck Amuck, 1953. Below left: Photograph, c. 1950, of Jones and crew. Left to right, standing: Phil De Guard, Lloyd Vaughan, Marilyn Wood, Paul Julian, Roy Laufenburger, Abe Levitow, Chuck Jones, Robert Gribbock, Michael Maltese, Keith Darling, Madilyn Wood, Ken Harris, Ben Washam. Crouching: Peter Alvarado, Richard Thompson, Phil Monroe. Bottom left: Cel from Chuck Jones' first cartoon,* The Night Watchman, *1938.*

DASHING THROUGH THE SNOW (FOOTED) YAH HAH HA[?] IN A ONE HORSE OPEN SLEIGH.— THROUGH THE FIELDS WE GO.

Chuck Jones:

"The difference between what we did at Warner Bros. and what's on Saturday morning is the difference between animation and what I call illustrated radio. For Saturday morning, they make a full radio track and then use as few drawings as possible to put in front of it.

"The best way to tell the difference is this: if you can turn off the picture and know what's going on, that's illustrated radio. But if you can turn off the sound and know what's going on, that's animation."

Right: *Layout drawing by Chuck Jones of Bugs and Elmer as Wagnerians, from* What's Opera, Doc? *1957. Above: Background painting by Philip De Guard from Chuck Jones'* Bunny Hugged, *1951, layout by Peter Alvarado.*

Below and opposite bottom: *Poses from a model sheet of Charlie Dog, drawn for Chuck Jones'* A Hound for Trouble, *1951. The story of a dog desperate to be adopted was introduced in Bob Clampett's* Porky's Pooch, *of 1941. Jones reprised this tale in 1947's* Little Orphan Airedale, *creating Charlie as a substitute for the earlier hound. Jones used Charlie in several subsequent and very funny cartoons in which the dog tries everything from swift-footed cunning to "the big soulful eyes routine" to land himself a home.* Bottom: *Coyote destiny: background painting by Philip De Guard from* Going! Going! Gosh! *(1952).*

*Furry-ous*, which introduced the Road Runner and Wile E. Coyote. For here was the fulfillment of the Jones aesthetic, and it succeeded with delectable hilarity. The Road Runner series was the ritual cartoon chase stripped down to bedrock fundamentals, reduced to the endless expression of animal appetite and animal evasion. No dialogue, no changes of setting, and no plot get in the way; character development never occurs; all there is is obsession. The self-defeating nature of one character—Wile E. Coyote—generates the entire film, and thereafter the entire series. Yet it is, at bottom, Jones' keenness at delineating the psychology of the Coyote that makes this series so memorable. Rather than the monstrous boomeranging disasters that the Coyote invariably inflicts on himself, it is his reactions to these disasters that count—when he opens a frail, would-be-protective umbrella as the shadow of a falling boulder begins to darken him, or his pained-incredulous "not again" grimace when he sees that somehow a canyon has once more appeared under his feet. In Jones' cartoons, physical pain never hurts nearly as much as the psychological devastation that precedes it—humiliation. His is a comedy, essentially, of reaction.

To a great extent, the Road Runner series—its effectiveness and popularity—set the tone for much of Warner's future. Soon many of the studio's other cartoons were marked by pared-down premises, simplified situations, and a kind of ritualized return of battle-mates—for example, Freleng's Tweety and Sylvester series, or McKimson's Sylvester and Hippety Hopper outings. As in the Road Runners, character conflict was elemental, direct, and unremitting. And the cartoons often adopted the structure typical of the Road Runner films—strings of blackout gags.

Yet Jones' questing intelligence continued to move in other direc-

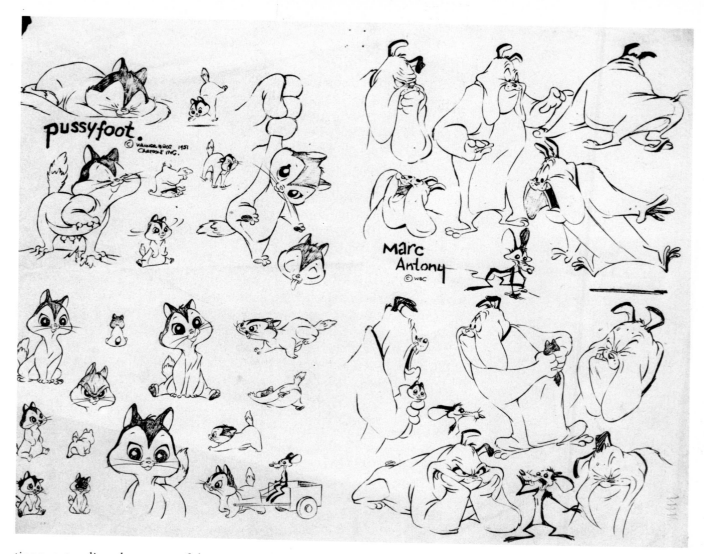

Above: *Model sheet drawn by Chuck Jones for* Feed the Kitty.

tions, extending the range of the animated short to precincts it had never visited before. Often, Jones' ideas could not all be accommodated by a single six-minute installment: Beginning in the 1940s, Jones launched several short series of cartoons—sometimes no more than three or four titles—in which he repeatedly returned to toothsome combinations of characters, so as to further investigate how their personalities would interact. By extending the canvas over additional cartoons, Jones gave his characters further opportunities to play off one another, and so illuminate new facets of their psyches. Some of these series involved new combinations of existing players, such as Porky with Sylvester, or Bugs Bunny and Wile E. Coyote. Other series, which resulted in some of the director's best and funniest work, featured characters of Jones' creation, including Charlie Dog, the Three Bears, a pair of impish mice called Hubie and Bertie, and a hyperactive, loud-barking little spaniel that was often referred to as Frisky Puppy.

A short series of tremendously accomplished cartoons began with one of Jones' most fetching efforts. In 1952's *Feed the Kitty*, a barrel-chested bulldog named Marc Antony adopts a teensy kitten called Pussyfoot, and tries to hide him from the woman who owns his suburban home. The cuddly kitty wins over the big dog's hard heart by hopping atop his back and gently pawing and purring him into submission, as the dog crunches through a hilarious series of grimaces, pouts, strains, shudders, sweats, smirks, smiles, and angelic grins. Later, when Marc Antony thinks his adored pal has inadvertently been baked into a kitty cookie, he balances the wafer on his back and slinks off, his tender bereaved sadness as funny as it is touching. It's a wonderful illustration of

Jones' notion that an animator is "an actor with a pencil," and a convincing display of Jones' use of the emotive power of drawing. Presented with such screen charisma, it's difficult to remember that the entire spectacle reduces to a rippling of graphite and paper.

Equally as successful is Jones' trilogy of cartoons—*Rabbit Fire* (1951), *Rabbit Seasoning* (1952), and *Duck! Rabbit! Duck!* (1953)—in which he sends hunter Elmer Fudd out to tussle with Bugs and Daffy. Throughout the films, sharpster Bugs tries to convince sappy Fudd that it's duck season, while devious Daffy struggles to persuade him to point his rifle at the rabbit. But Daffy's ploys never work, and he ends up getting his bill blown apart, askew, and asunder in more ways than any duck can be expected to tolerate. Working variations on a theme of frazzling the duck, the films are tremendously well honed and rippingly funny. And as written by Michael Maltese, the cartoons brim with layered and literate dialogue, from Daffy's pithy diagnosis of "pronoun trouble" as the reason for his gun-muzzle misfortunes in *Rabbit Seasoning* to his maniacal surrender near the end of *Duck! Rabbit! Duck!*: "Shoot me again! I enjoy it! I love the smell of burnt feathers and gunpowder and cordite! I'm an elk—shoot me, go on, it's elk season! I'm a fiddler crab! Why don't you shoot me—it's fiddler crab season!" Derangement has rarely been given such eloquent expression.

Interestingly, in the late 1930s and early forties, the Disney studio teamed its three leading characters—Mickey Mouse, Donald Duck, and Goofy—in some twenty cartoons. And invariably, in all of these films, the three come upon a situation, split up and become involved in individual business, then reunite at cartoon's end. In contrast, Jones thrusts his trio into continual confrontation, forcing the three characters to collide so that the sparks of personality can shower out. In Jones' work, plot is

*Character encounters. Above: From Friz Freleng's* Show Biz Bugs, *1957. Right: From Chuck Jones'* Rabbit Seasoning, *1952.*

substantially an outgrowth of character, not vice versa. And if Jones returns to similar situations in his series of related films, it is to continue with this process, to see what else about his characters can be discovered through their further engagement. Like Monet returning to Rouen Cathedral to capture the varying play of light upon its facade, Jones returns to his situations to capture the play of his characters' personalities, refracting in differing and beautiful ways.

But it needn't always be one character playing off another. It can also be an individual character at odds with his context. During the fifties, Jones directed a superb series of film-genre parodies starring Daffy Duck, in which much of the humor derives from the fact that the overemotional duck is the wrong "actor" for the job. Daffy's personality—what Jones created as the autonomous nature of the pen-and-ink duck, and what audiences have come to know and expect of him—undermines his attempts to play these parts. For example, in 1950's *The Scarlet Pumpernickel*, Daffy pitches a script he has written to studio chief "J.L." so he can star as a swashbuckling hero in a costume epic. But in his film, Daffy bungles the romantic mystique by, among others, having a fit when he samples a pinch of snuff, missing his horse whenever he tries to leap upon it, and by hopelessly overwriting the climax—adding bursting dams, cavalry charges, erupting volcanoes, and skyrocketing inflation that leaves kreplach selling for $1,000 apiece. Or in 1951's *Drip-along Daffy*, he plays a "Western-Type Hero" (as a subtitle informs us) intent on cleaning up a lawless town, but who can't even handle hardened bandit Nasty Canasta's favorite drink, much less a *High Noon*–style duel with him. (A tiny windup wooden soldier ends up doing Dripalong's job.) In

Above: *Background painting by Philip De Guard from* Duck Dodgers in the 24½th Century, *1953; layout by Maurice Noble.*

**Overleaf**
*Cel and background from* Drip-along Daffy, *1951.*

1953's famous *Duck Dodgers in the 24½th Century*, the would-be space-age Buck Rogers is sent to Planet X to find some "Aludium Phosdex—the shaving cream atom," because Earth's supply is "alarmingly low"; but instead, in his excessive gung-ho zeal, Daffy blows up that uncharted world. And 1958's *Robin Hood Daffy* casts the duck as a slipshod Errol Flynn, playing so unlikely a Robin Hood that he has to spend most of the cartoon convincing Fat Friar Porky Pig just who he is.

The supreme example, however, of Daffy at war with his context is 1953's *Duck Amuck*, for here he is at war with his entire world. The film begins with Daffy believing that he is in a conventional cartoon—lunging forth in French period costume, brandishing a sword and calling, "Stand back, musketeers! They shall sample my blade!" in front of a conventional background. But then Daffy's universe goes haywire. As he continues moving left, the background behind him loses detail, and eventually simplifies into blank whiteness. Daffy notices the change, becomes unsure, hides beyond the edge of the frame, then peeps in apprehensively: "Hey, *psst*! Whoever's in charge here. . . . The scenery! Where's the scenery?" The end of a large paintbrush swoops into the frame and paints a farmyard setting—whereupon Daffy rebegins his part in the musketeer picture, then confusedly notices his dislocation and falters to a halt. Sensing that it's better to switch than fight ("Ok—have it your way"), Daffy dons overalls and hayseed's hat and joins the new cartoon, singing happily, "Daffy Duck he had a farm"—whereupon the world goes out of control again, eventually becoming an Arctic snowscape, a tropical jungle, and others.

And like this it continues, with some unknown and capricious

*From* Robin Hood Daffy. Above: *Layout drawing by Chuck Jones.* Below: *Background painting by Philip De Guard; layout by Maurice Noble.* Opposite: *Cel of Daffy.*

creator-force switching backgrounds on Daffy, or making them infantile and absurd, or erasing Daffy's body and redrawing him as a cowboy (whose guitar at first emits nothing when strummed, then sounds like a Klaxon horn and a machine gun), or making him into a four-footed mutant monster, or painting his body with polka dots and stripes, or placing him into a crashing World War I plane and, when he bails out, redrawing his parachute to become an anvil. Finally, a frayed and distraught Daffy is left to splutter up to the unseen arbiter of his life: "All right—enough is enough. This is the final, this is the very very last straw. . . . *Who is responsible for this?* I demand that you show yourself! Who are you?! *Huh?*"

*Duck Amuck* has been seen as both a parable of modern man's powerless alienation from his environment and a hilarious "Merrie Melodie." Either way, it is one of the few unarguable masterpieces of American animation. For Chuck Jones, however, the film represents an attempt to explore the very limits of character within a cartoon: "What I want to say is that Daffy can live and struggle on an empty screen, without setting and without sound, just as well as with a lot of arbitrary props. He remains Daffy Duck."

*Duck Amuck* also stands in revealing contrast to Bob Clampett's seminal story of dystopia, *Porky in Wackyland.* In the 1938 Clampett film, the uncontrollable, bizarre, and often malicious world is set far away, and its events seem indifferent to whoever happens to wander into it; in the postwar Jones cartoon, it is Daffy's everyday reality that becomes denatured, and its cruelties seem to be responding to Daffy's particular anxieties. As always in Jones, character generates plot and conflict.

In 1955's *Rabbit Rampage,* Jones reworked the situation set out in

Above and opposite: *From* Duck Amuck, *1953.* Below: *Background painting by Philip De Guard from* Rabbit of Seville; *layout by Robert Gribbrock.*

*Duck Amuck*, with Bugs Bunny as the lambasted party. Yet the cartoon is not nearly as successful: the confident rabbit does not make a convincing victim. Even when he errs, Jones displays that personality is the well-spring of his genius.

Jones had other designs for Bugs Bunny, as a supremely capable leading man or a sharp-tongued jeerer who could put anyone and anything in its place. And in several cartoons, he used the bunny's irreverent streak to contrast with the sanctimoniousness of classical music. In *Long-Haired Hare* (1949), Bugs has a run-in with a pompous opera singer (named "Giovanni Jones") who doesn't appreciate the rabbit's disrupting his rehearsal by singing kitschy popular songs (such as "What Do They Do on a Rainy Night in Rio?") outside. Eventually, Bugs has his revenge by impersonating Leopold Stokowski at the baritone's Hollywood Bowl recital, and conducting him to sing the longest note in human history—a feat that brings about no little writhing, turning of motley colors, and shedding of formal attire. And in 1950's *Rabbit of Seville,* Bugs puts hunter Elmer through his maddening paces—making his bald scalp sprout flowers with the help of "Figaro Fertilizer," even going so far as to get him into drag and marry him—to the accompaniment of Rossini's opera "Il Barbiere di Siviglia."

But Jones' relationship to classical music is not, at bottom, satirical; rather, he often seems awed by its grandeur, and seeks to share in that glow. And nowhere is this more evident than in 1957's *What's Opera, Doc?* In this tour de force, Jones compressed the entirety of Richard Wagner's "Der Ring des Nibelungen"—a cycle of four operas that is

fourteen hours long—into six minutes, and threw in heavy doses of *Fantasia*-bashing besides. In an epic—but stylized—Valhallan setting, with thunderous mountains and impossible castles and otherworldly pavilions, Brunhilde Bunny and Siegfried Fudd enact their ritual hunt. Wearing heavy armor, complete with "spear and magic helmet," Teutonic warrior Elmer sings "Kill the wabbit! Kill the wabbit!" to the Valkyries' theme as he stalks his prey. But Bugs appears as a pigtailed Rhinemaiden, and inspires enraptured Elmer to join him in a languorous pas de deux—beautifully animated by Ken Harris—before they sing the melancholy duet "Return My Love" (whose lyrics were written by Jones and Michael Maltese). Then, when Bugs blows his disguise and flees, Fudd climbs atop a mighty tower and invokes the elements against him: "North winds blow! South winds blow! Typhoons! Hurricanes! Earthquakes!" and the coup de grace—"*Smog!!*"

By any standards this is an extraordinary cartoon, and for one made as late as 1957 it seems something of a miracle. In fact, Jones knew he was undertaking an unusual work, and so stole two weeks of production time from his other cartoons to lavish more attention on *What's Opera, Doc?*—thereby having all of seven weeks to devote to it. Whereas a typical cartoon might use about sixty different shots, *What's Opera, Doc?* required 106. And Maurice Noble's monumental designs and daring color-schemes sent the studio into a tizzy. "They thought I was bats when I put that bright red on Elmer with those purple skies," recalled Noble. "I had the Ink and Paint Department come in and say, 'You *really mean* you want that magenta red on that?' And I said, 'Yes, that's the way.' "

Above, bottom, *and* opposite: *Studies by Maurice Noble for* What's Opera, Doc?

*From* What's Opera, Doc? Above: *Layout drawings by Chuck Jones from the ballet sequence.* Right: *Color chart used by the Ink and Paint Department.*

1397
WHITES WHITE
COOL BR. 1
TC BUGS YEL.
GOLD YEL. 1/2
TC PALE CREAM
BUGS YEL. 1
LT. BL. VIOL. 1
Gold yellow 1/2
TC LT. BL. GRAY
Pale Cream 1
FL. 1
PALE CREAM 1
PINK 1/2
LT. BL. GRAY 1
WH.
GOLD YEL. 1/2
TC. DK. WM. BR.
LT. BL. GRAY 1
LT. BL. VIOL. 1
BUGS YEL. 1
S YEL.
BUGS NORMAL
GRAY 1/2
TC LT. BL. GRAY
WH
LT. BL. GRAY 1
TC LT. BL. GRAY
LT. BL. GRAY 1
CREAM 1
WH.
WH.
(FOOT PADS LT. BL. GRAY)
TC LT. BL. GRAY
BUGS AS BRUNHILDE

Above and opposite: *From* One Froggy Evening. *Below: Background painting by Philip De Guard from* One Froggy Evening; *layout by Robert Gribbrock.*

Alongside his several series of cartoons, Jones, like the other Warner directors, continued to make "one shots"—films featuring characters that never returned. And these cartoons often allowed different aspects of the directors' sensibilities to surface, working without the preconditions that established characters could impose. 1951's terrifically funny *Chow Hound*, for example, shows a rather gruesome side to Jones, one that is not seen elsewhere. It tells of an insatiable bulldog who enslaves a cat and a mouse and uses them in a scam to get food from several unsuspecting homes—"And don't forget the gravy!" he forever snarls to his helpless pawns. Ultimately, the mouse and cat get their revenge, on a dog too bloated to fight back, but who finally gets his gravy.

Of all of Jones' one-shot cartoons, though, none enjoys quite the renown as 1955's *One Froggy Evening*, which features a character that Jones has nominated as his personal favorite, and whom he later named Michigan J. Frog. This wicked little parable begins with a frumpy construction worker finding a box in the cornerstone of a just-demolished building. Opening the box, the worker discovers a croaking, regulation-style frog—who suddenly jumps up, produces a top hat and cane, and dances a spirited cakewalk as he grinningly belts out "Hello, My Baby." Dollar signs rise before the opportunistic worker, who sneaks away with the boxed frog and attempts to profiteer from his discovery—bringing him to a booking agent (the "Acme Theatrical Agency"), then spending his life's savings to present the frog in his own theater. The problem is, the frog won't sing when anyone else is watching—he drips back into being a floppy croaker. Yet he won't shut up when he's alone with the worker, smothering him with exuberant renditions of "I'm Just Wild About Harry," "Please Don't Talk About Me When I'm Gone," "Come Back to Erin," and others, including an original tune written by Jones and

Michael Maltese called "The Michigan Rag." Eventually, the situation reduces the worker to park-bench poverty and, finally, the madhouse, before he can dispose of the frog in a way that will make society safe again—or so he thinks.

Magnificently funny, the widely acclaimed *One Froggy Evening* says things about the power of greed, and hooks up with Jones' Road Runner films in looking at the mechanics of self-defeat. In a deft directorial touch, the entire film is done in pantomime (except when Michigan J. is singing) and uses many adroit devices for communicating its story line without dialogue. And it also exploits, to great comic effect, the difference between the frog's human-like movements while performing—strutting and crooning and high-kicking—and his naturalistic frog-like behavior when not doing what comes unnaturally. "We really had two frogs in the film, both stuck with the same anatomy, and we did a lot of studying of frogs to make the break between the two convincing," said Jones. "But in order to make the film work, you had to believe that the man was a real man—not a cartoon man, but someone who existed as a human being. So I looked through *The New Yorker* and studied some of their drawings, and tried to think in those terms." The director has also recalled that the voice of the frog was probably provided by a baritone named Terrence Monck.

In a 1973 *Time* magazine profile of Jones, film critic Jay Cocks wrote that *One Froggy Evening* "comes as close as any cartoon ever has to perfection." Presumably, it did so upon its release as well, eighteen years earlier. Yet there was nary a word written, nor an honor given, at the time. The cartoon's one tribute, in its brief lifetime—before television would immortalize it—was the laughter of a nation. It was all that was needed, and all that was asked.

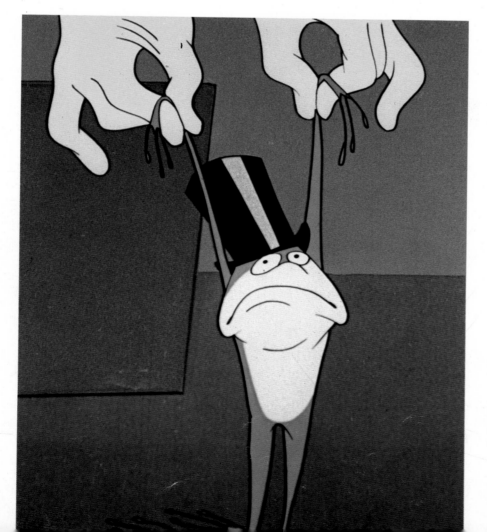

**Overleaf**
*Background painting by Philip De Guard and cel from* Lumber Jack Rabbit, *1954. The studio in part achieved its 3-D effects in this cartoon by preparing two nearly identical backgrounds for each shot, then combining them in the manner of a stereoscope.*

Jones also directed a film that qualifies as a one shot even though it starred Bugs Bunny: 1954's *Lumber Jack Rabbit*, Warner Bros.' sole cartoon to be produced in 3-D. The cartoon was commissioned by Jack Warner when Hollywood was in the middle of its 3-D craze. "He decided, I guess, that the entire world was going to wind up wearing Polaroid glasses," Jones once said. Yet Warner's cartoon plant had no real facilities for producing work in three dimensions, so it was left to veteran studio cameraman and business manager John Burton to improvise a technique. The result, however, does not make very effective use of the simulated depth. The one exception comes at the very beginning of the cartoon, when the Warner Bros. "W-B" shield, which normally races up from a distance, seems to spring far into the audience, before settling back into its customary position between the concentric circles. Nevertheless, *Lumber Jack Rabbit* is a nice cartoon, with Bugs ending up in Paul Bunyan's vast carrot patch and singing several spry choruses of "Jimmy Crack Corn and I Don't Care."

Yet 3-D had another consequence for the Warner cartoon shop: Jack Warner shut the shop down because of it. Studio head Warner thought that 3-D would soon become the norm in all movies, and that animated shorts would be too costly to produce in this process; he therefore let the majority of his cartoon staff go in the summer of 1953. Chuck Jones called Walt Disney, who invited him to the Disney studio and put him to work on *Sleeping Beauty* and the early television shows. But Jones lasted all of four months; at Disney, he found, every move and decision had to wait—sometimes for weeks—for Walt's approval. This proved intolerable for Jones' independent temperament, and so he left for greener pastures—the Warner Bros. cartoon studio, which Jack Warner was already reopening. In a rare instance of his foresight failing him, Warner had misjudged the durability of 3-D.

Although Jones won Warner Cartoons' second Oscar, for his 1949 Pepé Le Pew short, *For Scent-imental Reasons*, Friz Freleng proved to be the studio's resident Academy darling. In four years, Freleng won the award three times, for 1955's *Speedy Gonzales*, 1957's *Birds Anonymous*, and 1958's *Knighty Knight Bugs*. Fine films all—especially *Birds Anonymous*, the soulful tale of Sylvester's attempt to break his addiction to avian dinners (namely, Tweety)—they are nevertheless outshined by other Freleng efforts that were not acknowledged by the Academy. The 1951 *Canned Feud*, for example, is a handsome and skillful study of feline frustration, as Sylvester finds himself locked in a house with nothing to eat except food in cans, but no can openers beyond the one a little mouse keeps hiding.

Freleng also excelled in several films that featured pairs of supporting players that were his own. In 1952's *Tree for Two*, Freleng devised Spike and Chester, a gruff bulldog and his bouncy, adoring pal ("Spike's my hero!"). And in *Golden Yeggs* (1950), the director introduced Rocky and Mugsy, a hard-as-nails gangster and his oafish accomplice. Among their subsequent appearances, there is none so funny as 1954's *Bugs and Thugs*, in which the hoods inadvertently bring the bunny back to their lair. One famously clever sequence features an elaboration of a gag first essayed in 1946's *Racketeer Rabbit*: From another room in the gangsters' house, Bugs simulates with his voice the arrival of the police, producing sirens and catcalls and all. The rabbit then directs the scofflaws to hide in an oven, whereupon he acts out an encounter with an imaginary police chief who storms in the door:

1622 5/24/62

WHITE'S WHITE

INSIDE MOUTH-DK RED 1
TONGUE-PINK 1

© WARNER BROS. PICTURES INC.

MEDIUM INK LINES

TRACE OVERLAPPING BLACKS IN D

*Bugs:* Now look, would I turn on this gas if my friend Rocky was in there? (*He puts on the gas.*)

*Bugs (in Irish accent):* Ya might, rabbit, ya might.

*Bugs:* Well, would I throw a lighted match in there if my friend was in there? (*Match in; big explosion.*)

*Bugs (in Irish accent):* Well, all right rabbit, you've convinced me.

Then Bugs simulates the retreat of the police chief. But at that moment the real police pull in. They run upstairs and repeat exactly the same Bugs-and-Irish oven-and-gas routine—until Rocky and Mugsy crash out of the stove and beg the police to take them to prison's safety.

True to form, however, some of Freleng's strongest films from this period are his musicals. 1949's *Mouse Mazurka* sends Sylvester in pursuit of a Slavic mouse, in an elaborate pantomime set to a pastiche of Russian and Eastern European folk melodies. The charming *Pizzicato Pussycat* (1955) tells of a bespectacled little mouse who plays a mean piano—and who inadvertently launches the cat who is chasing him into a concert career. And *Show Biz Bugs* (1957) contains one of the neatest crystalizations of the 1950s Bugs vs. Daffy clash. Here, the two are vaudevillians, with Bugs instantly winning the audience's hearts and Daffy reducing them to indifference (and a silence so deep that crickets can be heard). So Daffy unleashes his jealous fury in some impassioned performances (to no avail), and tries to sabotage Bugs' acts (to even less avail). At one point, Daffy rigs a bomb to go off when Bugs hits a certain note while playing "Those Endearing Young Charms" on a xylophone; but when Bugs keeps missing the note, Daffy can not control himself, runs over, and shows him how to play it correctly—and receives a blast for his perfect performance. The insouciant Bugs and the splenetic Daffy are here keenly well captured. (The duo's tasteful soft-shoe duet in this film was animated by Gerry Chiniquy.)

But the most engaging of all of Freleng's late musicals is 1957's *The Three Little Bops,* which transplants the fable of the three little pigs to a 1950s nightclub setting. This time, the pigs play in a jazz trio, and the wolf

Above and opposite: *Sketches of Spike (later called Alf) from a model sheet for* Tree for Two. *Above left:* Color chart *from Friz Freleng's* The Unmentionables, *1963.*

is a sour, unhip trumpeter who "blows down" their act in three different clubs: The Straw House, The Dew-Drop Inn, and The House of Bricks. Bop veteran Shorty Rogers and his trio were brought in to handle the music for this cartoon, while comedian Stan Freberg sang Warren Foster's mirthful rhyming narration. Lively and unusual, it is an altogether winning effort.

Meanwhile, Robert McKimson entered the fifties riding on a series of briskly funny Bugs Bunny films, often casting him as an anarchist who delights in deviltry. In 1949's *Rebel Rabbit,* Bugs gets miffed when he finds that the bounty for shooting rabbits is a puny two cents, as these woodland creatures are believed to be harmless. Seeking greater recognition of his powers—"I'll show you a rabbit can be more obnoxious than anybody" he remonstrates to Washington's game warden—Bugs goes on a spree of destructiveness that includes shutting off Niagara Falls, filling up the Grand Canyon, and sawing Florida from the mainland (while shouting "South America, take it away!"). The story shows Warren Foster at his most cartoony and exuberant. And *Hillbilly Hare* (1950) brings the bunny deep into the Ozarks; there, he extricates himself from a local feud by impersonating a country fiddler and calling a would-be square dance that directs two yokels into all manner of mutual abuse ("Step right up, you're doing fine/I'll pull your beard, you'll pull mine. . .").

McKimson also showed strengths as a character creator. In 1948's *Hop, Look and Listen,* McKimson introduced Hippety Hopper, the playful baby kangaroo whom Sylvester is eternally mistaking for a giant mouse. And in 1950's *Pop 'im Pop,* McKimson supplemented this returning pair with Sylvester Jr., a scaled-down version of the daddy cat, who has become greatly popular in the United States and Europe. In 1953's *Cat-Tails for Two,* the director created Speedy Gonzales, although the high-octane Mexican mouse was taken over and redesigned by Friz Freleng as of his next appearance. And *Devil May Hare,* from 1954, saw the birth of McKimson's perhaps most memorable cartoon thespian, the growly and voracious Tasmanian Devil.

Principally, however, during this time McKimson emerged as a parodist. And the object, most often, of his barbed tributes was television. In nearly a dozen cartoons—with titles like *The Super Snooper* and *People are Bunny*—McKimson took on TV programs or genres, with help from writer Tedd Pierce; unfortunately, most of them have not aged well. Their satiric references have been lost in time, and their often lackluster production values deprive them of the period detail that makes so many of the cartoons from the 1930s so enjoyable.

But still, there are moments. 1956's *The Honey-mousers* and its two sequels have some vim in spoofing "The Honeymooners," with funny mouse versions of Jackie Gleason, Art Carney, and the rest of the cast. And *The Mouse that Jack Built* (1959) is yet another rodent parody, this time of "The Jack Benny Show." Pitting a resourceful house cat against cheapster mouse Benny—whose legendary vault is here stocked with cheese (and whose guard hasn't seen light of day since World War I)—the cartoon benefits from Benny, Mary Livingstone, Eddie "Rochester" Anderson, and Don Wilson providing the voices for their whiskered equivalents. The film was one of McKimson's favorites, and apparently it pleased Benny as well: as payment for his services, the comedian asked only for a print of the cartoon.

Above: *Detail of a background painting by Richard H. Thomas and cel from* Hillbilly Hare. Below: *Painting by Richard H. Thomas from* Pizzicato Pussycat.

**Opposite**
*Detail of a background painting by Richard H. Thomas from* Hillbilly Hare.

# Iris Out: 1959–63; 1963–69

For a Golden Age to exist, it must, at some point, end. There is no denying that, by 1959, the output of the Warner cartoon studio had suffered a decline in quality, caused in part by rising costs and inflexible budgets.

Of course, there were still some excellent cartoons. Chuck Jones' *High Note* (1960), for example, is a quite delightful novelty about a musical note that has the tendency to get a little tipsy, moving within a world of scores and staffs; the film exhibits a fine wittiness and crispness of execution. Likewise, several of Jones' last Road Runner cartoons, such as *To Beep or Not To Beep* (1963), were effective and energetic. But in many other corners of production, the spirit was gone.

Certainly contributing to the decline was the loss of some key creative personnel. In 1958 Carl Stalling retired, after several years in which he had shared the composing duties with Milt Franklyn. (Franklyn had also orchestrated Stalling's scores.) Familiar with the house style, Franklyn was an able hand. But Franklyn died in 1962 and was replaced by William Lava, whose work was decidedly more earthbound than what had preceded it. During a musicians' strike in the late 1950s, John Seeley

*Color chart for the opening dance of "The Bugs Bunny Show."*

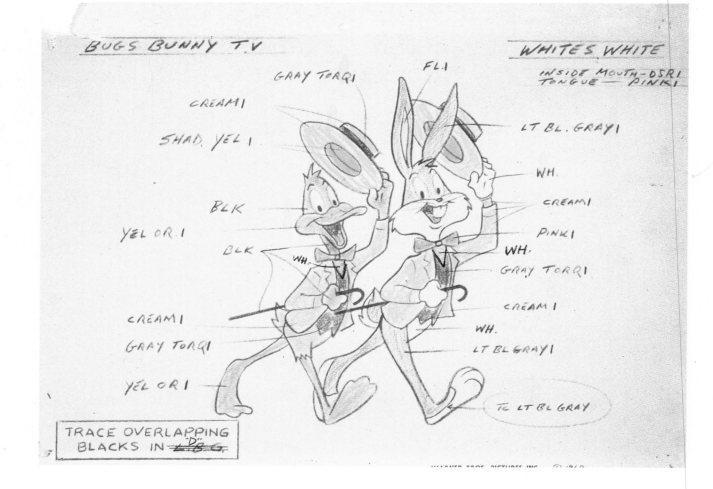

*From* High Note.

filled in by cobbling together scores from stock music.

Further, Warren Foster, Michael Maltese, and Tedd Pierce, Warner's long-time and very brilliant writers, left the studio around this period. Foster and Maltese joined the new Hanna-Barbera plant, where they again proved their abilities by writing such early Hanna-Barbera television productions as "The Flintstones" and "Yogi Bear," helping to make them into national favorites. Their replacement was former Disney storyman John Dunn, who ended up writing for all of the Warner directors without ever reaching the achievements of his predecessors. And 1959 saw the passing of Arthur Q. Bryan, the voice of Elmer Fudd. Other actors, including Mel Blanc and Daws Butler, tried to imitate the Fuddian sonority, but without capturing its simpy charm.

Other changes came to the studio's directing department. Beginning in 1959, several of Warner's premier animators—including Ken Harris, Abe Levitow, Phil Monroe, and Gerry Chiniquy—were given chances to direct cartoons while the shop's regular directors were diverted by outside projects, often for television. The results, however, were mixed. And Jones and Freleng began giving "co-director" screen credit to their long-standing layout artists, Maurice Noble and Hawley Pratt, respectively. According to Jones, this was done in acknowledgment of the growing importance of graphics in the Warner shorts; indeed, the layout men's striking colors and spatial compositions were often the strongest features of the later cartoons.

Less significant changes were administrative. In January 1958, Edward Selzer retired and was replaced by John Burton as Executive Producer of the Warner Bros. Cartoon Division; Burton, in turn, left in January 1960, passing the studio leadership to David DePatie. But even these shifts contributed to the scrambling of the studio's traditional

*Above, and below: Concept paintings by Maurice Noble from* Boyhood Daze, *Chuck Jones' 1957 sequel to 1954's* From A to Z-Z-Z-Z. *Animation's answer to Thurber's "The Secret Life of Walter Mitty," the cartoons feature Ralph Phillips, a quiet lad with an overactive imagination. In the initial film, Ralph daydreams his way out of his humdrum schoolroom, while in* Boyhood Daze, *he fantasizes himself to be an air ace, piloting his plane to thwart Martian attack and paying a visit to a lush jungle. Ralph's voice was supplied by Dick Beals.*

procedures, as well as disrupting the feelings of teamwork and unity that had inspired the Warner artists for decades. (There had also been a change of address: in 1955, the studio moved from its dilapidated home since the early 1930s, at 1351 North Van Ness Avenue in Hollywood, to a modern facility at 461 South California Street in Burbank.)

Further distraction from theatrical cartoons came from the studio's last major venture, a project prepared for what was then thought to be animation's destiny—television. "The Bugs Bunny Show" bowed on ABC on October 11, 1960, and its half-hour programs ran for two seasons in prime time. Produced, written and directed by Jones and Freleng in collaboration, the programs consisted of existing cartoons and new linking segments, which featured most of the studio's characters as showmen preparing to put on a revue, much in the manner of Freleng's cartoon *Show Biz Bugs*. Popular and praised, the program was a fine showcase for the older shorts, and began with an irresistible dance number sung by Bugs and Daffy ("Overture/Curtain! Lights!/This is it/The night of nights. . . ."); it was animated by Gerry Chiniquy. The show then moved to Saturday morning, where it has changed format several times while becoming the longest continuing Saturday-morning children's program in American network history (it later jumped to CBS, then returned to ABC).

In many ways, the rise of television contributed to the demise of

## Robert McKimson

Beyond his major contributions as an animator, director, and character creator, Robert McKimson brought enrichments to Warner Cartoons that were felt all through the studio. As animator and historian Mark Kausler has pointed out, McKimson's drawing style provided the foundation for virtually the entire Warner Bros. style of character construction. In the pivotal years of the early 1940s, McKimson was perhaps the studio's principal model-sheet maker, and his work on all of the shared characters, as well as many incidental players, strongly influenced Warner's overall graphic identity. Colleagues would marvel at McKimson's ability to draw a character "clean"—with no preliminary sketching or guide-lines to assist him. And around 1943, McKimson drew the famous pose of Bugs Bunny leaning on a tree, with carrot posed for chomping, that has remained the character's standard publicity image ever since. (It was originally drawn for an annual Easter show mounted by a Los Angeles department store after Bugs had become enormously popular.) When added to his many distinguished films, and his roster of original characters—Foghorn Leghorn, Hippety Hopper, Sylvester Junior, Speedy Gonzales, the Tasmanian Devil—McKimson's position in the history of Warner animation is unarguably of the first rank.

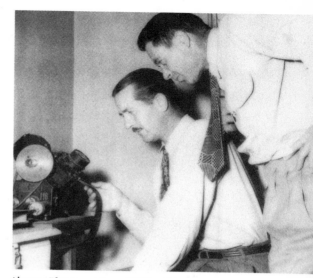

Above: *Photograph, c. 1950, of Robert McKimson (seated) and animator Rod Scribner,* Below: *McKimson's Bugs Bunny "Easter Greeting."* Left: *From* Rebel Rabbit, *1949.* Below left: *Model sheet by McKimson of Willoughby from* The Crackpot Quail, *1941.*

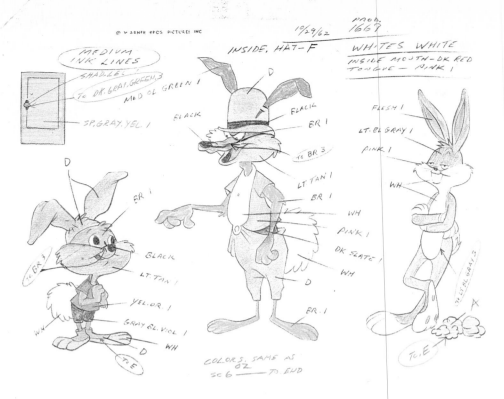

the Warner Cartoon shop, which came in 1963. Film attendance had dropped markedly by the early sixties, and theaters were closing all around the country. The double feature was in the process of vanishing, and along with it went the extensive screen programs—which had once included newsreels, comedy shorts, and other one-reelers—that cartoons had been a part of. Accordingly, theater owners wanted to pay less and less money for cartoons, and finally nothing at all. Meanwhile, television had emerged as a profitable outlet for cartoons, but Warner's

*That's all, folks.*
Above: *Layout drawing from Chuck Jones's last Road Runner cartoon,* War and Pieces, *1964, in which the Coyote's rocket blasts him through the Earth to China. It proves to be no vacation.*
Above right: *Color chart from the last Bugs Bunny cartoon,* False Hare. *Right: Layout drawing from the last cartoon released before Warner Bros.' 1963 closing,* Señorella and the Glass Huarache.

chose not to produce new work on the lesser budgets that television demanded (and which had led Hanna-Barbera to devise the cost-saving techniques of "limited animation"). Further, Warner's had hundreds of cartoons in its vaults that it could continually reuse for free, many of which boasted a quality that far outstripped what could then be attained.

The last Bugs Bunny cartoon, *False Hare*, was released in July 1964, and it was followed in August by the last Warner Bros. cartoon of all, *Senorella and the Glass Huarache*.

Above: *Background painting by Philip DeGuard from Chuck Jones'* Hare-way to the Stars, *1958; layout by Maurice Noble.* Below: *Model sheet of Don Knotts transformed into a fish, from* The Incredible Mr. Limpet, *a 1964 Warner Bros. feature film that made extensive use of animation provided by the cartoon studio. The film tells of a gawky devotee of his pet fish who turns pisciform himself. He goes on to become a World War II hero when he leads U.S. Navy submarine chasers to their targets.*

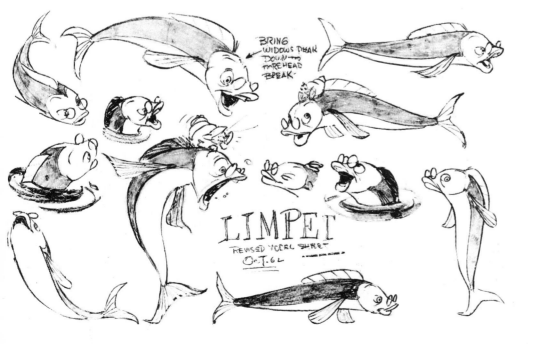

131

But like their characters, the Warner cartoonists were not to be knocked down for long. Soon after the studio's 1963 closing, Friz Freleng and David DePatie leased Warner's cartoon plant and formed an independent concern, where they went on to produce, among other projects, the much-enjoyed animated titles for the "Pink Panther" films, as well as the subsequent Pink Panther shorts. But then Warner Bros. decided that it wanted to get back into the theatrical cartoon business; in July 1964, it contracted with DePatie-Freleng Enterprises to make cartoons for release under the Warner name.

Beginning with the 1964 title *Pancho's Hideaway*, DePatie-Freleng produced some forty shorts for Warner's on tightly restricted budgets. The results reflected these cutbacks. Character movement was drastically slashed and repetitive canned music brought a tinniness to the sound track.

Yet these cartoons made money—and in response, Jack Warner decided in 1967 to open a new Warner Bros. cartoon studio. DePatie-Freleng moved off the Warner lot, and a new shop was organized under producer William L. Hendricks. Animation veteran Alex Lovy was hired from Hanna-Barbera to direct; he continued with the Daffy and Speedy series while introducing such characters as Cool Cat and Merlin the Magic Mouse. In 1968, Robert McKimson took over for Lovy, and soon added Rapid Rabbit and "Bunny and Claude"—outlaw rabbit derivatives of Warner's *Bonnie and Clyde*—to the stable. But in 1969, Warner's decided to discontinue its distribution of all short subjects, which led to the closing of its resuscitated cartoon division.

Periods of unevenness in no way tarnish the studio's earlier, formidable accomplishments. Rather, they might serve as a reminder that the happy confluence of elements that came together in Warner cartoons—involving production, distribution, and collective brilliance—should be cherished all the more.

Above: *A postcard with the whole gang, c. 1962.* Below: *Cel from the opening of "The Bugs Bunny Show."*

# CODA

I f television killed the cartoon stars, it just as certainly brought about their resurrection, and helped raise them to the position of cultural icons of a later day. By the late 1950s, television was aswarm with animated cartoons, as the movie studios dipped into their archives to exploit the profitability of this still-emerging medium; cartoons dating back to the silent years of the twenties were everpresent in morning and afternoon schedules.

And this included Warner's. In 1956, Warner Bros. struck an agreement for selling much of its back catalogue to Associated Artists Productions; the deal included all of Warner's color cartoons copyrighted before September 1, 1948. Thus, along with *The Maltese Falcon,* AAP got *Falling Hare.* And these cartoons—which have changed hands several times since, and are currently owned by Ted Turner—quickly became staples in syndication and on independent television stations around the country. By and large, the networks have leased Warner Bros. cartoons from Warner Bros. itself, which has retained the rights to its post-1948 films; this is why none of the earlier cartoons appear on the network Saturday morning "Bugs Bunny Show." However, Warner's does lease packages of the post-1948 films to syndication, so those cartoons are frequently presented off-network, as well.

With these two sources for television release, the Warner cartoons have remained in constant circulation. And beyond that, the characters have continued to turn up in other places, often in advertising. A notable example was the series of commercials for Kool-Aid in the 1960s, featuring Bugs Bunny—and directed by none other than Tex Avery, who directed the first real Bugs Bunny short in 1940. (After he left Schlesinger's, Avery continued his incandescent career in theatrical cartoons at MGM and Lantz; then he went into television production, where his work also included the popular early Raid commercials, with their screechy bugs.)

But television did bring some low moments. In 1972, Warner's leased a few of its characters to the Hollywood studio Filmation for an hourlong television special called "Daffy Duck and Porky Pig Meet the Groovie Ghoulies"; the less said about this work, the better. And from 1968 to 1970, Warner's had seventy-eight of its black-and-white "Looney Tunes" remade into color by Color Systems Inc., which is now known as Entercolor Technologies Corporation. (Warner's had also sold these early cartoons, but the company regained them through subsequent deals.) Using the same thinking that has led, more recently, to the "colorization" of such films as *It's a Wonderful Life,* the studio believed that the cartoons would be more marketable when Porky was pink, and not ashen gray. In the case of the "Looney Tunes," each cartoon's animated characters were traced, colored in, and then rephotographed over queasy-brownish reworkings of the original backgrounds; this copying was undertaken in Korea and New York. Sadly, these new versions are filled with technical errors, faultily executed "animation," clumsy colors, and other failings. Although in wide distribution, they should not be considered in any way representative of the cartoons they were intended to replace.

## Framing The Future

In 1984, Warner Bros. animation entered its latest phase, marked by the concerted expansion of all aspects of production. Growing in staff from a handful of contributors to more than forty, the studio has moved into a new facility in Burbank and stepped up its involvement with theatrical, television, and commercial projects. Under Producer Steven Greene, the studio began a policy of training new artists alongside some Warner veterans, giving the shop full production capability. And new writer-directors Greg Ford and Terry Lennon have brought an historical awareness to this new production that has let the studio's regenerated technical prowess meld with an informed and sophisticated sense of how to use the characters. This was clearly revealed in 1987's surprising release of the first Warner Bros. theatrical cartoon in almost two decades, a Daffy Duck one-reeler called *The Duxorcist.* The seven-minute cartoon received feature-length reviews and write-ups in, among others, *Time, Newsweek, USA Today,* and *People*—probably setting some kind of record in the ratio of screen-time to press attention. *The Duxorcist* and a subsequent short, *The Night of the Living Duck,* will both be incorporated into the upcoming feature *Daffy Duck's Quackbusters.*

And in the middle 1980s, Warner's moved into another field, when it began releasing compilations of its cartoons on videocassette. More than a dozen titles have been produced, many of which have qualified as gold or platinum sellers.

Above and opposite: *The Duxorcist.*

Yet nothing could staunch the international rediscovery of Warner Bros. animation in the early seventies. Among the surfeit of cartoons on TV, the Warner shorts were singled out—and when the people who had done the singling reached the age where they could act upon their affections, they did. Screenings and tributes were held in many countries. In 1975, Camera Three, an independent filmmaking group based in New York, produced "The Boys From Termite Terrace," an hourlong documentary about the Warner cartoon studio that was broadcast nationwide on CBS-TV. Also in 1975, filmmakers associated with the Orson Welles Cinema in Cambridge, Mass., produced *Bugs Bunny Superstar*, a feature-length film that includes a selection of the pre-1948 Warner cartoons along with interviews with Bob Clampett, Friz Freleng, and Tex Avery; in national release to theaters it earned lustrous reviews, and its advertising slogan—"You won't believe how much you missed as a kid"—captured the new generation's attitude toward its reclaimed cartoon heritage. New York's Museum of Modern Art held separate retrospective screenings of the work of Clampett, Jones, and Avery. And these were just the most conspicuous of the nation's showered honors.

Seeing the rising tide, Warner Bros. got busy. In the middle '70s, Warner's supplied CBS with five half-hour specials—consisting of three cartoons and opening and closing titles—to broadcast in prime time. The specials were so successful—each received above a 30 share—that CBS requested more compilations. But Warner's insisted that "new animation had to be done to hook the cartoons together and provide some continuity to the shows," said Hal Geer, Executive Producer at the time. CBS agreed, and from this has arisen, to date, nearly 20 specials with the Warner characters. Continually popular, these programs—most of them pastiches of older animation and new bridging footage—have become perennials in prime time.

Among the more highly regarded of the specials were two that Warner contracted from Chuck Jones, and which consisted entirely of new animation: "The Carnival of the Animals" (1976) and "A Connecticut Rabbit in King Arthur's Court" (1978). Returning to Bugs, Daffy, and cohorts was a welcome opportunity for Jones, who, after leaving Warner's, worked on MGM's last "Tom and Jerry" theatrical shorts before becoming about the last producer of programs in full animation for television. His half-hour specials include the acclaimed "How the Grinch Stole Christmas" and "Horton Hears a Who."

The natural next step, for all parties concerned, was to bring the characters back to the big screen. Again Chuck Jones was called upon, and his company produced *The Bugs Bunny/Road Runner Movie*, a feature-length assemblage of clips from Jones' Warner shorts along with over twenty minutes of new animation. The film was accorded the honor of opening the 1979 New York Film Festival, before beginning a nationwide theatrical run.

Buoyed by the performance of the Jones film, and by the unabating interest in their characters, Warner's decided to step up its involvement with animation by reviving its cartoon division in 1980. Friz Freleng was named Executive Producer, and with a growing complement of artists, the studio began work on television, theatrical, and commercial projects. Its first film, *Friz Freleng's Looney Looney Looney Bugs Bunny Movie*, is a sampling of Freleng's Warner shorts stitched with new footage, and was released to theaters in 1981. This was followed by *Bugs Bunny's 3rd Movie: 1001 Rabbit Tales* (1982) and *Daffy Duck's Movie: Fantastic Island* (1983).

While the post-1975 work may lack the eclat of the vintage Warner cartoons, it nevertheless brings welcome surprises. For starters, Chuck Jones was able to direct a "sequel" to one of his classic shorts, *Duck Dodgers in the Return of the 24-1/2th Century*, for television. And 1987 brought the first Warner Bros. theatrical cartoon in almost two decades, a Daffy Duck one-reeler called *The Duxorcist*, directed by Greg Ford and Terry Lennon. With a heritage so strong, there will always be movement. Immortal in spirit, the Warner characters have the advantage of being immortal in fact.

# PART TWO:
# THE STARS

# Porky Pig

A more unlikely hero there never was. Yet the pig known as Porky was the first character to put the Warner animation studio on the map, after five years and some one hundred cartoons of trying. Timid, varying in appearance, simpleminded, bloated, with a stutter you could drive a milk truck through, Porky nevertheless spoke, in his way, to moviegoers across America.

The epochal pig had his debut in Friz Freleng's 1935 *I Haven't Got a Hat,* as part of an ensemble of new schoolroom characters the studio was testing as replacements for the inefficacious Buddy. "When I was a kid, I had two playmates—a little fat kid called Piggy and his younger brother, who was called Porky," said Freleng. "I always wanted to do a comic strip with two kids with those names. But in animation, everything is animals, so when I had this classroom cartoon, I thought of Porky."

To give the character a gimmicky distinctiveness, Freleng decided

Above: *Layout drawing from* Gold-diggers of '49, *1935.* Below: *The first definitive Porky model sheet, 1935.*

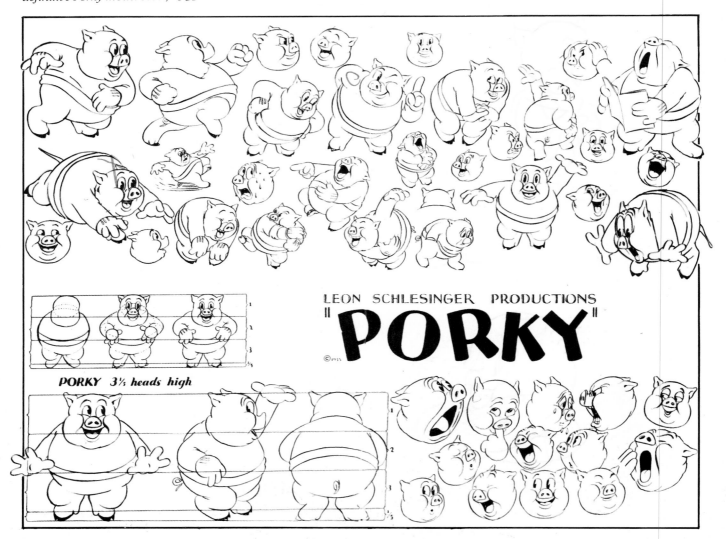

LEON SCHLESINGER PRODUCTIONS
"PORKY"

PORKY 3½ heads high

*Cel from Robert McKimson's* Boobs in the Woods, *1950.*

141

to endow him with a stutter. To this end, he engaged actor Joe Dougherty, who appeared as a dress extra in such films as *The Jazz Singer* and *Ziegfeld Girl,* to provide the voice. But Dougherty's stutter was genuine, making it impossible for him to control his delivery. "He would begin to recite, but then he'd get stuck," Freleng said. "He just couldn't get off certain words. We were recording on film at the time, and the film was running, and I figured, boy, if they find out how much film I used just to make a cartoon, they'll kick my ass off the lot."

Eventually, Dougherty became such a liability that new arrival Mel Blanc was asked to devise a controllable voice for the character. Blanc came up with a vocal caricature of a pig's stutterish oinking, and turned it to delightful comic effect. Explained Blanc: "I'd say things like, 'Say, have you got a nick-, eh-ni nick-, eh-ni-nick-, eh-ni- Spare five cents?'" Like Dougherty's, Blanc's voice was electronically speeded.

Porky's second outing, *Golddiggers of '49* (1935, Avery), was actually billed as featuring the cat called Beans, but the bit-part pig garnered the lion's share of the laughter. "We were searching for new characters," remarked Freleng, "and the audience told us Porky was the guy." Finally favored with a popular player, the Warner directors ran with Porky as

Above: *Opening Graphic.*
Top: *Model drawing by Vivie Risto from Bob Clampett's* Ali Baba Bound, *1940.* Right: *Layout drawing from Frank Tashlin's* Porky the Fireman, *1938.*

often as possible, and he quickly took over the "Looney Tunes" series. Yet the artists still didn't have a handle on the character, Porky's age, design, size, and face varied from picture to picture. In *I Haven't Got a Hat,* Porky is but a lad, while in *Golddiggers of '49* he is a full-grown father, with an appetite so ravenous that he is willing to marry off his daughter just to secure his lunch. Rather adolescent in *Boom Boom* (1936), he is a nubile suitor by the time of 1937's *Porky's Romance.* Physically, in these films, Porky passed through many shades of ugly, as the Warner artists labored to wrap an appropriate package around the appealing essence they had created.

The character achieved his first coherent identity when Bob Clampett took over a "Looney Tunes" unit in 1937. Clampett and his artists made Porky snappy and cute, downplayed his stammer, and cast him as an eager, if naive, delver into the world's wonders. Whether a visitor to a bizarro Garden (in *Porky in Wackyland*), a Sahara so sweltering that camels have hallucinating meltdowns *(Porky in Egypt),* an arctic area with ice sheets that mimic fun-house mirrors *(Polar Pals),* or a desert fort terrorized by a cross-eyed sheik with a bomb strapped to his head *(Ali Baba Bound),* Porky was an innocent observer, a surrogate for the

Above: *Porky and his horse are surprised by the mighty Injun Joe. Animation drawing from Bob Clampett's* Injun Trouble, *1938. Below: Promotional drawing by Mel Millar from* Porky and Gabby, *1937, Ub Iwerks' first cartoon for Leon Schlesinger.*

audience in looking at Clampett's wiggy visions. The wide-eyed pig played straight man to an entire unhinged cosmos.

But he also played straight man to Warner's unhinged characters. Cast as a simple, slow-witted hunter, Porky was set up as the comedic foil for the first appearances of that daffiest of ducks *(Porky's Duck Hunt,* 1937) and the germinal Bugs Bunny *(Porky's Hare Hunt,* 1938). Unprepared for personalities who flaunt convention and rationality alike, Porky becomes so bamboozled that, at one point, he turns to a higher authority: In the duck hunt film, Porky manages to maneuver quickly enough to shoot Daffy, who is lolling in the lake. He sends his dog to swim from the shore and bring the body back, but when he returns, it is Daffy who hurls the hound at Porky's feet. Lost, Porky pulls out a sheaf of papers and complains, "Hey! That wasn't in the script!"

There was something else in the script that Porky couldn't see. By the early 1940s, the characters whom Porky had helped introduce had

Above: *From Chuck Jones'* The Scarlet Pumpernickel, *1950.* Top: *Model sheet by Vivie Risto from* Ali Baba Bound, *1940.* Above right: *Porky does Oliver Hardy; model sheet from Norm McCabe and Bob Clampett's* The Timid Toreador, *1940.* Right: *From Chuck Jones'* Drip-along Daffy, *1951.*

COMEDY RELIEF

gone on to displace him as Warner's cartoon stars. Mild-mannered and boyish, Porky was out of tune with a wartime that favored the brazenness and power of Bugs, Daffy, Sam, and the others. Accordingly, the pig was used much less frequently; and because of his relative simplicity and reticence, he fell into resembling, personality-wise, the milquetoasty Elmer Fudd. Most of the time, the Fuddish Porky was paired with Daffy Duck, and often cast as a hunter—completing the parallel to the basic Bugs and Elmer situation. 1944's *Duck Soup to Nuts* (Freleng), for example, is an elemental hunter-and-hunted scenario, while the same year's *Tom Turk and Daffy* (Jones) entangles the two with a talkative Thanksgiving turkey (thereby letting Daffy reveal an uncontrollable fondness for cranberry sauce and candied yams). Where Elmer is undone by Bugs' razor smarts, Porky has no resources at all for dealing with the buggy duck.

Porky continued to languish through the late 1940s, until he was

Above: *Publicity drawing from Norm McCabe's* Who's Who in the Zoo, *1942.*
Below: *Animation drawings from* Duck Soup to Nuts.

*From cartoons directed by Arthur Davis in 1948:* Above: *The initial establishing shot from* Nothing But the Tooth, *in which Porky goes after California gold in 1849—although he must get past a Jewish-sounding little Indian who is intent on scalping him. Painting by Philip De Guard.* Below: *Layout drawing from* The Pest That Came to Dinner. *In several cartoons of the middle-late 1940s, Porky played a put-upon bachelor homeowner. Here he is plagued by a pesky termite.*

redesigned, recast, and resuscitated by Chuck Jones in his film-genre parodies starring the over-reaching Daffy Duck. Made more adult-looking and heavier on his feet, Porky injected a wry touch of the reality principle into Daffy's self-aggrandizing role-playing. In the mock-Western *Drip-along Daffy*, Porky—riding a miniature steed and sporting stubble on his cheek—is identified through a subtitle as "Comedy Relief." When Daffy falters in his big duel with Nasty Canasta, Porky turns a windup wooden soldier on the grisly villain and blows him away, then is hoisted heroically above the crowd of cheering townspeople and eventually elected mayor. Likewise, when Daffy Duck Dodgers goes overboard with his egomaniacal ranting, "eager young space cadet" Porky is so unimpressed that he can only mutter, "B-b-big deal." Or when Daffy's shrill and steely "Dorlock Homes" can't get that big Victorian brute the Shropshire Slasher to budge an inch, either with cunning or with jiujitsu, (in *Deduce, You Say*, 1956), Porky's dapper "Watkins" only makes a direct, understated appeal—"Now look, old boy, how's about returning to prison"—for the behemoth to willingly turn himself in. And when a smocked and booted Daffy Duck claims that he *really is* Robin Hood, then Friar Tuck Porky—tonsured, and in a clerical robe—can only reply with a fit of wiggly, blubbery giggles.

"I played Porky pretty square," said Jones. "He was an observer,

Below: *The initial establishing shot from Robert McKimson's* An Egg Scramble, *1950, painting by Richard H. Thomas.*

and he was in on the joke. I liked him, and I thought that it was a very important part to play."

But Jones does concede that, by the middle 1940s, Porky went through a long period of decline. "He was pushed back because he wasn't very interesting," the director said. "But he wasn't interesting because we didn't make him very interesting. You can hardly blame it on somebody else."

*Chuck Jones' later Porky: model sheet from 1947 with poses from* Scaredy Cat, *1948.*

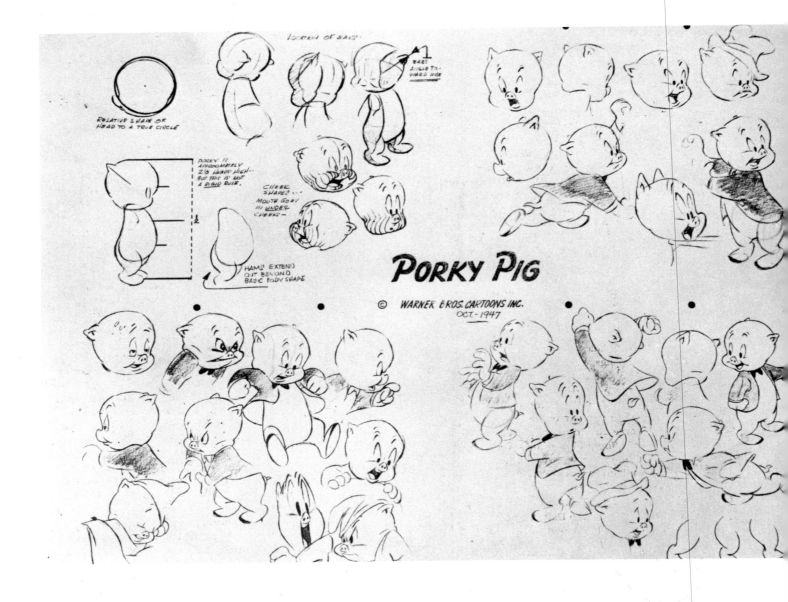

PORKY PIG

© WARNER BROS. CARTOONS INC.
OCT. - 1947

# A Warner Glossary

As part of Warner Bros.' attempt to bring animation from never-never land into the thick of contemporary culture, the studio used an unceasing stream of popular slogans in its cartoons, mostly in the latter 1930s and the 1940s. Sometimes these commonly known expressions let the cartoons comment on issues, personalities, and other referents of the day in ironic or sardonic ways; elsewhere, they provided another level of humor by giving the characters something familiar, but out of context, to say—a short cut to a sure laugh.

Some phrases spun off from political origins, such as the many War-related slogans in the cartoons of those years. These included "Turn off that light!" "Was that trip really necessary?" and references to gas rationing and to giving up meat. Other allusions were to advertising, such as Lucky Strike's "So round, so firm, so fully packed, so free and easy on the draw," which Daffy plays with in *Book Revue* (1946); and Ionized Yeast's "Have you had your iron today?," which is said in *The Goofy Gophers* (1947) and became "Have you had your Fluffies today?" in *Screwball Football* (1939).

But the most common sources for Warner's cross-cultural punning were films and, above all, radio, which had developed the technique of the catchphrase to give immediate recognizability to characters who, of course, could not be seen. Some of these phrases are as follows:

In the late 1930s, the comedian Joe Penner was Warner's most fertile source for appropriations. His "Wanna buy a duck?" occurs, for example, in *Porky's Duck Hunt* (1937) as delivered by a caricature of Penner himself, and among the recorded boxing-coach's babble in *Count Me Out* (1938). Penner's "Don't ever *dooo* that!" is pointedly cried by Egghead in *A-Lad-in Bagdad* (1938).

Later on, three other comedians were high on the hit list. Two of Jerry Colonna's turns were used repeatedly, as in Daffy Duck's "Greetings, Gate—let's osculate!" in *The Wise Quacking Duck* (1943), and Bugs' "Gruesome, isn't it?" from *Bugs Bunny Gets the Boid* (1942).

Red Skelton was also all over the studio. His character Clem Kadiddlehopper's drawn-out huckster's "Here I am!" is said by Bugs in *Stage Door Cartoon* (1944) and by Red Hot Ryder in *Buckaroo Bugs* (1944). And several lines originated with Skelton's Junior, the Mean Widdle Kid: "He don't know me very well, do he?" is said by Bugs at the bogus-cliffhanger conclusion of *Hare Trigger* (1945); "If I dood it, I gets a whippin'. I dood it!" was also given to Bugs, in *Case of the Missing Hare* (1942); and Daffy Duck's "You bwoke my widdle Daddy, you bwoke his widdle back, you bwoke his widdle head!" in *Ain't That Ducky* (1945) is a variation on Junior verbiage.

Lou Costello was caricatured in several cartoons, and his catchphrases were often heard elsewhere, such as his "I'm a baaaad boy!" wailed by Egghead from inside a lion's belly in *A Day at the Zoo* (1939). Bugs' perennial "Gee, ain't I a stinker?"—as used, for example, at the end of *Hare Force* (1944)—was taken from Costello, as was "I'm only three-and-a-half years old," which was spoken by one of the gremlins in *Russian Rhapsody* (1944) and by Bugs in *Falling Hare* (1943).

The high-pitched, Jewish-sounding "It's a possibility!," as said in *Russian Rhapsody,* as well as "Mmmmmm—could be!," as hummed by the pilot in *Ceiling Hero* (1940) and in *Russian Rhapsody,* came from the Mr. Kitzel character played by Artie Auerbach on "Al Pearce and his Gang" and the Jack Benny show. The Jewish-inflected "Were you expecting maybe Humphrey Bogart?" said by the little

Indian in *Nothing But the Tooth* (1948) was derived from Minerva Pious' Mrs. Nussbaum, on the Fred Allen show. Also on Fred Allen, Parker Fennelly's Titus Moody, a rustic New Englander, popularized the pronoun "Bub"—as in Daffy's roared "Watch it, bub!" in *The Wise Quacking Duck* and Bugs' "What's all the hubbub, bub?" in *Falling Hare.* Also in *Falling Hare,* the gremlin's scratchy laugh—"Heh heh heh" 's to the tune of "Yankee Doodle"—was taken from character actor Benny Rubin.

"I like him, he's silly," as intoned by the *Falling Hare* gremlin and by Tweety in *Birdy and the Beast* (1944), was based on Fanny Brice's Baby Snooks. And Tweety's "Aw, da poor puddy-tat—he fall down and go *BOOM!*" was derived from a 1928 song entitled "I Faw Down an' Go Boom." "Milkman keep those bottles quiet!," yelled by the cats in *Kitty Kornered* (1946), was the name of a 1944 tune performed in the film *Broadway Rhythm.* "The rabbits are coming, hooray, hooray," chanted by Bugs in *The Big Snooze* (1946), is a play on the traditional Scottish song "The Campbells are Coming."

The last line of *The Big Snooze,* Bugs' Southern "I *love* dat man!" was the catchphrase of Beulah, a black female character first played by a white man, Marlin Hurt, on "Fibber McGee and Molly." The phrase can also be heard in *The Great Piggy Bank Robbery* (1946). *Hare Ribbin',* from 1944, features a dog who speaks like Bert Gordon's The Mad Russian on the Eddie Cantor program; his line "Do you min it?" is also said by the homosexual Oscar statue at the end of *What's Cookin', Doc?* (1944), while his prim "How do you do!" is handled by the friendly gorilla in *Circus Today* (1940).

Tony Labriola's Oswald character on the Ken Murray program coined the long, low-toned "Wohhhh yeah!" sounded by the many hiding hunters in *Daffy Duck and Egghead* (1938) and by the film director's chorus of sycophants in *A Star is Hatched* (1938). "Well, now, I wouldn't say that," drawled by senior citizen Bugs at the end of *The Old Grey Hare* (1944) and three-and-a-half times by the little man from the draft board in *Draftee Daffy* (1945), started with Peavey the druggist, a part played by Richard Legrand followed by Forrest Lewis on the Great Gildersleeve show. Elmer Blurt, the timid salesman played by Al Pearce on his eponymous program, coined the quickly bounced "Nobody home, I hope, I hope, I hope" that the wolf says at the door in *Little Red Walking Hood* (1937). The genie character voiced by Jim Backus—before he became Mr. Magoo—in *A Lad in His Lamp* (1948) was based on his role as the rich Hubert Updike on the Alan Young program.

"Monkies is duh cwaziest people!" was Lew Lehr's handle in the Fox Movietone News, which he would conclude with comedy segments from the zoo. "Camels is duh cwaziest people" is said in *Porky in Egypt* (1938), pussycats become the cwazies in *Scaredy Cat* (1948), while Hitler declares the same of Nazis in *Russian Rhapsody.* "Confidentially, she stinks," was immortalized by Mischa Auer as the Russian ballet master in Frank Capra's 1938 film of Kaufmann and Hart's *You Can't Take it With You,* and the line was reworked in *Robinson Crusoe, Jr.* (1941), *A Wild Hare* (1940), *Hare Conditioned* (1945), and elsewhere.

But the preeminent Warner film borrowing must be "Which way did he go, George, which way did he go?" followed by "Well thanks a lot, thanks a lot." The dimwit Lenny's lines were from John Steinbeck's novel *Of Mice and Men,* but Warner's was specifically parodying Lon Chaney Jr.'s reading of them in Lewis Milestone's 1939 film. First appearing in Avery's 1940 *Of Fox and Hounds,* it was later mangled in *Falling Hare, Dough, Ray, Me-ow,* (1948), and scads of others.

Continued on page 152

Above: *Animation drawing by Bob Clampett from Daffy's first-scene getaway, from* Porky's Duck Hunt, *1937.*

**Opposite**
*Cel from Arthur Davis'* What Makes Daffy Duck, *1948, with background.*

**150**

# Daffy Duck

It is not a coincidence that Daffy Duck starred in many of the very greatest of the Warner Bros. cartoons—from *Book Revue* and *The Great Piggy Bank Robbery* to *Duck Amuck* and *Drip-along Daffy*. For the character seemed to be the agent through which the strongest of the Warner cartoon directors most robustly expressed their filmmaking personalities; each director found different aspects of the duck that powerfully articulated his individual temperament. In each of their very capable hands Daffy became a different entity, his character made more complex by the accretion of influences from his past performances. Whitmanesque in his way, Daffy contained multitoons.

The character was introduced in *Porky's Duck Hunt,* a black-and-white cartoon directed by Tex Avery and released in April 1937. Beginning as a more-or-less prosaic hunting film, the cartoon brings Porky, shotgun in hand, to a marshland with his loyal hound. But among the dozens of ducks in residence there, one refuses to play by the rules. Squat and rounded, the little black quacker quickly lets himself be shot; but when Porky's dog brings the carcass back to his master, who is whooping with joy, the duck turns the tables by tossing the dog's exhausted corpus at Porky's feet. He then breaks into a giddy laugh, goads Porky by saying, "Don't let it worry you, skipper—I'm just a crazy darnfool duck!" and makes a deranged, whirligig exit. As animated by Bob Clampett, the duck runs through every berserk movement in the inventory, while maniacally ululating "Woo-hoo! Woo-hoo!" like Hugh Herbert with a hotfoot.

A bit player, the duck returns only once during the story. When Porky aims at him with his rifle that refuses to fire, the duck glides to shore and shows him how to make it work. But when Porky senses something unusual in such thoughtful behavior, the duck only chuckles, "It's me again" and repeats his pixilated getaway. Yet Avery knew that he had hit the mark with this character and so arranged to give him an encore: At the cartoon's end, the duck returns, hooting and slithering through the lettering of the "That's all, folks!" title card—more infectiously flaky animation by Bob Clampett.

The effect was immediate. "At that time, audiences weren't accustomed to seeing a cartoon character do these things," Clampett told Mike Barrier. "And so, when it hit the theaters it was like an explosion. People would leave the theaters talking about this daffy duck."

Avery went on to direct two more cartoons with the screwloose duck, both in color and released in 1938: *Daffy Duck and Egghead,* a follow-up hunting film in which Daffy was christened; and *Daffy Duck in Hollywood,* where he skewers the pretensions of a huffy film director at "Wonder Pictures" ("If it's a good picture, it's a WONDER" reads a sign at the studio's entrance). At one point, Daffy grabs the director's cigarette and skywrites "Warner Bros." all through the sound stage. "Just givin' my bosses a plug," the duck cackles. "I've got an option coming up!" The character's gratuitous insanity fit well with Avery's desire to rupture the stultification that had come to animated cartoons; for Avery, having no reason for a character to act in this way was the perfect reason to make the character do so.

With such an origin, Daffy was someone whom Bob Clampett

Continued from page 150

**1951**
Rabbit Fire
Drip-along Daffy

**1952**
Rabbit Seasoning

**1953**
Duck Amuck
Duck Dodgers in the 24½th Century
Duck! Rabbit! Duck!

**1955**
Beanstalk Bunny

**1957**
Ali Baba Bunny
Show Biz Bugs

**1958**
Robin Hood Daffy

Above: *sketches from a Daffy Duck model sheet, c. 1941.*

could not resist. The studio's most passionate advocate of unmotivated lunacy, Clampett quickly started casting Daffy as a kind of oddball goofball, forever out of control, in several of his black-and-white "Looney Tunes" of the late 1930s and early forties. Clampett drew the character to accentuate his bizarreness, making him taller, skinnier, and more thin-limbed, crossing his eyes, and basing his design more on arc shapes than on rounded forms. His movements became staccato and erratic, and his getaways were usually preceded by little leg-swinging hops of no apparent purpose. Yet form accorded with function in Clampett's Daffy films, as the director used the goony-looking character to execute some of his most outrageous gags: In 1938's *The Daffy Doc,* Quack Doctor Daffy tries to perform surgery on Porky with a handsaw—but with no anesthesia—and relentlessly chases the terrified pig around the hospital with this in mind; elsewhere in the film, Daffy is thrown into an iron lung, which makes various parts of his body wildly swell and contract, like inflating balloons—an unstable character becoming a showcase for Clampett's love of elastic and unstable body proportions. In the following year's *Scalp Trouble,* Daffy, guarding a western fort and wearing a Napoleonic hat, unintentionally swallows a quantity of ammunition and is used by frontiersman Porky as a squeezable machine gun against an Indian attack.

Yet Warner Cartoons largely outgrew this kind of batty silliness by the early 1940s, and the studio adapted Daffy to its more sophisticated stylings of this period with finesse. For starters, the duck was re-designed—made rounder, weightier, and more solid, drawn with tailored, graceful lines that brightened his smile and made him handsome indeed; Robert McKimson was responsible for much of this new look. And the character also absorbed some of the intellectual ability that the studio, after the development of Bugs Bunny, seemed uniquely capable of infusing into its players. Daffy was still a child, but now he was a brilliant child—crazy and crazily articulate at the same time, flapping his mouth where before he had flapped his wings. Daffy was still daffy, but he had learned to harness his nuttiness, with a mental agility that matched his physical flexibility.

An example of this transmutation can be found in Friz Freleng's 1944 *Duck Soup to Nuts,* a Porky-hunts-Daffy picture made seven years after Tex Avery had minted this scenario. In this cartoon, Daffy bedevils the rifle-bearing Porky both with stuntwork and with lippy cleverness. At their first encounter, Daffy walks—on his hands, as it happens—out of the lake and brazenly stands up to the pig who has come to shoot him. "Drop that gun, son," he barks. "You're not blasting at no ordinary, everyday, meat-on-the-table duck. I'm gifted! I'm just thlopping over with talent! I can sing!" (Whereupon he breaks into a few manic phrases from "Laugh, Clown, Laugh.") "I can dance!" (Whereupon he wiggles through a torrent of rapid gyrations.) "And *I* am an actor! I got a contract with Warner Bros.!" (Whereupon he whips out the official document, begins to emote like a French lover, then dons top hat, cape, and thin mustache and, now a mad movie villain, proceeds to chase Porky around and around a boulder.)

When Porky and Daffy worked as a team, the interplay ran much the same way. One winning instance is Frank Tashlin's late masterpiece, *Porky Pig's Feat* (1943). Here, Daffy causes all the difficulty (by gambling away the money they need to pay their hotel bill, then by offending the hotel manager by pressing his head deep into the manager's face when he confronts them about their overdue bill); then Daffy devises all the

*Daffy says, "I can dance!" And proceeds to prove it. Animation drawings from* Duck Soup to Nuts.

Above: *Animation drawings from* Scalp
Trouble. *Right: Cel from Robert McKimson's*
Boobs in the Woods, *1950*.

154

hilarious ploys that the two attempt in order to escape, after they have been locked inside their room. Daffy instigates, then Daffy exacerbates; Porky just goes along with him, ballast for the drunken boat.

Sure of himself yet ungovernably flightly, Daffy also became the ideal vehicle for Bob Clampett during his most vibrant period, the middle 1940s, when his films combined surface chaos with a deep underlying control. The character's impulsiveness, gumption, and lack of inhibition made him just the one to handle Clampett's immoderate emotions; and the director's bristling and distortive character movement ably bespoke Daffy's uncontrollably turbulent inner life. And now that Daffy looked more substantial and more real, Clampett's shock humor registered even more forcefully. In 1943's *The Wise Quacking Duck,* for example, Daffy pretends that he has been decapitated by Mr. Meek's large axe; tucking his head into the lower part of his neck, the duck splatters ketchup about as he wails and thrashes through some truly horrific death-agony (although he does break the hysterics to poke his mug into the camera and offer a straight-faced "Gruesome, isn't it?"). Or, in Clampett's *Book Revue* (1946), when Daffy is startled to see his leg being held and salted by the hungry Wolf, he reacts by lunging into becoming one gigantic, disbelieving eye.

Indeed, in *Book Revue,* Clampett presents Daffy as a creature capable of doing almost anything, except controlling himself. In a matter of seconds, the duck does a dead-on impersonation of Danny Kaye's routine as a nostalgic Russian gypsy, as featured on Kaye's recording of

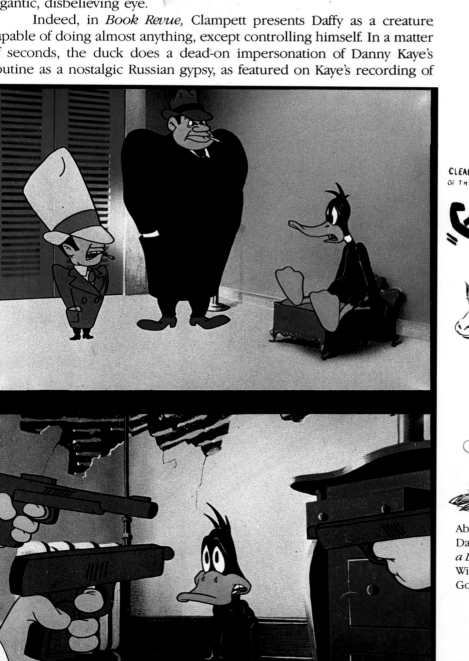

Above: *Model sheet from* Scrap Happy Daffy, *1943.* Top: *Animation drawing of a Daffy-terrorized Mr. Meek from* The Wise-Quacking Duck. Left: *From* Golden Yeggs.

155

*Above:* Daffy meets actor Victor Moore: story idea from Friz Freleng's Ain't That Ducky, *1945.* Below: *Model sheet used by the Jones unit, c. 1950.*

"Dinah" ("How different is my native willage," Daffy-Danny slurps. "Soft music; wiolins; the happy peoples sitting on their balalaikas, playing their samo*vahrs*"), performs a febrile "La Cucaracha," glides through a Kaye-inspired "Nothing Could be Feener Than to Be in Caroleener in the Morning," works his way into an excerpt from the "Little Red Riding Hood" story, and scat sings with the best of them—yet he also explodes into dippy "Hoo-hoo"-ing at several spots, once while bouncing on his rump deep into the reddened distance. For Clampett, Daffy was the character who best expressed the tension between his own freewheeling instincts as a filmmaker and the need to stay within the acceptable boundaries of Hollywood studio cartooning. Scratch the surface and a volcano erupts.

In fact, Daffy was so excessively energetic a character that he became a natural ally for the other Warner directors who were swept up in the Clampettian freneticism of the war years. In several of Frank Tashlin's very muscular efforts of the period, the character became heroic, a blaze of unstoppable spirit usable for patriotic ends. In *Scrap Happy Daffy,* the duck battles a plundering German goat, while in *Plane Daffy,* he undoes a Nazi duck spy-temptress called Hata Mari. If the duck's lack of self-restraint permits him to do anything, let him do it against the enemy.

Left: *sketches by Chuck Jones from* Rabbit Fire, *1951.* Below: *Layout drawing by Maurice Noble of where Daffy brings Elmer to have himself blasted ; from Chuck Jones'* Rabbit Seasoning; *1952.*

*Daffy by Chuck Jones.* Above: *Cel from Duck Amuck, 1953. Below: What Daffy wants to take home: Background painting from* Ali Baba Bunny, *1957*

Yet Daffy would again be transformed within the next few years. By 1950, the duck's psychobiography was being rewritten by Chuck Jones, who used the character with stunning effectiveness for nearly a decade. Jones made Daffy taller, beakier, scrawnier, and more angular, as edgy on the outside as he was within; he was more reminiscent of Jones' Wile E. Coyote than any other player. As for his character, Jones' duck is much more a creature of the mind, and has all but abandoned his penchant for speed gags. So undisciplined a character as Clampett's Daffy would have been unthinkable for a rationalist like Jones. Rather, Jones' Daffy has a root farther back, in Friz Freleng's 1940 *You Ought to Be in Pictures,* the film in which the plucky duck exhorts Porky to quit his career in cartoons so he can push out of his underling status, show his abilities, and grab some headlining glory. Jones' Daffy begins with this, but the director tinctured in some additional personality traits (read flaws) that endowed the character with a complexity and zest which made him perhaps the richest of all the studio's creations. Like such other 1950s antiheroes as Brando and Dean, Jones' Daffy is an outsider who both struggles to enter the mainstream and resists it, but who earns our sympathy for his conflicted ordeal.

In particular, Jones made Daffy what he described as a "self-preservationist," fighting furiously to preserve his skin or his dignity against a world that would rob them from him. Yet in Jones' work it is usually Daffy himself who triggers the processes that flay him. For Daffy,

Left and bottom: *From* The Scarlet Pumpernickel, *1950.* Below: *Daffy's subtle hints: Background painting by Philip De Guard from* Duck! Rabbit! Duck!, *1953.*

self-interest invariably becomes self-destruction; still impulsive, the duck acts before he thinks. A deeply funny example can be found in *Rabbit Seasoning* (1952), the middle of Jones' three celebrated cartoons in which Elmer goes hunting Bugs and Daffy. The film begins with series of mock Burma Shave road signs, seen in series along a woodland lane:

IF YOU'RE LOOKING FOR FUN—
YOU DON'T NEED A REASON
ALL YOU NEED IS A GUN—
IT'S RABBIT SEASON!

Thereafter comes a shot of a forest superfestooned with "Rabbit Season" signs, followed by knocking noises, and finally a glimpse of Daffy, industriously nailing the last of the signs to a tree. Immediately, then, the duck begins stamping a row of inked rabbit footprints right up to a hole in the ground—beside which stands a mailbox marked "B. Bunny"—and gives the camera a churlish grin: "Awfully unsporting of me, I know," he says, "but what the hey—I gotta have *some* fun." The duck ducks behind a nearby boulder, but cannot resist peeking out to add, "And besides, it's really duck season."

*Layout drawing by Chuck Jones from* Robin Hood Daffy, *1958.*

First flaw: That Daffy's suppression of the fact that it is duck season will go forever undetected. Second flaw: That he believes he can outwit Bugs Bunny, that supreme swifty, with this ruse. Result: A duck debeaked, in very many very degrading ways.

"Daffy has courage that most of us just don't have," said Jones. "He will continue to try and try again where we would have given up, because failure is unknown to him. No matter how badly things have worked out, he's always going to come back."

Thus irrepressible in his ambitions, the duck became in many Jones films a kind of unleashed id (stripped of sex, of course—these *are* animated cartoons, of course). "Daffy expresses all of the things we're afraid to express," Jones says. At one point or another, the duck embodied such qualities as malicious evil, shameless self-promotion, pure hate ("You're dethpicable!"), and, most of all, insatiable greed. In 1957's *Ali Baba Bunny,* for example, Bugs and Daffy mistakenly tunnel into a secret treasure cavern being guarded by the immense and sword-bearing Hassan. When the two pop up through the ground, Daffy sees the mountainous heaps of gold and jewelry in the cave and becomes possessed by covetous thoughts. Quickly he pounces on Bugs: "It's mine, you understand! Mine! All mine!" Daffy yells, battering Bugs back into the ground. "Get back in there! Down down down! Go go go! Mine mine mine!" Daffy emits a demonic chuckle, then dives into the booty. "I'm rich! I'm wealthy! Ya-hoo!" he exults, when he surfaces from the golden sea. "I'm comfortably well-off!" But then knuckleheaded Hassan hits on the magic phrase that lifts the stone covering the cave's mouth ("Er...Open septuagenarian? Uhh...Open saddle soap? Open sesame?"—and he is startled) and he goes after the unwelcome intruders ("Hassaahhn *chop!*"). Eventually, Daffy is diminished in size, if not in selfishness. Daffy is greedy, even when living within an oyster shell.

Such compulsive negative emotions are never simple. And it was Jones' particular gift in animation to be able to delineate, with adroitness, the intricate psychological equation that gave rise to such feelings. With ongoing humor, Jones showed how all of Daffy's emotional wrenchings were frantic overcompensations for his fundamental sense of insecurity. Daffy *needs* the love of an audience (in Freleng's *Show Biz Bugs*), or a Rockefellerian fortune (*Beanstalk Bunny, Ali Baba Bunny*), or certification from a supreme being (*Duck Amuck*) because he believes, at bottom, that he is unworthy of them. Fearful that he counts for nothing, Daffy must prove that he is capable of anything.

Thus, the black, beaked cartoon character envisions himself as a Romantic Hero (in *The Scarlet Pumpernickel*), a Western Hero (*Drip-along Daffy*), a Space Hero (*Duck Dodgers*), an Intellectual Hero (*Deduce, You Say*), and as Errol Flynn (*Robin Hood Daffy*). The duck is blind to the fact that he is flatly ridiculous in these roles, much less that he can not handle their requirements. "When Daffy pleaded with 'J.L.' to put him in a serious part [in *The Scarlet Pumpernickel*], he actually believed that he could do it," said Jones. "It never occurred to him that he couldn't."

And it was this tricky interrelationship between desire and failure—a subject also explored in the Road Runner films—that made the duck so resonant a character for Jones. "I'm probably closer to Daffy than to anyone," he said. "He was one of the great comedians, and I was lucky to be associated with him."

*Promotional drawings from some key performances.*

161

*From Chuck Jones'* Rabbit Seasoning, *1952.*

# Elmer Fudd

That sap for all seasons, that schlemiel nonpareil, Elmer Fudd is the archetypal wimp. Soft and round, pink and lumpy, epically bald, the befuddled one was Warner Cartoons' all-purpose dupe. And if one look at him doesn't establish that fact, just wait until he opens his mouth. Soon enough, the pwobwem is obvious.

In fact, the Fudd voice preceded the character. Physically, Elmer evolved from a character called Egghead, an even more highly caricatured mincer introduced in Tex Avery's *Egghead Rides Again* (1937). With his balloon nose and his vast flat feet, Egghead played such parts as duck hunter (in *Daffy Duck and Egghead*), fairy-tale crasher *(Cinderella Meets Fella),* and amateur boxer *(Count Me Out)* in some dozen cartoons. And although his personality varied from role to role, Egghead was a

*Cel from* Slick Hare, *1947.*

kind of hybrid of some of the comedians of his day: His voice, supplied by Cliff Nazarro, was often an impersonation of Joe Penner, and his typical attire—loose suit, high collar, derby hat—was in large part derived from that of nightclub comic Ben Blue.

But Egghead was rather too bizarre to generate any real popularity. In the thirties, however, an actor named Arthur Q. Bryan was freelancing in films and radio; perhaps his best-known part was that of Doc Gamble on the "Fibber McGee and Molly" radio program. Bryan was called down to Warner Cartoons, and one of his voices conveyed such world-class milksoppiness that it immediately suggested itself for a character; it was first used in Tex Avery's 1939 *Dangerous Dan McFoo*. The studio then decided to restyle Egghead to complement this stwiking new sonority. In Chuck Jones' *Elmer's Candid Camera* (1940), Fudd made his screen debut; yet he still showed vestigial traces of his Egghead origins, including the bulbous nose, the stiff collar, and the derby. (Interestingly, the name had been auditioned earlier: In Avery's 1938 *A Feud There Was,*

*Egghead becomes Elmer, as seen in model sheets from cartoons directed by Tex Avery.* Right: *From* Egghead Rides Again, *1937.* Below: Daffy Duck and Egghead, *1938.* Opposite Top: *From* Little Red Walking Hood, *1937. Bob Clampett: "Tex and I and one of the gag men had a session in which we talked about how to 'cuten up' [Egghead]. . . . We used an earlier model sheet, and as we talked, checks were put by the derby, the high collar, and the clothes, indicating they should be kept. But . . . Tex sketched a smaller nose and indicated other changes. This was the beginning of the final, 'cuter' Elmer."* Opposite bottom: *From* A Wild Hare, *1940; drawn by Robert Givens.*

Egghead appears as a yodeling peacemaker between two warring back-water clans, but his motor scooter identifies him as Elmer Fudd.)

*Elmer's Candid Camera* finds Fudd as a numskull naturalist, inno-cently going after "wildwife" with his tripod and box camera. Coming upon "wabbit twacks," he has his first encounter with a developing version of Bugs Bunny, who proceeds to con, hector, and heckle him until he is reduced to stumbling wild-eyed around the forest wailing "Wabbits! Wabbits!" Naturally, Elmer ends up shoulder-deep in a lake.

But it was in Avery's 1940 *A Wild Hare*—the cartoon that also crystallized Bugs Bunny—that the definitive Elmer was realized. Here he is a hunter, with floppy hat and long rifle; based on a model sheet drawn by Robert Givens, his nose is smaller, his head rounder, and—most importantly—he has a chin. And he delivers all the telltale lines. After a moment of concentrated stalking at the film's outset, Elmer turns to the audience: "Be vewy vewy quiet," he says earnestly. "I'm hunting wabbits." He continues, looks down, and sees pawprints: "Oh, boy—wabbit twacks!"—then the legendary laugh. Coming upon the rabbit hole, he baits it with a carrot; when the temptation is swiped by a gloved hand, Elmer rams his gun into the hole, only to become deflated when its two barrels are tied into a bow knot. Later, he sets up a trap that involves a carrot, a box leaning on a stick, and a glaring neon sign advertising the prize; and his benighted belief that this ploy will actually work lets Bugs

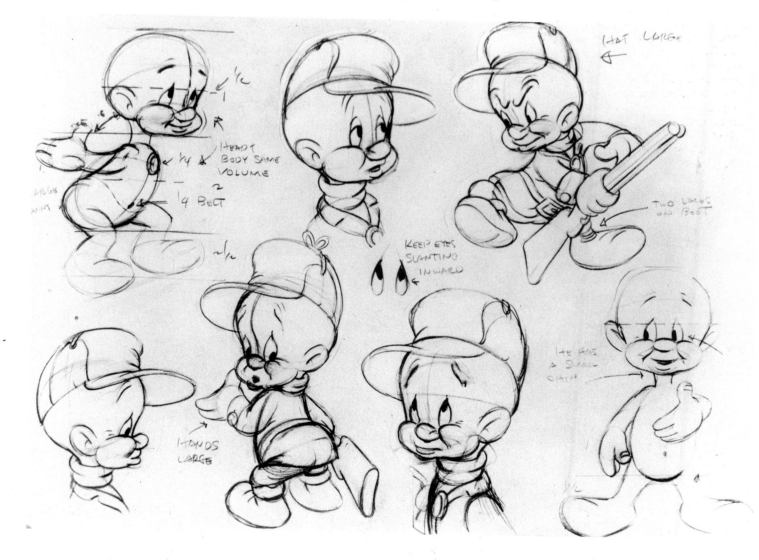

Above: *Publicity drawing for Bob Clampett's* Wabbit Twouble, *1941. Below: December, 1940 publicity photograph of Arthur Q. Bryan (left) with Artie Auerbach, taken at the "Al Pearce and his Gang" radio program.*

know that Elmer is the kind of guy whom he can have a field day with. It was a pairing that would last for better than twenty years: dolt versus sharpster.

In 1941, however, Fudd took a detour of sorts. Beginning with Bob Clampett's *Wabbit Twouble* and continuing in three subsequent cartoons and the fund-raiser in which Bugs sings "Any Bonds Today?" Elmer became exceedingly portly, although the voice and the personality remained. Fudd was plumped, according to Clampett, because he and his artists weren't pleased with the character in his current dimensions—he wasn't funny-looking enough—and so they decided to make him resemble the man who provided his voice, the dumpling-like Arthur Q. Bryan. But the bloated Elmer proved even less amusing when he was animated; accordingly, in 1942's *The Hare-Brained Hypnotist* (Freleng), the svelte Fudd was back for good, once again as the quintessential hunter. The Warner cartoonists' attitude toward hunting was perhaps expressed in a Fuddian line from Chuck Jones' *Duck! Rabbit! Duck!* (1953). After a spurt of smoke has cleared, Elmer, with gravest concern, consoles victim Bugs: "Golly, Mr. Wabbit, I hope I didn't hurt you too much when I killed you." The wabbit is not comforted.

Left: *Layout drawing from* The Old Grey Hare, *1944.* Below: *Cel from* Elmer's Candid Camera.

Nevertheless, for Fudd, once a hunter, always a hunter. Bob Clampett's roguishly funny *The Old Grey Hare* (1944) establishes this point by considering the course of Elmer's unchanging life from infancy until doddering, wrinkled senility. In a flashback, Baby Elmer chases Baby Buggsy (who sucks a bottle of carrot juice through a nipple) in wildly paced crawling hops, then in heavily motorized prams. And through a flash–forward (after a God-like voice intones, "Let us look far into the future: 1950, 1960 . . ."), Elmer is still going after the rabbit well beyond what should rightly be retirement age. In the year 2000, however, he shoots him not with a rifle, but with his "Buck Wogers Wightning Quick Wabbit Killer." And after Elmer thinks that he has finally finished off his prey, Bugs ultimately turns the tables and buries Elmer alive (rasping, "So long, Methuselah!"). Adding insult to infamy, Bugs plants a bomb down in the ground with Elmer, timing it to go off during the cartoon's closing and shake up the "That's all Folks!" end title.

Yet even within his role as hunter, Elmer had his moments to shine. In *The Hare-Brained Hypnotist*, Elmer learns some mind-bending techniques from a book on hypnotism and exchanges identities with Bugs Bunny; now gleefully able to outsmart the rabbit, Elmer even takes

Below: *Animation drawing from* The Hare-Brained Hypnotist, *1942.*

*Three stages of Elmer.* Opposite top: *Model sheet by Vivie Risto, 1942.* Opposite bottom: *Sketches from Arthur Davis'* What Makes Daffy Duck, *1948.* Below: *Sketches from Chuck Jones'* Rabbit Fire, *1951.*

*Background paintings by Richard H. Thomas from* What's Up, Doc? *Above: Railroading in to conquer the Big Town. Below: A marquee from a stage triumph.*

the opportunity to kiss him wantonly on the cheek ("Who's the comedian in this picture, anyway?" an irked Bugs protests). And this idea was taken further in Freleng's 1955 *Hare Brush*. Here, Elmer begins as a wealthy business magnate with a problem: He thinks he is a rabbit. Committed to a sanitarium, he spots Bugs ambling by and entices him to take his place in return for the institution's generous ration of carrots. Soon Bugs is led to a psychiatrist for therapy and forced to repeat, very many times: "I am Elmer J. Fudd, millionaire. I own a mansion and a yacht." Eventually, Bugs comes to believe that he *is* Fudd; in time he puts on Elmer's clothing and goes out hunting wabbits, until he chances upon Elmer hopping around a woodside dressed as one. But in the middle of this reversed hunt, an IRS agent taps Bugs on the shoulder and leads him away, citing a problem with back taxes. "I may be a scwewy wabbit," happy Fudd then tells us, "but I ain't goin' to Alcatwaz!"

In several cartoons, Elmer was allowed to leave behind his typecasting as hunter. And in many of these instances he became Warner Cartoons' Everyman, a dullardly bourgeois unable to perceive even the simplest of the cartoon world's scams. In the early *Elmer's Pet Rabbit* (1941, Jones), he brings a vexatious Bugs back to his house for some gratuitous abuse (and delivers the infinitely contented line, "That was weawwy a awfuwwy good weg of wamb"). In *An Itch in Time* (1943, Clampett), Elmer is a homeowner who threatens his dog with a dreaded bath if he ever again scratches himself, while in *Hare Tonic* (1945, Jones)

Bugs paints polka dots all over Elmer's living room, impersonates the bearded "Dr. Killpatient," and convinces panicky Fudd that he has the hideous disease "Rabbititus." (Later, Bugs tries to convince the audience that it has come down with the same affliction by making the screen swirl with colorful dots.) And in *Slick Hare* (1947, Freleng), Elmer is an employee in a tony restaurant to which Humphrey Bogart has come to eat, demanding a rabbit dinner. In this cartoon, beleaguered Elmer must set some sort of record for most pies in the face per interval of six minutes.

Yet Elmer did have his moments of apotheosis. Sometimes they end in humiliation, as they did in 1950's *What's Up, Doc?* (McKimson). Here, Elmer is a vaudeville bigwig who rescues Bugs Bunny's fizzling career, but who ends up getting razzed on stage when the rabbit proves to be the more capable entertainer. But in Chuck Jones' *What's Opera, Doc?* (1957), Elmer knows genuine glory. Playing a resplendent Wagnerian, in impenetrable armor and shining helmet, Elmer dances a graceful *pas de deux*, sings stirring mock-arias, and controls the tempestuous elements with waves of his hand. So what if, after Valkyrie Elmer believes he has finally slayed his rabbit adversary, Bugs raises his head and offers, "Well, what did you expect in an opera—a happy ending?" Into fields of golden color, Elmer strides somberly away, entering, magnificently, cartoon Valhalla.

Above: *Layout drawing by Chuck Jones. From* What's Opera, Doc? *Below: Concept painting by Maurice Noble.*

# Bugs Bunny

The criteria for greatness in animated cartoons are several. Bugs Bunny easily meets them all: He was the star of his own long-running series of shorts, in this case numbering more than 160; he became the internationally recognized symbol of an animation studio; he has won more popularity polls than anyone cares to count; hit recordings, sheet music, comic books, newspaper strips, and feature films have carried his name; his image embellishes merchandise ranging from jewelry to toothpaste; he has not been absent from television for one day in more than 30 years; his mention brings a pleasant tension to the corners of the mouth.

Of course, a few other cartoon characters can support such claims. But in one intangible but critical way, Bugs rises above the pack: Perhaps more so than any other cartoon creation, Bugs is the character whom, if he were to come to life, you would want to spend time with. There would be much to say.

Yet he didn't begin that way. Bugs' first unequivocal ancestor—for the rabbit's parentage has been the source of much debate and controversy—appeared in a 1938 cartoon called *Porky's Hare Hunt*. This black-and-white film was directed by Ben Hardaway and is essentially a retread of the situation established in the first Daffy Duck cartoon, *Porky's Duck Hunt,* which was directed by Tex Avery and released slightly more than one year earlier to a reception so strong that it all but mandated sequels. "Hardaway needed a story," said Friz Freleng, "and I remember that he told me, 'I'm just going to put a rabbit suit on that duck.'" In addition, Bob Clampett said that he contributed story and gag suggestions to this first rabbit short. Recapitulating the first Daffy plot, it finds a nincompoop-ish Porky encountering an unpredictable and sassy sprite who whips around the forest spouting wisecracks and irreverence, and who forever confounds Porky's earnest attempts to conform to his role as hunter. If the character seems to be a graduate of the Daffy Duck finishing school, it is no accident: Hardaway received screen credit for writing the second Daffy cartoon, and probably had a hand in the first. (And if both characters seem to anticipate Walter Lantz's Woody Woodpecker, again Hardaway is the key: Two years later, in 1940, he wrote the first Woody cartoon.)

Physically, the unnamed rabbit is drawn more naturalistically than the final Bugs; totally white, he has long, slender ears and a cottony tail, with just a slight overbite and a coffeebean nose. His speeded voice has a throaty, sloshing tone, somewhat reminiscent of Disney's Goofy, and his cackly laugh would soon be made famous by a woodpecker working across town. (Again, no accident: Mel Blanc, who performed for all the proto-Bugs Bunny's, also originated the Woody Woodpecker voice at Lantz's, repeating this ricocheting laugh.)

Juvenile, aggressive, and purposefully screwy, the rabbit in *Porky's Hare Hunt* has an altogether different personality than the mature Bugs Bunny. Indeed, the rabbit's defining line in this cartoon—"Don't let me worry ya, chief; I'm just a trifle pixilated"—would have made Bugs gag. In fact, it is an echo of the first line spoken by role-model Daffy in *Porky's Duck Hunt.* The Hardaway rabbit hops about frantically, clicks his heels,

Bringing Bugs to maturity: Above: *Animation drawing from* Porky's Hare Hunt, *1938.* Below: *Model sheet by Charles Thorson from* Hare-um Scare-um, *1939. When Thorson labeled this model sheet for the director, Ben "Bugs" Hardaway, the character got a name.* Above right: *Model sheet by Robert Givens from* A Wild Hare, *1940.* Right: *Model sheet by Robert McKimson, drawn after the release of* A Wild Hare, *c. 1941.* Bottom right. *The full-grown bunny: the 1943 model sheet by Robert McKimson, then one of Bob Clampett's principal animators.*

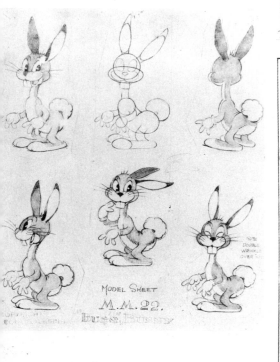

turns pirouettes, and even spins his ears like propellers to make himself fly.

But many of Bugs Bunny's most characteristic bits were first essayed in this film, albeit to different effect. The hunted hare engages in such business as pulling out a picture of his multitudinous rabbit family, so as to appeal for sympathy; drinking "Hare Remover" to become invisible; chomping on a carrot with serene disregard for a nearby menace; faking a death scene; and delivering the filched-from-Groucho line "Of course you know that this means war!"—all of which would be repeated, with drastically different valences, over the next twenty-six years. And it is just these character-determining gags that give the lie to the contention that Warner's rabbit was based on Disney's Max Hare, star of the 1935 cartoon *The Tortoise and the Hare*. Disney's rabbit was a show-offish speed freak, but Warner's bunny was born with his own slapsticky shtick.

*Porky's Hare Hunt* was a substantial success on the screen— "People were stopping on their way out of the theater to ask the manager when they could see the next rabbit cartoon," Bob Clampett once reported—and so follow-up films in color were undertaken. The next to arrive was Chuck Jones' 1939 *Prest-o Change-o,* in which the rabbit plays against the two naive dogs that the director featured in several cartoons of the time. But Jones concentrated on only one aspect of the Hardaway bunny, that being when he acted like a magician's rabbit. Here, the still nameless hare inhabits a haunted house into which the puppies flee to evade a dogcatcher; the rabbit then subjects them to a series of magician-like stunts—making himself disappear, doing tricks with wands and ropes, performing "nothing up my sleeve" gags—with no apparent motivation beyond exhibiting his mischievous ability to do such things. Physically recalling the *Porky's Hare Hunt* rabbit, Jones' bunny does not talk, although he still has the Woody laugh. Perhaps the rabbit's only significant contribution to Bugs' development comes when he coolly, archly, arrogantly plants a kiss on one of the perplexed dogs. Another component.

Schlesinger's subsequent rabbit cartoon, *Hare-um Scare-um,* was directed by the team of Hardaway and Cal Dalton, who had begun collaborating immediately after Hardaway made *Porky's Hare Hunt.* But for this August 1939 release, the character was physically overhauled. Charles Thorson, the Schlesinger studio's principal character designer of the time, was asked to revise the rabbit, and he composed a model sheet that made him squatter, curvier, and more chipper-looking, with gray top–fur, bent legs, an articulated muzzle, and large buck teeth. Director Ben Hardaway's nickname happened to be Bugs, so Thorson informally labeled the model sheet "Bug's Bunny." The possessive apostrophe was mistakenly placed, but no matter: soon it was dropped altogether, and Schlesinger's rabbit had a name.

Yet *Hare-um Scare-um* does not represent much of an advance on the pioneering Hardaway cartoon. The rabbit is perhaps even more flippy and assertive in this film, as he makes a mockery of a round-headed hunter who has been driven by an economic downturn to go after something to eat ("Meat Prices Soar," reads a headline in his newspaper. "Consumers Also Sore!" adds a subhead). Madly tittuping through a forest, "Bug's" bunny pulls pranks compulsively while mouthing off with the same Goofy-ish chortle and pre-Woody laugh. His props include a joy buzzer, a motorized surfboard, an impossible elevator built into a ridge of land, and an invisible policeman's motorcycle,

*Sketches of Cecil Turtle by Robert Givens from* Tortoise Beats Hare, *1941. Tex Avery's second Bugs Bunny cartoon, it was also the first of Warner's three demolitions of the* "Tortoise and the Hare" *fable. It was followed by Bob Clampett's* Tortoise Wins by a Hare, *1943, and Friz Freleng's* Rabbit Transit, *1947.*

175

and he at one point costumes himself as a female dog to short-circuit the hunter's pup—the initial instance of the rabbit's cross-dressing. But his centerpiece is a rather self-serving original song, which at first plugs Leon Schlesinger's wares (as the bunny comes across a billboard advertising "Looney Tunes" and sporting a picture of Porky Pig) and then promotes himself: "I'm so goony, looney-tuney, tetched in the head/Please pass the ketchup, I think I'll go to bed." Clearly, this unruly hare still had some growing up to do.

Essentially the same character, however, reappeared in the next rabbit cartoon, *Elmer's Candid Camera,* which was directed by Chuck Jones and released in March 1940. In accord with all of Jones' work of this period, the bunny has slowed down considerably in this film; no longer does he uncontrollably caper around the woods, but he is no less malicious, and he trots out yet another sham death scene ("Gimme air! Gimme air!" he groans, with just a wide-webbed hunter's net covering him). But in this cartoon, the rabbit has his first encounter with a schlump called Fudd, who has taken to the green to photograph "wildwife." Wholly unequipped to handle the scalawag bunny, Elmer is driven to attempting suicide by tossing himself into a lake; the rabbit rescues him, makes sure that he is all right, then kicks him right back in.

The one cartoon, however, that must be singled out as the birth of Bugs Bunny is Tex Avery's *A Wild Hare,* released four months later, on July 27, 1940. For Avery assimilated all of the best of the existing rabbit ingredients for this hunt film, while refashioning the character mentally and physically and bequeathing to him the most crucial of his trademark bits. According to Robert Givens, Avery thought that the rabbit that

Below: *Model sheet by Jean Blanchard for The Robert McKimson unit, c. 1947. Poses from this sheet appear in* A Lad in His Lamp, *1948 and elsewhere.*

Left: "Gimme air!" Cel from Chuck Jones' Elmer's Candid Camera. Below: Animation drawing from Friz Freleng's The Wabbit who Came to Supper, 1942.

Charles Thorson had devised "didn't have any personality, and was too cute," and so assigned Givens—who had succeeded Thorson as Schlesinger's leading character designer—to draw a reworked model sheet. Accordingly, Givens made the character look hepper and more clever, with a snappier smile and devilish eyes and a more substantial feeling of weight.

But it was what Avery did with these drawings that counted. Most importantly, Avery jettisoned Bugs' bugginess and made him the brainiest wiseass on the block. Taking a cue from Jonesian slowness, Avery converted the rabbit's new deliberateness into a show of imperturbability under pressure. Whatever the challenge, whatever the threat, Bugs maintained total composure, insouciantly chewing his carrot and thereby defusing those who would harm him, waiting for them to exhaust themselves with their feckless displays of aggression. A perfect master of comic control, Avery's bunny knows that he can take his time. For Bugs has already read the script; he understands that *he* is the star, and therefore is aware of what must happen. He needn't put himself out just for purposes of drama; rather, he will make his intent antagonist do things *his* way.

So, for example, when Elmer shoves his gun right into the rabbit's chest, Bugs indifferently pushes it aside. But then he decides to toy with the hunter by making him happy. "To show you I'm a sport," he says, "I'll give you a good shot at me." Unsuspecting, Elmer backs off and takes aim—until his target practice is interrupted when Bugs hears chirping birds on a branch directly over his head and cries "Whoa! Hold it!" Delicately, Bugs steps aside, out from under genuine harm's way. Only then can Elmer proceed with firing. A single blast—and more bogus death histrionics.

**Overleaf**
*Cel and background from Frank Tashlin's* The Unruly Hare, *1945.*

Above: *Animation drawing from Chuck Jones'* Hold the Lion, Please, *1942.* Top: *Layout drawing from Frank Tashlin's* The Unruly Hare, *1945.*

With wonderful aptness, Avery found ways for Bugs to express his new impudence and impenetrable cool. The first thing Bugs says in this film, upon meeting his would-be assassin, Fudd, is "What's up, Doc?"—a line from Avery's Texas boyhood. Audiences "expected the rabbit to scream, or anything but make a casual remark," Avery told Joe Adamson. "It got such a laugh that we said, 'Boy, we'll do that every chance we get.'" And in *A Wild Hare,* Avery had Bugs kiss Elmer with sufficient frequency to seem positively promiscuous—twice on the mouth and once, with slurping tenderness, on the nose. Even without talking, Bugs gives Elmer lip.

Moreover, it was for this cartoon that Mel Blanc coined Bugs' razzy voice. "They showed me the storyboard and told me that this rabbit was a real tough little stinker," said Blanc. "So I thought, 'What are the toughest voices I know?' They've got to be Brooklyn or the Bronx"—and, switching to his Bugsian dialect, he added, "So I put the two of 'em tagedda, Doc."

With these pieces in place, Bugs' identity largely solidified—a street-smart scrapper who would always stand his ground. Yet the rabbit's confidence and self-possession were also revealed through other cues. After the release of *A Wild Hare,* Robert McKimson executed a series of model sheets that progressively refined the rabbit's physical expressivity and character, bringing him through a rather rat-faced phase until he came to life in drawings that definitively captured the essence of Bunnyhood. "I drew him so he could react to any situation, do anything most people would love to do, if they had the nerve," McKimson said. Chuck Jones elaborated: "Hardaway's Bugs would stand in a crouched, ready-to-leap fashion, like somebody who's afraid and prepared to get the hell out of there. The Bugs that evolved stood upright, a guy who's not going to go anyplace—sure of himself."

Yet Avery's Bugs did go places—anywhere, in fact, that a cartoon character can go. *A Wild Hare* was nominated for an Academy Award, and Bugs went on to become the most popular cartoon player in the land. Quicker than Groucho and tougher than Cagney, the rabbit who stood up to ostensibly overwhelming opponents became America's mascot during World War II. "Bugs Bunny has been loved for over a quarter of a century now, but he has never been loved the way he was during those war years," Bob Clampett said to Mike Barrier. "Just as America whistled the tune from Disney's *Three Little Pigs,* 'Who's Afraid of the Big Bad Wolf?' in the dark days of the Depression...so, Bugs Bunny was a symbol of America's resistance to Hitler and the fascist powers. In both instances, we were in a battle for our lives, and it is most difficult now to comprehend the tremendous emotional impact Bugs Bunny exerted on the audience then."

How to account for the rabbit's powerful appeal? Part of it certainly has to do with the wittiness and sharpness that the Warner writers and directors gave the character in his first years: Bugs became a Bowery Boy with Oppenheimer's intellect. In 1939's *Hare-um Scare-um,* the embryonic bunny sings of how "goony, looney-tuney" he is; in 1941's *Hiawatha's Rabbit Hunt* (Freleng), the post-Avery Bugs states, matter-of-factly, "Imagine a joik like that tryin' to catch a smart guy like me." And the brainy bunny would, over and over again, prove it, with a verbal deftness that made it all the more convincing—as in when he japes his farewell to evil scientist Peter Lorre with "And don't think it hasn't been a little slice of heaven—'cause it hasn't!" (in *Hair-Raising Hare*), or when he taunts Nero the lion for his caged condition with "Iron bars do not a prison make—but they sure help, ay, Doc?" (*Acrobatty Bunny*), or when he pleads with Elmer not to abandon their act, because "We're like Rabbit and Costello!" (*The Big Snooze*), or when he impersonates The King and knights the Sheriff of Nottingham "Sir Loin of Beef" (*Rabbit Hood*), or when he, before going into his wind-up on the mound, confides, "Watch me paste this pathetic palooka with a powerful, paralyzing, perfect,

Below: *Cel of the Sherriff of Nottingham, from Chuck Jones'* Rabbit Hood, *1949.* Bottom left: *Model sheet by Robert Givens from Friz Freleng's* Hiawatha's Rabbit Hunt, *1941. Givens says that Hiawatha is a caricature of the long-time Disney artist Ward Kimball.*

181

pachydermous, percussion pitch" (*Baseball Bugs*). Effortlessly, Bugs makes an ally of language, playing with it as he makes it play with his opponents.

Another source of Bugs' popularity must lie in his cavalier disregard for scruples and moral conventions. Gleefully, he gets away with doing things that society debars, glorying in his unfettered freedom with a self-congratulatory "Gee, ain't I a stinker?" Bugs acted out society's repressions—nowhere more so than in the almost incalculable number of times he went in drag. As a saucy mermaid (in *Hare Ribbin'*), a meek geisha (*Bugs Bunny Nips the Nips*), a mock Carmen Miranda *(What's Cookin', Doc?)*, or a buxom fleshpot who "would just love a duck dinner" *(Rabbit Seasoning)*, Bugs used sex as a weapon, driving his opponents to pop their corks while he jockeyed for position. In few other instances of the cinema of the time was eroticism expressed so directly.

That Bugs has a mercurial side, however, is revealed not only in his taste for transvestism. Nearly incessantly in his films, the bunny hops from disguise to pose to put-on, exchanging identities with a quickness and ease that can only provoke wonderment. Bugs, it seems, lives without the limitations and weight of a self; he can be all bunnies to all people, and he uses this infinite adaptability to escape troublesome situations or to locate the precise point of attack against his enemies. Childlike in this way, Bugs play-acts in a world that, all too grown up, can only take itself seriously. This is wonderfully displayed in a number of funny and important bunny cartoons that Friz Freleng directed in the 1940s. In them, Bugs role-plays with a conviction and gusto that makes it seem as if he is testing the frontiers of what he can do, joyfully exploring the possibilities still latent within himself. In *Baseball Bugs* (1946), for example, the

Right: *Dancing with Gruesome Gorilla: Animation drawing from* Gorilla My Dreams. Below: *With Count Bloodcount; color chart from* Transylvania 6—5000, *1963.* Above: *With floorwalker "The Great Gildersneeze." Animation drawing from* Hare Conditioned, *1945.*

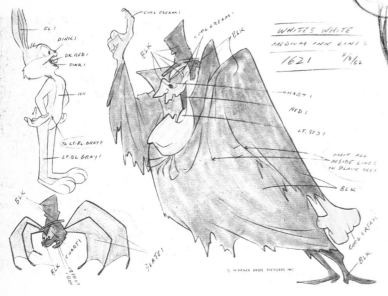

The handwritten inscription on the image reads: *This is an original painting I used in "Looney Tunes" and "Merrie Melodies" © Leon Schlesinger*

rabbit single-handedly plays all the positions on a big-league team, including—simultaneously—the hard-throwing pitcher and the gabby catcher ("*That's* the old pepper, boy; that's the old pitchin'..."). And in the same year's *Racketeer Rabbit,* Bugs acts out a confrontation with a non-existent policeman while gangster Rocky (a caricature of Edward G. Robinson) hides in a nearby trunk. When Bugs speaks the copper's lines, he jumps into costume for the role—derby, shoes, cigar; yet this is totally unnecessary, as the hidden Eddie G. cannot see him. Then, when Bugs stages a fight between himself and the imaginary policeman, the rabbit actually takes a punch. He so delights in his role-playing that he must follow it through to its furthest point, even if it means superfluous activity or self-inflicted pain.

Yet there were other structures at work within the bunny's world. Most commonly, Warner's directors placed Bugs in adversarial situations where the deck was stacked against him, making him seem to start in the position of the underdog. Then the rabbit's startling resourcefulness could be activated to counter his disadvantage—cunning trumping brute force. In his two archetypal confrontations, for example, Bugs has to deal with guns pointed by a blockhead, Elmer Fudd, or a hothead, Yosemite Sam—each more dangerous than the other. One needs be mighty quick to outmaneuver a bullet.

But where there were no firearms, the adversaries were made perilous in other ways. Usually they were huge and powerful and possessed by violent emotions; in contrast, Bugs was sleek and lithe and small, capable only of mobilizing his feet and his intellect. And in short notice, Bugs' coolness would melt his opponents' heat, his imagina-

Above: *With Elmer Fudd. Cel from Chuck Jones' Elmer's Candid Camera, 1940. This cel contains a screened endorsement and signature by Leon Schlesinger; it was part of a short-lived marketing of artwork undertaken around that time.* Below: *Manicuring a monster: Promotional drawing from Hair-Raising Hare.*

A bunny's anima: Animation drawings. As Carmen Miranda from Bob Clampett's What's Cookin' Doc? *1941. As a flirty mermaid from Clampett's* Hare Ribbin', *1944; animation by Robert McKimson. As a blushing bride from Friz Freleng's* Hare-Trimmed, *1953; animation by Virgil Ross. As a geisha, from Freleng's* Bugs Bunny Nips the Nips, *1944.*

tiveness puncture their thundering rage. Examples are numerous: In two splendid Chuck Jones cartoons staged in the ring, 1948's *Rabbit Punch* and 1951's *Bunny Hugged,* Bugs TKOs two fighters whose muscles can be made to engulf their entire bodies. Or in Jones' 1945 *Hare Conditioned,* the rabbit makes porridge of a department-store employee whom he calls "The Great Gildersneeze" by impersonating an elevator operator and—natch—dressing as a female shoe-buyer and giving the big masher an artificial leg to flirtatiously tickle. Or in the very funny *Gorilla My Dreams* (McKimson, 1948), Bugs exhausts gigantic Gruesome Gorilla in "Bingzi-Bangzi" jungleland after the hairy ape's childless wife mistakenly adopts Bugs, and the big-hearted rabbit hasn't got it in him to disillusion her ("That's my soft spot—dames cryin'"). Alternately, *Baseball Bugs* finds the rabbit outscoring the entire goon team called the "Gas-House Gorillas," one of whom uses a tree for a bat and blasts a ball higher than the flagpole atop the Umpire State Building (although Bugs still manages to catch it). And in 1946's savory *Hair-Raising Hare* (Jones), the rabbit is lured into mad scientist Peter Lorre's castle by a mechanical, but shapely, female rabbit; there, he's set upon by a roaring monster who looks like a

tremendous tooth covered with orange hair and wearing sneakers. At one point, the monster chases Bugs up to the edge of a deep water-bottomed pit and, lightning quick, Bugs is a chatty manicurist, filing away across a table: "My, I bet you *mahn*sters lead *inn*teresting lives. I said to my girlfriend just the other day, 'Gee, I'll bet monsters are *inn*teresting,' I said. The places you must go and the things you must see—*myyy* stars. And I'll bet you meet a lot of *inn*teresting people, too. I'm always interested in meeting *inn*teresting people. Now let's dip our paddies in the *wa*-ter," and SMACK: two paddy-mousetraps. Indeed quick himself, Jones brought this priceless orange monster back in 1952's *Water, Water Every Hare,* where his master's castle bears a sign that flashes "Evil Scientist," then "Boo."

  Of course, not every Bugs outing reduces to such stratagems. In Jones' 1954 *Baby Buggy Bunny,* for example, the rabbit runs up against a gangster named Ant Hill Harry, whose entire career is based on the fact that he is abnormally small. Wearing an inordinately tall cloak and a hat, Harry sticks up a bank; then he ducks around a corner, tosses aside his disguise, removes his stilts, puts on a baby's bonnet and sleeper, and

*Cel from Robert McKimson's* Now Hare This, *1958*.

settles into a waiting stroller. Now a woozy-eyed toddler, he is ignored by the cops when they rush by. But his bag of loot inadvertently gets thrown into Bugs' rabbit hole, so the con impersonates an abandoned baby named Finster to get Bugs to take him in. Touched and paternal, the rabbit is pleased to spend quality time with him—until he catches the tot shaving and smoking a cigar in the bathroom, wearing a tattoo that reads "Maisie, Singapore 1932."

Neither huge nor immediately threatening, Babyface Finster, like most of Bugs' antagonists, has provoked him—in this case, has tried to dupe him to get the stolen money. Unlike in his early days, the mature Bugs never fought, but fought back. He unleashed a kind of controlled anarchy in his efforts to counter some form of encroachment. "That sense of sympathy is vital," said Chuck Jones. "I felt that somebody should always try to impose his will on Bugs. That gave him a reason to act, and I couldn't understand the character unless he had a reason for what he did."

In 1953, Jones directed a cartoon that synopsizes virtually all of the motifs that sustained the later bunny series. *Bully for Bugs* takes place in Spain, a locale that is both exotic and incongruous for a rabbit; Bugs has burrowed his way into a bullring there, popping out and proffering the scantest of excuses: "I knew I shoulda taken that left turn at Albuquerque." He then crosses paths with a quintessential antagonist, a tremendous and bellowing black bull who snorts sparks and smoke and sharpens his horns on a grindstone. The muscular bull soon charges up behind the rabbit and begins huffing and puffing. "Stop steamin' up my tail!" Bugs protests. "Whaddaya tryin' to do, wrinkle it?" The bull backs off and butts Bugs far out of the ring and, in midair, "Of course you realize this means war." Between frames, Bugs becomes Juan Belmonte, the legendary matador; and, before long, the bull is receiving a boulder between the horns and Bugs is taking bows.

How did so finely realized, so classically correct a cartoon come about? As Jones told Peter Bogdanovich: "One time, I was drawing a bull—just for the fun of it—when [Warner cartoon producer Eddie Selzer] came in, looked over my shoulder, and said, 'I don't want any bullfights—bullfights aren't funny.' Now, I had no intention of making a bullfight picture, but after he said that I went ahead." Like his long-eared hero, Jones doesn't fight, he fights back.

Almost from the outset, the Warner 'toonsmiths knew they had a star in Bugs Bunny, and treated him appropriately—having other characters refer to him admiringly in their cartoons, letting him make cameo appearances, designing a brassy capital-letter logo for him to recline on at the beginning of his cartoons. And in several instances, the Warner directors treated Bugs as if he was an autonomous entity, casting him in roles in which he played off of his own celebrity status. Two examples of such metacartoons are fabricated "biographies" of the bunny: Friz Freleng's *A Hare Grows in Manhattan* (1947) begins with the voice of a sycophantish female gossip columnist scanning the estates in the "fabulous Hollywood movie stars' colony" before dropping in on Bugs' digs: a "scrumptuous" place complete with swimming pool, ornate statuary, formal gardens, and Bugs' home, a hole in the ground. Wearing smoking jacket, ascot, beret, and dark glasses, Bugs fawns, "You know how I hate to talk about myself," before quickly proceeding to narrate his childhood experiences on New York's Lower East Side (where he sings "She's the Daughter of Rosie O'Grady" while tap dancing his way to school). Three

Below: *Cel from Chuck Jones'* Operation Rabbit, *1952.* Left: *From* Long-Haired Hare.

Above: *Animation drawings by Virgil Ross from* A Hare Grows in Manhattan. Below: *Study for the title card of* Bully for Bugs, *1953.*

years later, Robert McKimson again began *What's Up, Doc?* at Bugs' Hollywood manor, this time with the rabbit at poolside on a chaise longue. With an equal lack of reluctance, Bugs tells of his early work on stage (as part of a black-tie ensemble that sings, "Oh, we are the boys in the chorus, we hope you like our show/ We know you're rootin' for us, but now we have to go"). And then it's on to his dire years down and out (collapsed on a park bench beside such other derelicts as Jack Benny, Al Jolson, and Eddie Cantor), his chance meeting and recruitment by mega-star Elmer Fudd, his eventual upstaging of Fudd, and his big break in the movies—where he ends up performing the same "boys of the chorus" number. Memorably done, *What's Up, Doc?* was excerpted in Peter Bogdanovich's 1972 feature film of the same name.

Perhaps more sassily, a third cartoon deals with Bugs' aspirations in show business. Bob Clampett's very funny *What's Cookin', Doc?* (1944) finds the rabbit beaming with confidence that he is going to win that year's Oscar—an award he had not yet achieved. After a narrated live-action montage of sites in Hollywood and scenes from the Oscar ceremony, the film cuts to the animated Bugs, sitting in clover at a swank table, greeting several of his good friends—Katharine Hepburn, Bing Crosby, Edward G. Robinson—by doing overbaked impersonations of them. But when the Oscar is eventually given to James Cagney, Bugs is crushed; "It's sab-o-tah-gee!" he hollers, and petitions the crowd to reconsider. Finally, to prove his worthiness, Bugs whips out several cans of film to show the Academy "some of my best scenes"—footage from his past cartoons (although the projection mistakenly begins with a "Stag Reel" that Bugs shrieks at and rushes to the screen to cover).

It would take another fourteen years for Bugs to persuade them.

For with Friz Freleng's 1958 *Knighty Knight Bugs,* the rabbit won his first and only Oscar. The film situates the bunny in the role of King Arthur's court jester, endeavoring to rescue the fabled "Singing Sword"—a quivering blade that makes like a soprano—from Black Knight Yosemite Sam. It is a pleasant cartoon, and the acknowledgment was most welcome by the studio; yet it does seem regrettable that the Academy never cited any of the very many truly stellar bunny cartoons that preceded this choice.

Yet there is some justice in the cartoon universe, for the rabbit eventually did receive his just desserts. On December 21, 1985, Bugs became the second cartoon character (after Mickey Mouse) to be given his own star on the Hollywood Walk of Fame. Before a large gathering of admirers and the press, Bugs was honored with an underfoot plaque in front of 7007 Hollywood Boulevard. Finally, the rabbit has an appropriate canopy for his subterranean home.

Above: *Cel from Chuck Jones;* Rabbit Hood, *1949.* Top: *Painting by Richard H. Thomas from* What's Up, Doc?

# Tweety and Sylvester

L ike Rodgers and Hammerstein, Tweety and Sylvester had enjoyed accomplished solo careers before they worked together. But it was only when they were paired that they reached the most rarefied levels of cultural achievement.

Tweety was the first to arrive, in Bob Clampett's 1942 *A Tale of Two Kitties*. He began life high atop a spindly tree, sleeping in a nest—a bitty speck of a bird who, with huge head and pinkish tint, looks positively fetal. Unofficially called Orson in this cartoon, the tiny, featherless thing is tantalizing a pair of loquacious cats named Babbitt and Catstello—funny feline caricatures of the Abbott and Costello team. Bouncing on a pair of springs up to the sky-high nest, Catstello wakes the big-eyed bird and, right off, "I taut I taw a puddy-tat!"—a line of baby talk coined by Clampett several years earlier.

"All the time I was growing up, my mother insisted on keeping out a baby picture of me . . . in the nude," Bob Clampett told Mike Barrier. "I detested that picture all my life. So when I was making the first sketches of Tweety in his nest, completely naked, I was actually satirizing my own baby picture." Clampett also pointed out that the character's name was

Tweety and Sylvester

**1947**
Tweetie Pie

**1948**
I Taw a Putty Tat

**1949**
Bad Ol' Putty Tat

**1950**
Home Tweet Home
All Abir-r-rd

**1951**
Tweety's S.O.S.
Tweet, Tweet, Tweety

**1952**
Ain't She Tweet

**1953**
Catty Cornered

**1957**
Birds Anonymous

Left: *From* Bad Ol' Putty Tat, *1949.*
Below: *Model sheet from* A Tale of
Two Kitties.

**Opposite**
*Concept sketch for the opening of* Birdy
and the Beast, *1944.*

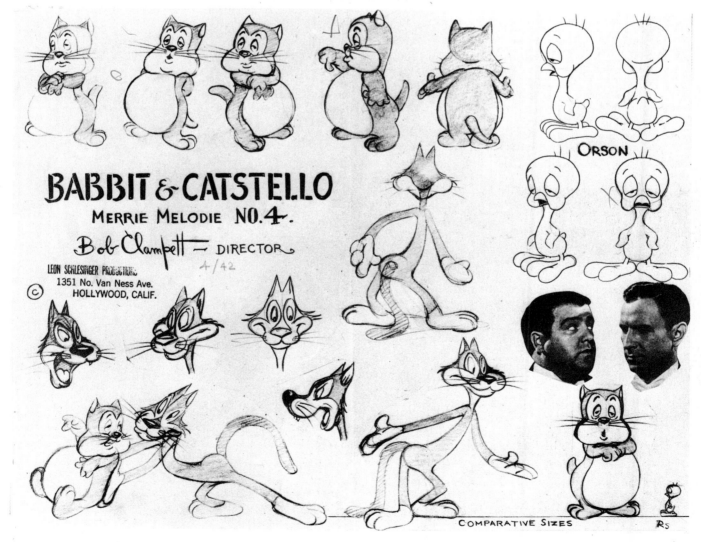

ORSON

BABBIT & CATSTELLO
MERRIE MELODIE NO. 4.
Bob Clampett — DIRECTOR
LEON SCHLESINGER PRODUCTIONS
1351 No. Van Ness Ave.
HOLLYWOOD, CALIF.
A/42

COMPARATIVE SIZES

derived from those of "Twick 'n' Tweet," "two little newly hatched baby
birds" that Clampett had once drawn, and whose names were a play on
the Halloween phrase "Trick or treat."

In that first cartoon, Tweety eventually gives the cats their comeup-
pance—once, when Catstello dons a pair of wooden wings and flaps up
to the nest ("Hey, Babbitt! I'm a Spitfire!"), Tweety puts on a helmet
labeled "Air Raid Warden," telephones an alert, and has Catstello very
explosively shot down. And Tweety went on to comport himself with
similar blithe nastiness in his next two cartoons, both directed by Clampett. In 1944's *Birdy and the Beast,* in which he was first named, Tweety
lights a match in a cat's mouth and cries, "Help! Help! Da puddy-tat is on
fire!"—and then extinguishes the blaze by pumping him with gasoline.
And in the smashing *A Gruesome Twosome* (1945), Tweety zaps a pair of
cats, one of whom is a caricature of Jimmy Durante; when the cats don a
floppy horse costume and try to sneak up on him, Tweety whips out a
bee, slaps it around to·make it buzzing mad, then shoves it inside the
costume. The horse begins to writhe and gallop so quickly that Tweety
grabs the reins and rides it like the Lone Ranger.

Meanwhile, elsewhere on the lot, Sylvester first picked through back-
alley garbage cans—lifting out fish skeletons and other scraps and placing them gently into an upside-down trash can lid—in Friz Freleng's 1945
*Life With Feathers.* Eternally hungry, the splattery Sylvester in this cartoon
is confronted by a lovelorn lovebird who has been spurned by his
shrewish wife. Disconsolate, the bird decides to take his own life, and his
method is to fly into Sylvester's mouth. But Sylvester is so skeptical about
this inversion of the natural order that he concludes the bird must be
poisoned. He rids himself of the heartsick one, leading the bird to

marshall all of his resources in the hope of getting digested. The first thing Sylvester says is "Sufferin' succotash!"

Working with layout artist Hawley Pratt, "I designed Sylvester to look subtly like a clown," said Freleng. "I gave him a big red nose and a very low crotch, which was supposed to look like he was wearing baggy pants. But gradually he was changed, because the construction restricted his animation." Mel Blanc's voice for the "big sloppy cat" was actually the same as Daffy Duck's early voice, except not speeded.

Sylvester next appeared in Freleng's *Peck Up Your Troubles* (1945), going after a redheaded little woodpecker. And his subsequent film was Bob Clampett's *Kitty Kornered* (1946), where he plays the ringleader of a quartet of cats attempting to crash Porky Pig's warm house during a winter's night. ("Are we men—or *arrre* we mice?" Sylvester orates to his fellows. "I like cheese," squeaks the smallest puss.)

The fateful collision came in *Tweetie Pie,* a film on which some preliminary work had been done by Clampett, but which was taken over and directed by Freleng. Released in 1947, it became the first Warner cartoon to win an Oscar. In retrospect, it seems a natural pairing, as house cat Sylvester—called Thomas in this film—is introduced to a gamin-like canary who has been taken in from the cold by a thoughtful housemistress. Rousingly funny, the cartoon features many typifying gags, including Sylvester's attempts to get to Tweety's cage by strapping an electric fan to his body (to make himself float) and by building a mountain made of furniture.

For Freleng, this cartoon began when Michael Maltese and Tedd Pierce "did a storyboard with the woodpecker" from *Peck Up Your*

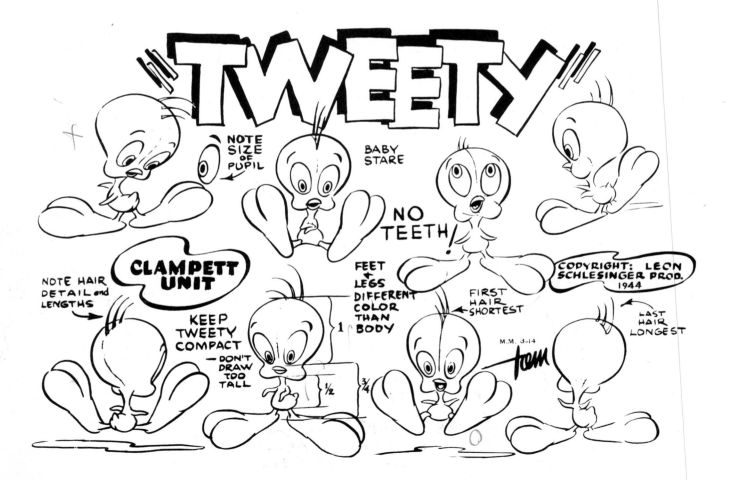

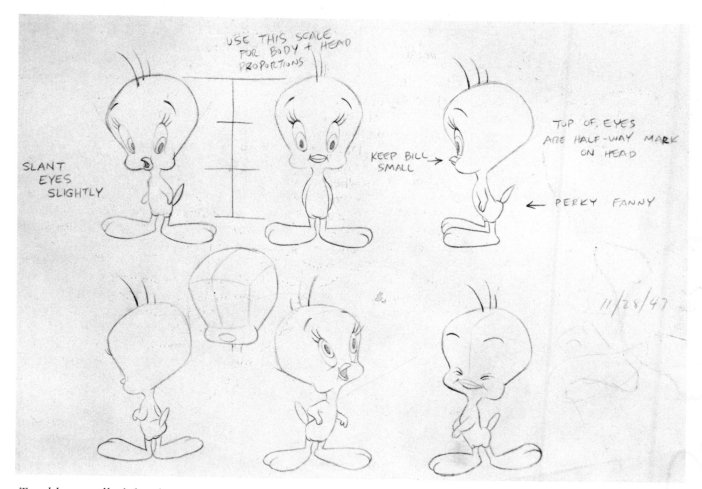

Troubles, recalled the director. "But Clampett had left, and so I decided I might as well put Tweety in there instead of the woodpecker, because he already had a following. But [producer] Eddie Selzer came in and said he wanted me to use the woodpecker. We began to argue about the point, until finally I said, 'If you know better, you should be doing it.' I handed him my pencil, walked out, and went home. That night, he called me at home and said, 'All right, do it your way.' Then, when it won the Academy Award, Selzer went up and took the honors."

A new design for Tweety was unveiled in this cartoon, following objections from movie censors that the pink bird looked naked. After rejecting the possibility of putting Mickey Mouse–ish short pants on Tweety, Clampett gave him a yellow coat of feathers and officially made him a canary. Further refinements were made by Freleng and Hawley Pratt. "I gave him big blue eyes and tried to give him a baby look, to appeal to women," said Freleng. "I also calmed him down from what Clampett had. Clampett went to extremes on everything." Yet Freleng's Tweety was no pacifist, and the director drew great slapstick from contrasting the bird's minuscule size and toddler's babble with his guiltless striking back at bruisable Sylvester (using, for example, a bat, dynamite, a spritzing seltzer bottle, and a boxing glove on a retractable frame in just one scene of 1949's *Bad Ol' Putty Tat*).

Encouraged by his first-time success with the Academy, Freleng went on to employ Tweety with Sylvester for fifteen years. (The duo's final film, however, 1964's *Hawaiian Aye Aye*, was directed by Gerry Chiniquy.) The characters continued their attacks and avoidances in such settings as a city park (*Home Tweet Home*, 1950), a train to Pasadena (*All Abir-r-rd*, 1950), an ocean liner (*Tweety's S.O.S.*, 1951), a national park (*Tweet, Tweet,*

Above: *A 1947 model sheet of Tweety.* Below: *Model sheet of the non-Jimmy Durante cat from* A Gruesome Two-some, *1945.*

**Opposite**
Top: *Animation drawing by Virgil Ross from* A Mouse Divided, *1953.* Bottom: *Model sheet by Tom McKimson from* A Gruesome Twosome.

*Tweety,* 1951), a beach (*Sandy Claws,* 1955), and Venice (*A Pizza Tweety Pie,* 1958). In many of these films, Tweety was put under the ownership of Granny, a gingerly matron still strong enough to take a whack at Sylvester with a broom or an umbrella. (Granny's crinkly voice was supplied by Bea Benaderet, followed by June Foray, then Julie Bennett; all three contributed other female voices, such as Miss Prissy's, during their stints with Warner Cartoons.)

Freleng also stirred the characters' chases into several parodies, including ones of "Dragnet" (*Tree Cornered Tweety,* 1956) and Jekyll and Hyde (1960's *Hyde and Go Tweet*). But the clincher of these parodies is certainly 1957's *Birds Anonymous,* with its lovely story by Warren Foster: Just as Sylvester has finished some elaborate preparations to grab Tweety, a gentle-voiced cat turns up and says, "I wouldn't do that if I were you. . . . It can only lead to self-destruction." Eventually, the cat talks Sylvester into attending a Birds Anonymous meeting in an alleyway, where he hears such confessions as "I was a three-bird-a-day pussycat—until B.A. helped me," and "Being on a bird kick cost me five homes." Sylvester swears off his feathery habit ("Fellow members, from now on my motto is: Birds is strictly for the birds!") and tries to make peace with Tweety—until his resistance agonizingly crumbles in the face of overpowering temptation. "One little bird . . . just one! *Just one!*" he blithers. And later, pounding the floor: "I—I—I can't stand it . . . I gotta have a bird . . . I'm weak . . . *I'm weak!* . . . But I don't care! I can't help it! After all, I *am* a pussycat!" The film brought the Tweety and Sylvester team its second Academy Award.

Above: *Background painting by Paul Julian from* All Abir-r-rd, *1950. Julian often put the names of Warner artists— or plays on those names—into his backgrounds.* Below: *Publicity drawing from* Ain't She Tweet, *1952.*

**Opposite**
*"Cute? He's delithious!": Sylvester sees the baby mouse—and pounces; from* A Mouse Divided, *animation drawings by Virgil Ross.*

Sylvester—good-natured, but none too quick—was sufficiently appealing for the Warner directors to cast him in many sidelines to his Tweety series. Often these were one-shot films, such as Friz Freleng's charming *A Mouse Divided* (1953), in which a besotted stork mistakenly brings a baby mouse to Mr. and Mrs. Sylvester's home. Papa Sylvester must then defend his diapered kid from the swarming alley cats who come to welcome him.

But Sylvester also starred in several parallel series. In 1955's *Speedy Gonzales,* the cat moved to Mexico and began a mouse chase that didn't stop for ten years. An earlier and even longer-running series, however, originated in 1948, when a baby kangaroo first escaped from a zoo and was believed by Sylvester to be a titanic mouse. Called *Hop, Look and Listen,* and directed by Robert McKimson, this first Hippety Hopper cartoon set a pattern that would continue for sixteen years. The bouncing Hippety is smiling and innocent, and acts as if Sylvester's predations are all part of a carefree game. Sylvester, however, continually has his dignity deflated by the silent, almost ungrabbable kangaroo; even when Sylvester manages to get him in his grasp, Hippety only has to rear back and use his powerhouse legs to kick the cat clean out of the frame (or into a garbage can, or against a fence). And with every new failure, Sylvester's determination escalates; soon that determination becomes desperation. At first fighting the kangaroo, Sylvester ends up fighting his own self-image.

The premises varied somewhat in the films with the springy Hippety. For example, in 1954's *Bell Hoppy,* Sylvester, in order to gain a dearly sought-after admission into the "Loyal Order of Alley Cats Mousing and Chowder Club," must hang a bell around the neck of any giant mouse he happens to come across. But the final assault on Sylvester's sense of self-worth came when Robert McKimson made the character fail—over and over again—in front of his own son. In 1950's *Pop 'im Pop,* McKimson introduced Sylvester Jr. and had him function as a kind of one-kitten Greek chorus for the indignities befalling his father. After proclaiming to Junior that he is "the world's greatest mouser," Sylvester invariably has an encounter with Hippety Hopper, and invariably ends up the tattered worse for it. The series is a fairly brutal satire of the idealized father–child relationships that prevailed in such 1950s television sit-coms as "Father Knows Best," as the boastful father's comforting omnipotence is slaughtered right in front of his hypersensitive son. After registering pained dismay in his high-toned lisp—"Oh, the shame of it!"—Junior then has the habit of slipping a paper bag over his head, to hide his face. He acts out what Sylvester feels—leaving Sylvester to feel all the worse for it, and hardening his resolve to restore his pride yet again.

Above: *Model sheet of Granny from 1952.* Top: *Publicity drawing from* Pop 'im Pop. Right: *Color chart of Sylvester and Son, 1961.*

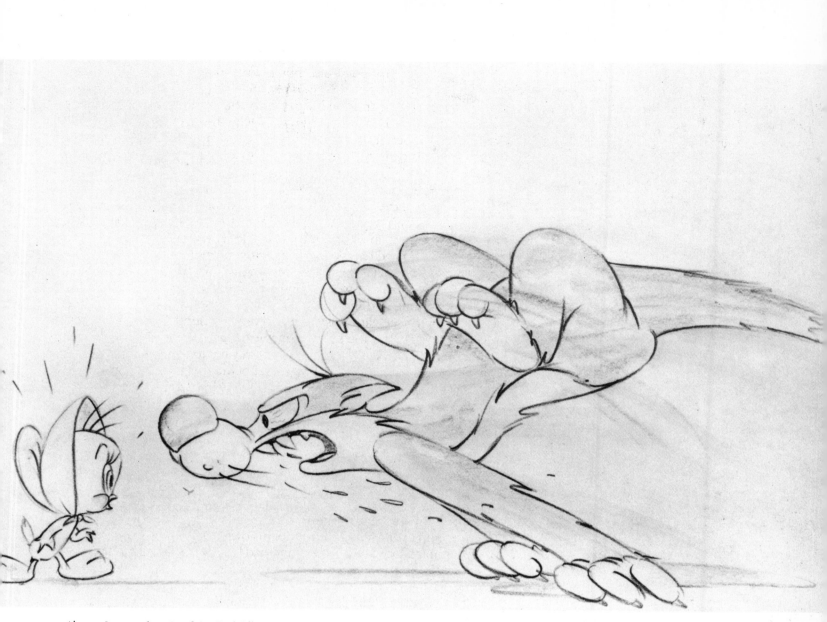

Above: *Layout drawing from* Bad Ol'
Putty Tat, *1949. Below:* Layout drawings
*by Hawley Pratt from* Canned Feud,
*1951, a Sylvester solo outing.*

# The Three Bears

It is perhaps surprising that the institution of the family survived Chuck Jones' cartoons featuring the Three Bears. For these five films are among the flat-out funniest animations ever made, in their excoriating depiction of the tensions and insipidities that underlie the roles of Father, Mother, and Child in the American domestic mythology. Yet, Jones may just have been ahead of his time here, because, as the director likes to point out, his Three Bears cartoons almost startlingly anticipate the dynamics that made "All in the Family" the most popular and controversial program on television, decades later.

"It is exactly the same structure," said Jones. "Both of them involve a smaller, volcanic character in the father, a big, slatternly mother, and a huge child who acts like a monstrous baby."

Moreover, the two treatments of family life look at individuals coming to terms with roles that are changing, or at least under question. The cartoon characters' first film, for example, 1944's *Bugs Bunny and the Three Bears,* finds the bears coping with hunger by deciding to enact the Goldilocks fable in order to lure in an edible victim. "But when Goldilocks goes upstairs to sleep," schemes Papa Bear, *"WWWHAM!"* Unfortunately, Mama Bear has no porridge, only a bunch of carrots, so Papa agonizingly screams at her to make carrot soup. The meal cooked, the three sit down to table to enact the ritual. But they deliver their lines half-heartedly, forced into their roles but incapable or unwilling to play them fully. Quavery-voiced Mama Bear begins, slurping her soup and saying, "Ahem....Oh! My soup's...uh, my porridge...is too—hot." Papa cuts in with an irate and perfunctory "Uh, my soup's too hot," before lamebrain Baby Bear slurps, belches, and says, "Eh...eh, Somebody's been sleeping in my bed"—and, immediately, *WHAM!,* the assault on Goldilocks becomes a fist on Junior's noggin.

Eventually, the scent of the carrot soup brings Bugs Bunny floating in and the melee begins, and the rabbit, at one point, extricates himself by charming the mother. But Bugs' savoir-faire in this case works against him, as Mama becomes instantly smitten—sighing the unforgettable "Tell me more about my eyes"—and goes after him for other purposes.

As written by Tedd Pierce, this cartoon is one of the finest of Warner's many revisionist fairy tales; it's a story told of characters out of step with assigned roles, made by the studio that had labored to unshackle cartoons from their Disney-derived expectations. Interestingly,

**The Three Bears Filmography**

**1944**
Bugs Bunny and the Three Bears

**1948**
What's Brewin', Bruin?

**1949**
The Bee-Deviled Bruin
Bear Feat

**1951**
A Bear for Punishment

Above and right: *Animation drawings from* Bugs Bunny and the Three Bears.

**Opposite**
*Detail of the initial establishing shot from* A Bear for Punishment; *painting by Philip De Guard.*

*Model sheet by Arthur Heinemann from*
*The Bee-Deviled Bruin.*

the Three Bears films are among the very few multiple-character Warner cartoons that do not employ the services of Mel Blanc. Papa's voice was provided by Billy Bletcher, whose growling gruffness was used for bad-guy characters as far back as Disney's Peg Leg Pete; Mama Bear was done by Bea Benaderet; and Junior was handled by Stan Freberg. "The picture didn't seem to call for Mel," said Jones. Clearly, he was after voice work that seemed somewhat at odds with typical "Looney Tunes."

When Jones brought the Three Bears back, in 1948's *What's Brewin', Bruin?,* Warner Cartoons was established at the top of the heap; the director could then settle in to directly exploring the self-defeating workings of this dysfunctional family. Here, the Bears attempt to hibernate, with Papa blowing his fuse because of Junior's snoring and the unendurable noises of nature. 1949's two cartoons with the Bears involve them in family projects, and show their assumed cohesiveness disintegrating in the face of the slightest task: nuclear family fission. In *The Bee-Deviled Bruin,* the three try to gather honey, but Papa only gathers bruises and bandages. And *Bear Feat* finds them rehearsing vaudeville acts in the hope of earning money as entertainers; after Junior stupidly sabotages every stunt—by, among others, drinking all the water in the tank that Papa is using for his high dive—Papa is driven to attempt suicide (although, alas, Junior also frustrates this plan).

Finally, 1951's incomparable *A Bear for Punishment* makes Father's Day into an unbearable ordeal for Papa—no sentimentalist, he—as Mama and Junior undertake tributes and pamperings. Junior expresses his filial devotion by insisting on filling Pa's favorite pipe (mistakenly, however, with gunpowder) and performing the tender favor of giving him a shave (with a straight razor that he has dangerously smashed). Thereafter comes an elaborate pageant of songs and recitations, and an egregiously overdone wild-stepping dance performed by Mama with Keatonesque deadpan; it was superlatively animated by Ken Harris.

"The Father's Day picture was simple," said Jones. "One Father's Day, when my daughter was about six years old, she insisted that I have breakfast in bed. Of course, when you're that age you don't do so well on that sort of thing. And so, although I admired her and love her for doing it, it wasn't my favorite occupation."

# Pepé Le Pew

A more delicious premise is hard to find. A suave French skunk oozes amour and is ready to run after every female of his kind that crosses his path. In the tradition of great French lovers, he believes—he *knows*—that he is irresistible. If there is the occasional setback, it never daunts him; the problem is only the timidity of his overwhelmed partner. Little does he know that he is so offensive that his presence evacuates buildings, much less that he uniformly traumatizes those he would woo. Love may be blind, but there are other senses to consider.

Yet, Pepé Le Pew, the ultra-confident stud unaware of his innate repulsiveness, held a special charm for his director, Chuck Jones. "He's the man I always wanted to be," said Jones. "I never had much luck with girls when I was in school. But there is somebody who is absolutely certain about his own sexuality, who's so secure with women that it's inconceivable to him that he could offend them. So Pepé was something very personal to me. I tried to get some of his personality inside me so I could draw on it in my relations with women."

Yet Pepé's essence took years to fine-tune after the skunk had originally been conceived by Michael Maltese. A close forerunner of the character had its debut in Jones' 1945 *Odor-able Kitty*. Written by Ted Pierce, the cartoon centered on an orange tomcat who grows tired of the world's abuses (from boots and bulldogs and the like) and so decides to disguise himself as a skunk to achieve some solitude; his tools include white paint, black paint, Limburger, onions, and garlic. But soon enough a real skunk catches his scent and leaps upon him with pants, French coos, and caresses, showing him that there are worse alternatives than the life he had known. But at cartoon's end, the anonymous skunk turns out to have kids and a wife—a wife with a rolling pin—and to be shamming about his Frenchness. More weasel like in appearance than the final Pepé, the skunk in this film is no more than a housebroken American.

Above: *Animation drawing from* Scent-imental Romeo. Below left: *Animation drawing from* For Scent-imental Reasons.

**The Best of Pepé Le Pew**

**1945**
Odor-able Kitty

**1947**
Scent-imental Over You

**1949**
For Scent-imental Reasons

**1954**
The Cat's Bah

**1955**
Past Perfumance

**1959**
Really Scent

Two years passed before Jones again worked with the character. But in *Scent-imental Over You* the hallmarks began to fall into place: A hairless Mexican dog, female and petite, is laughed at by the luxuriantly-coated pedigrees on New York's Park Avenue, and so she obtains a skunk fur to dress up in. But a French skunk—identified on a mailbox as "Stinky"—mistakes her for the real thing, and immediately begins "zee woo-eeng" all through a city park. Ultimately, however, when the Mexican hairless reveals herself to be a dog, Pepé also transforms himself into a hound—at least for an interval. Jones still had not found the precise formula.

But the components of the Pepé series were locked in with the character's next film, *For Scent-imental Reasons* (1949). Set in France, this roundly funny cartoon begins with Pepé in a perfume shop—a sight that drives the shop's aghast owner to paint a stripe down the back of a curvy pussycat in the hope of luring Pepé away. In the space of a single heartbeat it is libido on parade, as Pepé lunges after the terrified cat with clutches and tender words ("Ah, c'est l'amour. . . . Ahhh, c'est tou*jours!*"). Her writhing horror doesn't stop Pepé for an instant; for example, when the cat tries frantically to pry open a window in order to escape, Pepé

Below: *Color chart from* Louvre Come Back to Me, *1962.*

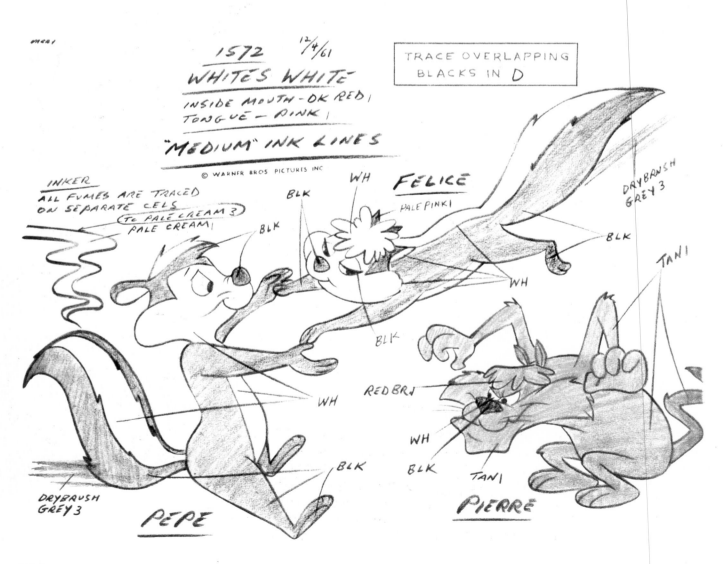

204

stands coyly back and rhapsodizes, "Zees leetle luff bundle—now she is seeking for us a trysting place" (and adds, for the benefit of the audience, "Touching—is eet not?"). More than in the previous cartoons, nonsensical Gallic babble is part of the soundtrack, from the human shouts of "Sacré maroon! Les help! Gendarme! Gendarme! *Avec*!" to the pussycat's "Les meow. . . . Les purrrr. . . ."

Repeating a familiar scenario, Producer Eddie Selzer "said that all that fractured French wasn't funny—that *nobody* would think it was funny," Jones recalled. "We really battled on that. Then, when *For Scent-imental Reasons* won the Academy Award, he went up and took it anyway!"

According to Jones, the skunk's name was derived from that of Pepe Le Moko, a character played by Charles Boyer in the gurgly love–classic *Algiers* (a 1938 remake of a 1937 French film named for the character, which was again remade in 1948 as the musical bauble *Casbah*). But the skunk's unctuous accent, Jones said, "is patterned not only on Boyer, but on all the French actors. They all used the same thing." In particular, Jones had the sound of Maurice Chevalier in his ear when he worked with Mel Blanc on developing Pepé's fetid Franglais. And the tribute is made explicit in 1951's *Scent-imental Romeo*, when Pepé appears with straw hat and cane and sings "Baby Face" à la Chevalier.

Above: *Background painting from* The Cat's Bah, *1954. Layout by Maurice Noble.* Below: *From* For Scent-imental Reasons.

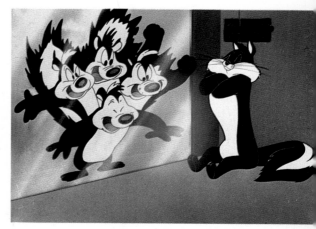

Above: *Model sheet from* Scent-imental Over You, *1947. Below:* Pepé crashes a Sylvester and Tweety cartoon: a surprise cameo in Friz Freleng's Dog Pounded, *1954. Layout drawing by Hawley Pratt.*

Another ingredient in the Le Pew series is the structure of the love-struck chase; typically, the panicky cat frantically scrambles away as smiling Pepé hops along with leisurely aplomb (and Carl Stalling sounds little curlicue figures in the orchestra). "Pepé would always be slower than the cat at the beginning, and faster at the end," Jones has said; "it was a tortoise-and-the-hare type of thing." And the later films regularly feature handsome French designs by Maurice Noble. "My approach was to get books out of the research library, thumb through them, and then put them away and never look at them again," said Noble. "Then I would strongly exaggerate what I remembered—shapes, atmosphere, colors, all of it. You had to exaggerate. On a fast cut, if you put all the grain in the wood and all the noodles in the carving, it would never be seen. But with the exaggeration, the effect would be captured."

The Pepé cartoons continued until 1962's *Louvre Come Back to Me,* in locations that included New Orleans, the French Alps, the Sahara Desert (home to the French Foreign Legion), and the Louvre museum. And in these many locations, setting up the films' rather artificial mistaken-identity situations required some cleverness. In 1955's *Two Scents Worth,* for example, the pussycat is given a white back by a bank robber who wants to use her to clear out the site of his next hit. Or in *Touché and Go* (1957), the story gets under way when the cat is inadvertently slathered by a highwayman painting stripes down the middle of a road.

For Jones, the Pepé series had another distinguishing feature. While the history of animation is indeed clogged with chase cartoons— cat and mouse, cat and canary, Road Runner and Coyote—they usually had one thing in common. "It was a matter of eating somebody," Jones has said. "Nourishment. Sustenance. Survival. But the skunk Pepé was unique in that he was after the cat, well,…"

## A Warner Bros. Chronology

**1930**

Harman and Ising sign with Schlesinger. Release of first "Looney Tune," starring Bosko and Honey.

**1931**

Release of first "Merrie Melodie."

**1933**

Harman and Ising part company with Schlesinger, who forms his own studio. Last Bosko cartoon released by Warner Bros. Introduction of Buddy and Cookie.

**1934**

Friz Freleng's first screen credit for direction. First color "Merrie Melodie"; series goes all-color by end of year.

**1935**

Introduction of Porky Pig. Last Buddy cartoon released. Tex Avery joins studio, releases first cartoon.

**1936**

Frank Tashlin rehired to direct. Carl Stalling and Mel Blanc join studio. Treg Brown joins Schlesinger from Warner Bros. main studio.

**1937**

Introduction of Petunia Pig, Daffy Duck, and Egghead. Ub Iwerks makes two cartoons for Schlesinger. Bob Clampett directs first cartoon for Schlesinger. Friz Freleng leaves for MGM, is replaced by Hardaway and Dalton.

**1938**

Introduction of proto-Bugs Bunny. Tashlin leaves and is replaced by Chuck Jones.

**1939**

Jones introduces Sniffles, Inki, Minah Bird. Freleng returns, takes over for Hardaway and Dalton.

**1940**

Introduction of Elmer Fudd, followed by true Bugs Bunny.

**1941**

Avery leaves for MGM; Clampett takes Avery's unit, McCabe takes Clampett's.

**1942**

Last Avery cartoon released. Introduction of Beaky Buzzard, Henery Hawk, Tweety. First color "Looney Tune."

**1943**

Introduction of Hubie and Bertie. Tashlin returns, takes over for McCabe. Last black and white "Looney Tune" released.

**1944**

Introduction of the Three Bears. Schlesinger sells out to Warner Bros.

**1945**

Introduction of Pepé Le Pew, Sylvester, Yosemite Sam. Tashlin leaves, is replaced by Robert McKimson.

**1946**

Clampett leaves, is replaced by Arthur Davis. Foghorn Leghorn introduced.

**1947**

The Goofy Gophers and Charlie Dog introduced. *Tweetie Pie*—first pairing of Tweety and Sylvester—wins Warner Cartoon's first Academy Award.

**1948**

Hippety Hopper and the Martian introduced.

**1949**

Introduction of Road Runner and Wile E. Coyote. Arthur Davis' unit discontinued. *For Scent-imental Reasons* and *So Much for So Little* win Academy Awards.

**1950**

Introduction of Rocky and Mugsy, and Sylvester, Jr.

**1952**

First pairing of Wile E. Coyote and Bugs Bunny.

**1953**

Introduction of Ralph Wolf and Sam Sheepdog, and Speedy Gonzales.

**1954**

Introduction of the Tasmanian Devil and Witch Hazel. Cartoon released in 3-D.

**1955**

*Speedy Gonzales* wins Academy Award.

**1957**

*Birds Anonymous* wins Academy Award.

**1958**

*Knighty Knight Bugs* wins Academy Award. Carl Stalling retires.

**1963**

Studio closes. DePatie-Freleng leases Warner Bros. cartoon plant.

**1964**

Last pre-shutdown cartoon released. Warner Bros. contracts with DePatie-Freleng to produce cartoons.

**1967**

Warner Bros. discontinues relations with DePatie-Freleng and reopens own studio. Cool Cat, Merlin the Magic Mouse introduced.

**1968**

Introduction of Bunny and Claude.

**1969**

Closing of Studio.

---

## Academy Awards

Based on the inscrutable logic of the Motion Picture Academy, the following is a list of the Warner Bros. cartoons nominated for Academy Awards; those marked with an asterisk were Oscar winners. Warner Cartoons also produced an Academy Award-winning documentary, *So Much For So Little.*

*It's Got Me Again,* 1932, Ising
*Detouring America,* 1939, Avery
*A Wild Hare,* 1940, Avery
*Hiawatha's Rabbit Hunt,* 1941, Freleng
*Rhapsody in Rivets,* 1941, Freleng
*Pigs in a Polka,* 1943, Freleng
*Greetings Bait,* 1943, Freleng
*The Swooner Crooner,* 1944, Tashlin
*Life with Feathers,* 1945, Freleng
*Walky Talky Hawky,* 1946, McKimson
\**Tweetie Pie,* 1947, Freleng
*Mouse Wreckers,* 1949, Jones
\**For Scent-imental Reasons,* 1949, Jones
*From A to Z-Z-Z-Z ,* 1954, Jones
*Sandy Claws,* 1955, Freleng
\**Speedy Gonzales,* 1955, Freleng
*Tabasco Road,* 1957, McKimson
\**Birds Anonymous,* 1957, Freleng
\**Knighty Knight Bugs,* 1958, Freleng
*Mexicali Schmoes,* 1959, Freleng
*Mouse and Garden,* 1960, Freleng
*High Note,* 1960, Jones
*The Pied Piper of Guadalupe,* 1961, Freleng
*Beep Prepared,* 1961, Jones
*Nelly's Folly,* 1961, Jones
*Now Hear This,* 1963, Jones

# Yosemite Sam

"The roughest, toughest, he-man stuffest hombre as ever crossed the Rio Grande—and I ain't no mamby-pamby" (a Yosemite Sam self-portrait, from *Bugs Bunny Rides Again*) first blazed his guns and bellowed his voice in 1945's *Hare Trigger,* directed by Friz Freleng. His appearance is foreshadowed by a grim-visaged poster:

> WANTED FOR TRAIN ROBBERY
> YOSEMITE SAM
> $5000 REWARD

Well, there *is* a train chugging through the dusty ochre countryside and the brush. And one of its passengers is Bugs Bunny, lazing about the mail car, strumming a banjo and singing, "A boy's best friend is his mudder." But Sam moves in. Fearlessly, he takes a position square in the middle of the train tracks, his pistols drawn, his countenance severe, staring down the train that is bearing down directly at him. He will hold his ground until the onrushing train halts before his eyes. It is a moment of electric suspense—until the train passes clean over the tiny Sam, leaving him all afluster.

"I was looking for a character strong enough to work against Bugs Bunny," Freleng recalled. "For me, Elmer Fudd wasn't it—he was so

Right: *Animation drawing from Yosemite Sam's first scene in* Hare Trigger.

208

Above: *Animation drawing by Virgil Ross from* Hare Trimmed, *1953.* Left: *Animation drawing of Red Hot Ryder and horse, realizing that they can't complete their jump across the Grand Canyon; from* Buckaroo Bugs, *1944.*

"YOSEMITE SAM"
(AS PIRATE)
© WARNER BROS. CARTOONS

*Sketches from* Buccaneer Bunny, *1948.*

dumb a chicken could outsmart him. So I thought to use the smallest guy I could think of along with the biggest voice I could get. Tex Avery had made a picture set in the Yukon, with a character who just yelled as loud as he could all the time [*Dangerous Dan McFoo,* 1939]. To me it was funny, so I adapted that idea."

Yet there were other contributions to the development of the firebrand Sam. Most significantly, Red Skelton fashioned a persona called Sheriff Deadeye—a hot western blowhard with a droopy moustache that flapped when he roared his words—in radio and, later, on television, and there is much of him in the cartoon character. Within the Warner studio, Bob Clampett's *Buckaroo Bugs* (1944) features a sawed-off gunslinger based both on Deadeye and on the comic-strip character Red Ryder; named Red Hot Ryder, he gallops in to save the West from the ravages of the Masked Marauder. Brave but boneheaded—he at one point loses his fillings to a magnet aimed by Bugs, then is instructed by the rabbit to attempt to vault the Grand Canyon—Red anticipates Sam's diminutive size, his hair color, and his overlarge hat. And he also uses a bit that originated with Skelton's Deadeye: When, in mid-gallop, Red's horse will not heed his commands to slow down, the cowboy is reduced to begging the dumb animal—still charging at full tilt—to hit the brakes ("Whoa! Whoa! . . . Aw, c'mon now, horsey, whoa! Please, horsey, please whoa. . . . Purty please?"). It is a routine from which Sam would get much mileage.

In Freleng's own *Stage Door Cartoon* (1944), a walk-on part is played by a Deadeye-like sheriff who looks and sounds a lot like the imminent Sam. But the foremost source for Sam may have been Freleng himself: Writer Michael Maltese said that he patterned the character on the short-tempered, short, and risible Friz. "Friz *was* Yosemite Sam,"

MODEL SHEET
PROD #1019

Above: *After Sam's introduction in* Hare
Trigger, *the character's design was next
used for an identical pair of starving
Arctic denizens, in Freleng's 1947* Along
Came Daffy. Left: *Publicity drawing for*
Bugs Bunny Rides Again, *1948, Sam's
first return in a Western setting after*
Hare Trigger.

Above: *Background painting from* Rabbit Every Monday. *Near the end of this cartoon, Sam succeeds in getting Bugs Bunny into his oven—only for the rabbit to discover a genuine live-action party taking place in it.* Below: *by Paul Julian from Mutiny on the Bunny, 1950.*

agreed Hawley Pratt, who worked on the character's design with Freleng. The identification was so strong that, until near Warner Cartoons' closing, no other director called on the services of Sam.

Over the next nineteen years, Freleng placed the character in a broad variety of settings, deriving much comedy from this unlikely casting. But throughout, Sam maintained a gruff and endlessly aggressive bluster, with a competitive streak that compelled him to take on any challenge. When Bugs makes a mark with his foot and dares him to "step across this line," Sam must reply, "Ah'm a-steppin'"—right off a high-diving board and down to a theater stage (in *High Diving Hare,* 1949). Or, in *Bugs Bunny Rides Again* (1948), Sam sprays bullets around the rabbit's feet and, asserting his dominance, commands him to dance. But after Bugs hoofs through some snazzy tapping, the rabbit calls out, "Take it, Sam!" and Sam jumps right in, even whipping his hat around during his spirited stepping. Yet Sam gets so carried away in his performance that he makes a would-be show-stopping vaudevillian exit by briskly dancing to his right—and plummets crashingly down a mine shaft, whose door Bugs has courteously opened.

Left: *From* Rabbit Every Monday *1951.*
Below: *Sam sees that his bride-to-be is a bunny. Animation drawings by Virgil Ross from* Hare Trimmed, *1953.*

Some of Sam's funniest moments come in a trio of films—*Buccaneer Bunny* (1948), *Mutiny on the Bunny* (1950), and *Captain Hareblower* (1954)—in which he plays a pirate (or "Sea-goin' Sam!"). Throughout these cartoons, he displays substantial gifts for opening gunport covers and getting blasted by Bugs' cannons. Yet Sam's analytical abilities often seem lacking. In *Buccaneer Bunny,* he needs to use a lifeboat to chase the rabbit from the shore to his ship, but Bugs has already made that crossing and taken the only set of oars; so Sam dives into the water, swims to his ship, grabs the oars, swims all the way back, and climbs into the lifeboat with the reclaimed equipment. Only then can he return to the ship on his terms.

In *Hare Trimmed* (1953), Sam plays an opportunist who reads of an elderly widow who has inherited $50 million (giving her so much "money to burn" that she warms herself by tossing stacks of bills into the fireplace). So Sam goes a-courting, drunk on thoughts of affluent matrimony ("When I get my hands on that money," he growls, "I'll buy the old ladies' home and kick the old ladies out!"). But Bugs learns of his rapacious intentions and manages to deflect him—impersonating Granny and getting Sam to take him all the way to the altar, where the horrified groom finally catches on.

But it's in the Oscar-winning *Knighty Knight Bugs* (1958) that Sam rises to his highest point. After his fire-breathing dragon sneezes in a turreted castle tower filled with explosives, the tower launches like a rocket into orbit. Even when Sam displays his bravado by shooting his six-guns into the ground and lifting himself into the air, he never rises quite that high.

Above: *Promotional art for* From Hare to Heir, *1960.* Right: *Animation drawing by Virgil Ross from* Hare Trimmed.

214

By the early 1940s, Warner Bros. had a full and thriving program of character merchandising. Currently, the studio licenses over 300 products, including jewelry, framable graphics, apparel, and accessories. Sales have exceeded $200,000,000.

# Foghorn Leghorn

**The Best of Foghorn Leghorn**

**1946**
Walky Talky Hawky

**1947**
Crowing Pains

**1948**
The Foghorn Leghorn

**1949**
Henhouse Henery

**1950**
A Fractured Leghorn

**1951**
Leghorn Swoggled

**1953**
Of Rice and Hen

**1956**
The High and the Flighty

The loudmouthed southern rooster—I say, the loudmouthed southern rooster called Foghorn Leghorn is the lone major Warner character to be wholly derived from personalities outside the studio. Most directly, the great white bird's unstoppable Dixie yapping is a parody of the "Senator Claghorn from Bighorn" character played by Kenny Delmar on the old Fred Allen radio program. But director Robert McKimson—who introduced Foghorn and managed the barnyard for all of his subsequent outings—also cited the sheriff character on an earlier radio show, "Blue Monday Jamboree," as a source. Meanwhile, Mel Blanc recalled that he "took that voice when I was just a kid from a vaudeville show of a hard-of-hearing sheriff." Nevertheless, this stew of inspirations resulted in one of the most likable of Warner's cartoon stars—an effusive, big-smiled, and jaunty-stepping cock o' the walk powerless to resist a practical joke.

Foghorn first appeared in McKimson's 1946 *Walky Talky Hawky*, a cartoon intended to be a star vehicle for Henery Hawk; the diminutive chicken hawk had been introduced by Chuck Jones and had reached his final form in Jones' 1942 *The Squawkin' Hawk*. But in *Walky Talky Hawky*, Henery was immediately reduced to having the career of a supporting player, so thoroughly was he upstaged by the voluble rooster. Setting the premise for many future installments, the cartoon begins with youthful

Above: *Cel of Foghorn Leghorn, c. 1950.*

**Opposite**
Above: *Cel of Miss Prissy, c. 1951.* Right:
*Cel of Henery Hawk from* Leghorn
Swoggled, *1951.*

Henery being told by his melodramatic father that what the boy craves is chicken; the spunky hawk immediately sets out to bring back a meal, without, however, having a shard of an idea what a chicken is. In the barnyard Foghorn discovers this ignorance and quickly turns Henery into an unwitting pawn in his never-ending prankish battles with the gravel-voiced dog who is on guard. Foghorn tells Henery that the dog is a chicken, and sics the scrappy hawk on him; the rooster then uses the resulting confusion to also take a few swipes at his canine nemesis. Eventually, the unnamed dog diagnoses the problem and manipulates the persistent Henery into becoming part of his revenge.

And so it continued in the seventeen years of follow-up films to this artful short, which was nominated for an Academy Award. Throughout, Foghorn shows an undying affection for the song "Camptown Races" (although he usually glosses over most of the words, as in: "La da dee da dee dee da, DOO DAH, DOO DAH"). And his unending blabbering is laden with all kinds of chummy asides about the gullible, ankle-high hawk ("Nice boy, but he's got more nerve than a bum tooth"). Indeed, when Foghorn gets into gear, his mouthings-on can take off like verbal cadenzas, such as this unprovoked extravaganza from 1948's *The Foghorn Leghorn:* "That Rhode Island Red turned white—then blue!

FOGHORN LEGHORN
© WARNER BROS. CARTOONS, INC. 1953

Rhode Island! Red, white, and blue! That's a joke, son, a flag-waver! You're built too low! The fast ones go over your head! You got a hole in your glove! I keep pitchin' 'em and you keep missin' 'em! You gotta keep your eye on the ball! Eye! Ball! Eyeball! I almost had a *gag,* son—joke, that is."

While Henery remains folded in the barnyard feud, Foghorn usually finds time for some favorite stunts. Often the rooster reaches inside the dog's house, silently lifts out a pointy tail, and proceeds to thrash the hound's hindquarters with a plank. And when the dog regroups and races after the fleeing rooster, invariably he reaches the end of the rope attached to his collar, resulting in some knotty body-crunchings and short-term stranglings. Usually, in films that feature this gag, the story hits a turning point when Foghorn comes upon the dog standing quietly, his expression one of smiling menace, with the collar swinging from his hand, detached

Some cartoons throw the series' premise funny curves. In 1947's *Crowing Pains,* Foghorn convinces Henery that guest-star Sylvester is a chicken; he has Henery get inside an eggshell, then sneaks him under the sitting cat, leading to a momentary identity crisis ("Thufferin' thuccotash—I'm a mother!"). And the film ends with Henery so far at sea in

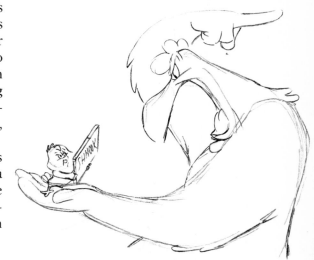

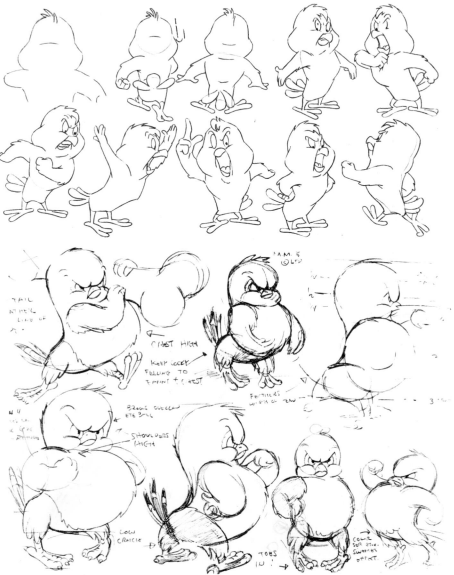

Top: *Concept sketch from* The Foghorn Leghorn, *1948. Above:* Sketches of Henery Hawk by Robert McKimson, *from* The Foghorn Leghorn. Left: *Model sheet by Robert Givens of an ancestor of Henery Hawk, from Chuck Jones'* Stage Fright, *1940.*

**Opposite**
*Model sheet of Foghorn Leghorn, 1953*

219

his attempts to identify which creature is a rooster that he decides to wait until dawn to see who crows. In a well-evoked sunrise setting, Foghorn, the dog, and Sylvester stand in a row, nervously awaiting the involuntary event. Suspense grows for Henery—until, unexpectedly, Sylvester lets out a full-throated "Cock-a-doodle-doo!" that seals his fate. Henery hauls off the nonplussed pussycat—and we cut to a close-up of Foghorn, smiling into his book on ventriloquism.

In later entries, Foghorn crossed paths with several other returning characters. One was Miss Prissy, a spinsterish hen who first appeared in 1950's *An Egg Scramble.* The skinny, bonneted bird schemes to wed Foghorn in 1953's *Of Rice and Hen,* eventually creating an imaginary rival that sends the rooster down the aisle with jealousy. *Little Boy Boo,* from 1954, introduced Prissy's round-headed son (or nephew, in later films); in this cartoon, the distracted little scientific genius would rather work on "splitting the fourth dimension" than go out and play. And 1953's *Plop Goes the Weasel* brought a buck-toothed, slavery weasel into Foghorn's life; the goony weasel's attempts to steal chickens from the coop extended through several films. But Foghorn, with keener cunning, was always there to turn him back—prevent him, that is.

Below: *Cel of the barnyard dog from* Leghorn Swoggled, *1951, with background.*

**Opposite**
*Painting by Richard H. Thomas from* Walky Talky Hawky, *1946.*

# The Road Runner and Wile E. Coyote

It began as a parody and ended as a paradigm. Like much else in the Road Runner series, plans just seem to backfire.

"Mike and I thought it would be funny to do a parody of chase cartoons," said Chuck Jones, referring to the writer Michael Maltese, "because everybody was always chasing everybody else—dogs chasing cats, cats chasing mice. Then we would become the Dean Swifts of our day. So, as Mike said, we tried things like an anteater chasing a dugong, a giraffe chasing a snail—things like that. But we realized that there's logic at work in chases like cats and mice; they're natural adversaries, so you don't have to establish their motivations.

"So we tried to find a more logical chase. I came up with coyotes because I had read Mark Twain's *Roughing It* when I was a kid, and he has a whole chapter on the coyote—what kind of person the coyote actually is. And he also has a chapter on jackrabbits, in which he gives a description of their speed. That's what gave me the clue to the speed of the Road Runner: I thought of roadrunners—they're all over southern California—and then I remembered how fast Twain said the jackrabbit is. The roadrunner seemed funny, anyway—a bird that runs. They're like flying fish of the land.

ACCELERATII INCREDIBILUS '72

**Opposite**
*The first sketches of the Road Runner and the Coyote, c. 1948*

*By Chuck Jones. Layout drawings of the Coyote trying the "Acme Earthquake Pills"—and discovering that they do not work on his intended victim, the Road Runner; from* Hopalong Casualty, *1960.*

"They can run about twenty-one or twenty-two miles an hour. They spread their little stubby wings and shoot up to the top of a big swirl of cactus and vibrate to a stop. I always thought they were funny—funny by the way they move, not by what they look like. And the coyote, by his very nature, and by how Mark Twain described him, is never well-fed—he's always hungry. So you don't have to explain it. You come across a coyote chasing a roadrunner—he'd chase anything."

Other influences, however, fed into the creation of the Road Runner and Wile E. Coyote, whose disaster-laden desert scrambles were first revealed in Jones' 1949 *Fast and Furry-ous*. For its structure, Jones has cited Frank Tashlin's 1941 Columbia cartoon *The Fox and the Grapes* as a model, with its tale of Aesop's fox desperately attempting every means he can to obtain some grapes from high in a tree, as told through a sequence of blackout gags. Another source was autobiographical, as Jones worked out his own shortcomings as a handyman through the Coyote's determined tinkerings: "Give me any tool and I'm in trouble," he has said. "I have yet to learn the mysteries of a screwdriver. My wife and daughter would go hide when I'd start to hang a painting."

And a third antecedent can be found in Jones' 1946 *Fair and Worm-er,* a zestily funny, velocity-filled film that represents an earlier satire of formulaic cartoon chases. In it, a worm goes after an apple, a crow goes after the worm, a cat goes after the crow, a dog goes after the cat, and a dogcatcher goes after the dog, all of which is intermixed with a mouse chasing the dogcatcher's wife and hop-ons by a small, Le Pew-like

Above: *Cel of the Road Runner, c. 1955.*
Below: *Painting by Philip De Guard from* Beep, Beep, *1952.*

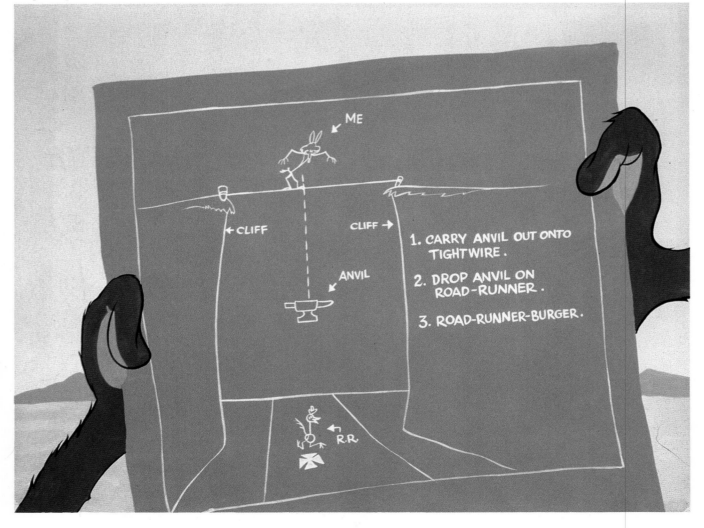

ME

CLIFF

CLIFF

ANVIL

1. CARRY ANVIL OUT ONTO TIGHTWIRE.

2. DROP ANVIL ON ROAD-RUNNER.

3. ROAD-RUNNER-BURGER.

R.R.

skunk who convolutes the entire proceeding. It was perfectly consistent for the reductivist Jones to boil this baroque spoof down to a single pair of speeding adversaries.

From these disparate sources, Jones fashioned fifteen years of cartoons that have become perhaps the most critically lauded animated series ever. In part, this has to do with the director's exquisite control of his material—his ability to weave elaborate comic structures from pure gags, dispensing entirely with the need for narrative. The Road Runner cartoons are the distilled culmination of the slapstick tradition—comedy with zero concessions to the traditional demands of storytelling.

In place of traditional narrative conventions, Jones established a framework for the Road Runner cartoons that gave them resilience and coherence. He called this the "disciplines" that operated within these films, restrictions that he consciously applied after the cartoons had found their groove. The director has enumerated five: The cartoons are set in the desert of the American Southwest; the Road Runner never leaves the road; never is there dialogue; the Coyote is never injured by the Road Runner; and the audience's sympathy must remain with the Coyote.

Beyond these, there are other constants and returning elements in the series, themes upon which the Coyote can create variations of self-destruction. Among them are the cartoons' props, both personal and geographical—all the boulders, cannons, ropes, rifles, precipices, and abyss bottoms. But other components are structural: After beginning

*From* Fast and Furry-ous: Above: *A film frame from the first encounter.* Below: *Model sheet by Chuck Jones.*

ACME
*ROCKET POWERED*
ROLLER SKATES

their cartoons with heated action, the Road Runner and the Coyote usually hit freeze frames for formal introductions, with mock Latin genera and species superimposed (*Accelleratii incredibus* and *Carnivorous vulgaris,* respectively, in the first few cartoons (although the spelling varied), later moving to such appellations as *Burnius roadibus* and *Famishius famishius)* The cartoons are always seen from the point of view of the Coyote. The Coyote brings about all of the films' mayhem, as the schemes he concocts to catch the Road Runner misfire and make him the victim of his own machinations. Indeed, the Road Runner does nothing to antagonize the Coyote, beyond merely existing (although he occasionally startles him into smashing up into an overhang with a well-timed "meep meep!" or plunks his little tongue at him when a chase temporarily closes in—before the Road Runner hops into high gear and shoots away, making the blacktop ribbon up from the ground and the Coyote's jaw drop down to it). And the Coyote's nutsy gadgetry is usually acquired, with no indication of how, from a company known as ACME; its products include Rocket Powered Roller Skates, Triple-Strength Battleship Steel Armor Plates, Dehydrated Boulders, Do-It-Yourself Tornadoes, and Axle Grease (Guaranteed Slippery). "When I was a kid, we called everything the ACME Corporation," Jones says. "I adored the idea that there was a factory someplace that supplied nothing but things for coyotes."

Further, all of the cartoons progress through series of discrete blackouts. Yet even within this unvarying pattern, their humor is carefully orchestrated. "There *is* a structure," Jones told Greg Ford. "It isn't, as it may appear in the beginning, a series of spot-gags without relationship to one another. I'd alternate, say, a gag which would let the audience in on what was going to happen, where the surprise might be *how* it would happen, with a scene that would get a laugh from something that the audience couldn't have the remotest idea would happen." Elsewhere, the gags' rhythms would change, from abrupt to developed and sustained, or gags would play off one another, or a setup planted early in a cartoon would surprisingly reappear and pay off later. Jones has said that he learned that about eleven gags were correct to fill out and pace each Road Runner cartoon.

Yet all this complex comic architecture—disciplines, frameworks, themes, props, gag stuctures—served an immediate purpose. For the director's rigorous adherence to them powerfully heightened the qualities of obsession that lie at the center of the Road Runner series. Indeed, "We found that the more disciplines we applied, the better it got," Jones said. In these cartoons, form strongly reflects content, reinforcing its comedic purpose and harmonizing the whole effect. And the content of these films is largely determined by the personality of Wile E. Coyote—the character whose self-defining but self-defeating hungers occasion everything that matters on screen. In each gag in every cartoon, we know what the outcome will be: the Coyote will fail. What is unknown about each gag is its apparatus—*how* the Coyote will fail. Locked in an unending cycle in which the beginning and the terminal points are foreknown, the Coyote is a Sisyphus-figure condemned to his toil only by himself. Comedy as repitition-compulsion.

In the Coyote, Jones created a great comic persona, the definitive cartoon antihero. Through Jones' drawings and direction, Wile E. has a purely physical expressivity that makes him as rounded and real as any flesh-and-blood actor, fully capable of engaging our affections—even though his ostensible goal is to murder a carefree bird. As rendered by

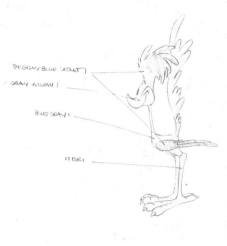

**Opposite**
*Background paintings by Philip De Guard.* Top: *From* Beep, Beep, *1952; layout by Robert Gribbrock.* Bottom: *From* Zip 'n Short, *1961; layout by Maurice Noble.*

*Concept painting by Maurice Noble from* Zoom and Bored, *1957.*

*Layout drawings by Chuck Jones.*
Above: *From* Rabbit's Feat, Top: *From*
Zoom and Bored, *1957.*

Jones, the Coyote's facial expressions of pure desolation or his dwindling pupils or his momentary flashes of triumphant inspiration—his giddy belief that he has found the reason to try *just one more time*—carry more comedic clout than the biggest boulder. Yet fundamentally the Coyote is so successful a character because his conflicts seem to spring from such deep and true psychological sources. He is a Ralph Cramden-like Everyman whose deluded schemes for accomplishment or advancement eternally crash back down upon him—eleven times per outing. But Jones also made it clear that the Coyote was no longer at war with the bird, but with himself, for the payoff for actually catching the Road Runner—gristly, meatless thing—could in no way justify what had gone into achieving it; rather, each effort to get the bird became foremost an attempt by the Coyote to salvage his own dignity. And his extension of these efforts through increasingly farfetched mechanical aids is a tragicomic expression of the powerlessness he feels in his pursuit, and his desperation to overcome it. It is intellect losing out to instinct, a mind destroying itself in its thought-driven attempts to conquer a force of nature.

In explicating the Coyote's psyche, Jones often mentions a quotation from George Santayana: "A fanatic is someone who redoubles his effort when he has forgotten his aim." For Wile E., this redoubling is most tangibly expressed in his use or construction of cockamamie destructive devices—often ingenious, but more often flawed. The result, inevitably, is self-inflicted disaster. For example, in his first film, *Fast and Furry-ous,* the Coyote straps a refrigerator, a meat grinder, and an electric motor to his back, rigging them so that the fridge's expelled ice cubes will form a snow path in front of him on which he can ski. And the ploy works—until he skis right past the Road Runner and out over an abyss on a machine-made ice-bridge; when the motor falters, down he goes. Or in *Zoom and Bored,* we see, climbing up and around a mountain, a very long and rickety trough that the Coyote has built; at the top of the mount, he stands about to light the bomb that will roll down it—until it explodes as soon as he touches his match to its fuse. In *Lickety Splat,* it is little sticks of dynamite that the Coyote has equipped with wings; early in the cartoon, he lets them loose from a balloon, and they drift in to pulverize him all throughout the film. And in *Hopalong Casualty,* Wile E. piles Acme Earthquake Pills on the road and labels it Free Bird Seed; disappointed when the Road Runner pecks them up and scoots away with nary a tremor, the Coyote samples some himself—but then reads on the label that Road Runners are immune to the pills' effects. Soon he is Coyote-quaking enough to grind boulders into pebbly dust.

The Road Runner series was also distinguished by its venturesome backgrounds and unique use of space. As first designed by Robert Gribbroek and painted by Peter Alvarado, the series' desertscapes conveyed a strong sense of depth and distance through mostly realistic details; boulders and buttes had real heft, lending the characters greater feelings of weight. But after a few years, layout artist Maurice Noble and painter Philip De Guard began to make the desert vistas lighter-seeming and more abstract—reactions to the desert's brilliance and heat rather than depictions of them. Their backgrounds envisioned deserts of pastel yellows, lavenders, oranges, and pinks, conveying sun and sultriness without heaviness. Similarly, the impossible rock formations that Noble constructed were both massive and airy, impressive but non-intrusive; the ways in which they seemed to defy gravity—with boulders perched atop slender spires of rock, and the like—also made the characters seem fleeter and more buoyant. And in these wide-open settings, often extending unto a far horizon, the characters became the only measure of depth and distance. According to Chuck Jones, the esteemed drawing instructor Don Graham said that "the Coyote and Road Runner pictures were the only films in which forms moved in pure space—where perspective was determined not by the drawing or the backgrounds but by the movement of the characters." And Jones has compared the spatial arrangements of the Road Runner films to Japanese prints.

There was a gap of nearly three years before Jones made the second Road Runner cartoon. The director says that he decided to revive the characters after he had received a letter from a Captain in the Naval Air Force; it stated that some of the pilots participating in flight training had begun calling "Beep Beep!" to one another during maneuvers, after having had seen *Fast and Furry-ous*. That, for Jones, provided part of the incentive to return to the series. But before the Road Runner returned for his second appearance—1952's, what else, *Beep, Beep*—Jones cast the Coyote in a different role, beginning the first of two additional series in which the scraggly creature would star. Released earlier in 1952, the hilarious *Operation: Rabbit* introduced a series of a few films in which the Coyote set his sights on Bugs Bunny. Here, the Coyote is a crackpot intellectual sealed in the hothouse of his cerebrum; even more obsessed with his own gizmos than in the Road Runner cartoons, the Coyote takes an almost erotic delight in the brilliance of his brainworks. A pure rationalist, he fully expects everything to work out in accordance with the logic that only he is sharp enough to see. And in this series he was given a

*Animation drawings by Ken Harris from* Gee Whiz-z-z-z, *1956.*

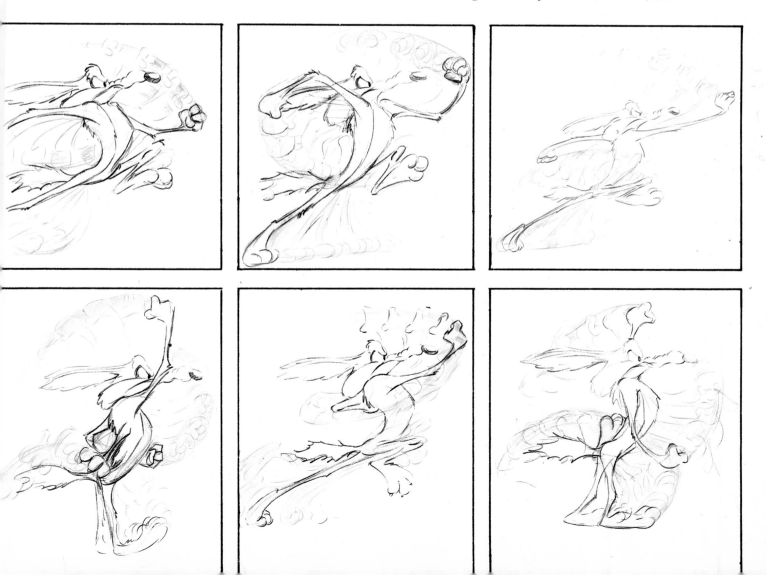

Above: *The initial establishing shot from*
Operation: Rabbit, *1952; painting by*
*Philip De Guard.* Below: *Color chart*
*from* Hopalong Casualty, *1960.*

voice with which to sing his own praises. The cartoon begins with the Coyote scurrying from his cave to Bugs' rabbit hole, unfolding a portable door, knocking on it smartly, and waiting for the bunny to emerge and answer it. "Allow me to introduce myself: Wile E. Coyote—genius," he says elegantly, and shows Bugs a business card that contains the same information. He goes on: "I am more muscular, more cunning, faster, and larger than you are—*and* I'm a genius, while you could hardly pass the entrance examinations to kindergarten. So I'll give you the customary two minutes to say your prayers." When Bugs instead gives him guff, the Coyote confidently retreats to his cave. "Why do they always want to do it the *hard* way?" he wonders.

Then the Coyote begins his schemes, all the while mouthing delight for his own cleverness. "Gad—I'm *such* a genius," he says, while putting together a pressure-cooker device that he is ultimately fried by. Or later, when working in a shed stocked with explosives, he delightedly fills a few carrots with nitro: "Brilliance!" he revels. "That's all I can say—*sheer unadulterated brilliance!*"—just before Bugs tows the shed into the path of an onrushing train. As in the Road Runner series, the Coyote maintains a neurotic belief in the mind's ability to overmaster instinct.

This theme was given a corkscrew twist in 1953's *Don't Give Up the Sheep,* the first cartoon in Jones' third series with the Coyote—or a

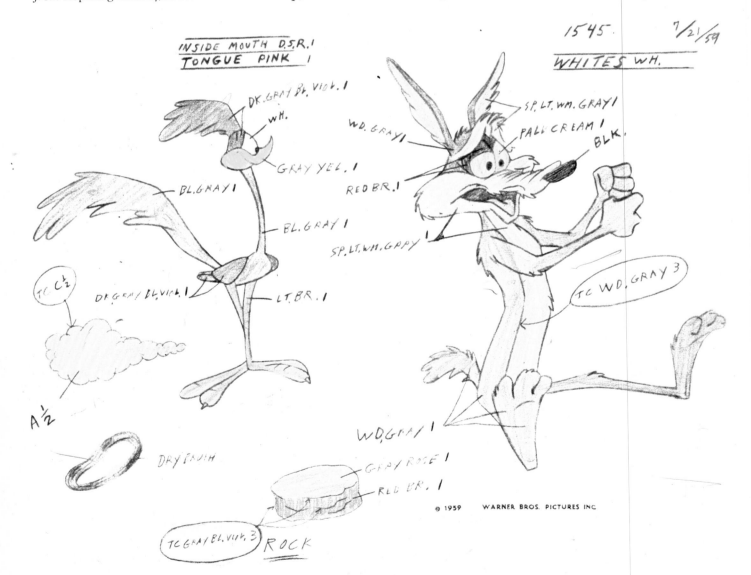

230

character who distinctly resembles him. For in these cartoons, the Coyote has been reclassified as a Wolf, a distinction that is only visible in that the Wolf's nose is usually red. He has also picked up a new name, Ralph Wolf (the name of a veteran studio artist), and a new adversary, a chunky sheepdog named Sam whose eyes are entirely covered by his bangs. For the most part, these several films consist of blackout vignettes in which the Wolf tries—and fails—to steal sheep from the white dog's flock; the Sheepdog is an even-tempered and stolid guardian, presiding over his herd from atop a cliff, who does not hesitate to violently punish the Wolf for his attempted poachings.

But what sets these cartoons apart is their frames. (Indeed, Friz Freleng had made a wolf-and-sheepdog cartoon as early as 1942, *The Sheepish Wolf.*) The Jones films typically begin and end with the Wolf and Sheepdog not as adversaries at all, but as friendly working stiffs. At the beginning of the day, on the way to their battlesite, the two meet and mutter tired and indifferent small talk—"Mornin', Sam." "Oh, uh, good morning, Ralph"—before they punch a clock and begin their allotted tasks: systematic mutual antagonism. Occasionally, the Sheepdog will be in the middle of pummeling the Wolf when the lunch whistle will sound; the two stop their assault, walk off and share coffee and sandwiches (with the wolf reeling a bit), and vacuously banter; when the whistle toots to indicate the end of the break, they return to exactly the same place and position in which they had been interrupted and recommence the beating. Later, after hearing the whistle that concludes their work day, the two salaried opponents walk into a sunset, carrying their lunch pails, and one platitudinously hums, "Great to be alive."

Incisive and very funny, the Wolf and Sheepdog cartoons sound a note about contemporary alienation and role playing, the consequences of the suppression of instinct, and the role of the workplace in channeling certain aggressive instincts. While the series clearly reflects some of the tensions of the Cold War, Jones says that the cartoons relate to a remark by the writer Lewis Browne in his 1934 book *How Odd of God.* "He said something along the lines that there are no judges, only people judging; no tramps, only people tramping; no high-jumpers, only people jumping high," Jones said. "So I drew the conclusion that there are no sheepdogs, only dogs who tend sheep during the day. They only become sheepdogs when they punch in in the morning."

As in the Road Runner cartoons, the Sheepdog series is propelled by the never-ending hungers of one character. But, in terms of mechanics, "It's the exact opposite of the Road Runner and the Coyote," Jones said. "The Sheepdog is not fleet, indeed he hardly moves at all; all the movement is done by the Wolf. I was trying to find out what kind of gags we could come up with within the situation of an immobile character. The dog *appears* in different places, but almost magically—seldom do you see him moving."

Yet moving, eternally, is the Coyote, compelled to act by his own needs and desires. And through three series, this ever-needy, ever-failing character cast a powerful spell on his creator-director. "All of us have things that we love to pursue so much that we hope we don't catch them," Jones has said. "Anybody who draws knows that drawing or writing or composing or anything is an elusive goal. There's no way you can win. So, in a way, the Road Runner is to the Coyote what a blank piece of paper is to an artist. It's unattainable. It's unachievable. Do you think it satisfied Hillary to climb to the top of Mount Everest? Not at all. What he's hoping is that somebody would find a mountain that is bigger than that."

*Poses of Sam Sheepdog from a 1960 model sheet drawn by Chuck Jones.*

# The Goofy Gophers

Take politeness to the point of pathology, mix in healthy measures of inquisitiveness and, occasionally, maliciousness. The contradictions inherent in such a combination account for the peculiar charms of the Goofy Gophers, who were introduced in a 1947 cartoon of the same title. Something of a Warner reply to Disney's supersaccharine Chip 'n' Dale, the mischievous chipmunks with speeded voices, the Gophers were later even given the tweaking names Mac 'n' Tosh.

Yet the Gophers had a history at Warner's. In 1942, Norm McCabe directed a black-and-white cartoon called *Gopher Goofy*, but if the characters in this rural tale are as impish as the later gophers, that is where the similarity ends. Rather, Bob Clampett rethought and redesigned a pair of gophers for the 1947 film, and herein lies the reason for their continuing appeal. But Clampett left Warner's after finishing only the story and the soundtrack of *The Goofy Gophers,* and it remained for director Arthur Davis to complete the cartoon. And he completed it with admirable élan, as it tells of a limber hound who speaks the King's English, guarding a vegetable garden late one night.

After the dog paces military-style in front of his house, he curls down to relax for the evening—until the sound of crunching vegetables provokes a widely opened eye. Eventually, the veggies begin disappear-

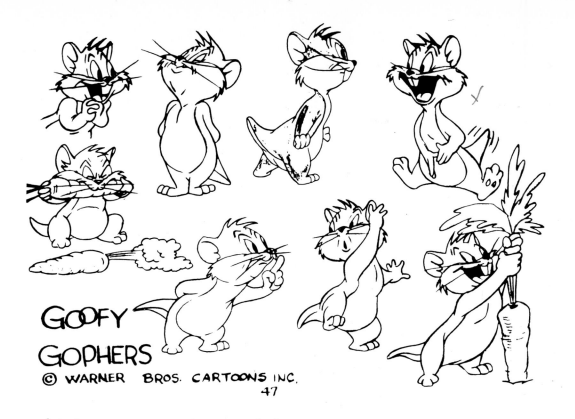

GOOFY GOPHERS

© WARNER BROS. CARTOONS INC.

47

ing at an alarming rate, at one point even whisking into the ground in time to a conga rhythm. The dog tries all manner of devices and ploys—even dressing as a scarecrow—to catch the very proper gophers, but they continue their depredations both ruthlessly and politely.

"Their speech pattern was a takeoff on a comic strip from years ago called 'Alphonse and Gaston,'" said Davis. "They would constantly go on saying things like, 'But you first, my dear.' 'But no—it must be *you* who goes first.'" Beyond that, Bob Clampett told Mike Barrier that the gophers' rather effeminate demeanor was derived from two like-mannered character actors of the time, Edward Everett Horton and Franklin Pangborn. Mel Blanc and Stan Freberg provided the gophers' voices.

And so the gophers vex the dog while maintaining perfect decorousness among themselves. Before they light a book of matches that they have secretly slid under the hound's paw, they make sure there is mutual approval: "Shall we?" inquires one; "Surely," affirms the other. A blazing hotfoot ensues. And before cartoon's end—when the gophers finally rid themselves of the dog by launching him to the moon—they display their abilities in mimicry. Mac (or is it Tosh?) grabs two carrots, points them up like a pair of ears behind his head, chomps on a third, and burbles, "Who am I making like? Who am I making like?" Warner's self-conscious tribute to its lead rabbit is completed when Carl Stalling fills the soundtrack with a tinkly version of the "Merrie Melodies" theme.

The gophers later played in more than a half dozen cartoons, including the funny *I Gopher You* (1954, Freleng), in which their veggie supply is carted off by a produce company. They follow the company's truck back to the canning factory and mistakenly get caught in its massive machinery; one gopher accidentally ends up in a can himself, while the other must open every tin in the house to find him. Perhaps their finest hour, however, is Robert McKimson's *A Ham in a Role* (1949), in which they addle a pompous, Shakespeare-spouting dog who grows disgusted with his "degrading occupation" of appearing in animated cartoons. But if the gophers are tough on those they take as foils, they can also be hard on themselves. In Friz Freleng's *A Bone for a Bone* (1951), the pair are happily playing cards. "You've lost five in a row. Would you like to lose another?" asks one. "Oh, yes, yes, very much, quite," is the reply.

**Opposite**
*Background painting by Philip De Guard from* The Goofy Gophers.

Above: *Model sheet, 1947.* Below: *Layout drawing by Hawley Pratt from* A Bone for a Bone.

# Marvin the Martian

He has no mouth, but he must blow up the Earth.

He is Warner's little Martian, unnamed during his tenure at the studio but later christened Marvin by his director, Chuck Jones. He was created for 1948's *Haredevil Hare,* a cartoon that begins with two newspaper headlines: "Scientists to Launch First Rocket to Moon," followed by "Heroic Rabbit Volunteers as First Passenger"—followed by a shot of Bugs madly clawing the ground and howling his protests as he is dragged to the gigantic rocket ("No! You ain't gettin' me into that flying cigar!").

But when a passel of carrots is dumped into the spaceship, Bugs decides to snuggle in and is launched aloft. After a terrifying journey and a bumpy crash landing, Bugs grows proud of being "the foist living creature to set foot on the moon"—just as another space vessel, labeled "Mars to Moon Expeditionary Force," smoothly lands right nearby. The oblivious Martian skitters out and, for no stated purpose, aims a vast destructive weapon at the Earth.

"I patterned him after the god Mars," said Chuck Jones, who devised the character with writer Michael Maltese. "That was the uniform that Mars wore—that helmet and that skirt. We thought that putting it on this ant-like creature might be funny." Funny, too, are the Martian's sneakers—apparel that he shares with the orange monster in Jones' *Hair-Raising Hare*—and his meek and creamy voice (which innocently intones that he wants to blow up the Earth because it obstructs his view of Venus). And funnier still is that the Martian's "reserves"—a gangly, greenish dog—is attired just the same way.

The Martian returned for four more cartoons, perhaps most celebratedly in 1953's *Duck Dodgers in the 24½th Century.* Here, he voyages in his "Martin Maggot" spacecraft to Planet X, to claim it "in the name of Mars," and shows a knack for wielding an "A-1 Disintegrating Pistol" (which makes Dodgers go from duck to dust). His most stylish film, however, may be 1958's *Hare-way to the Stars,* for which Maurice Noble designed a sleekly visionary space-city—transparent panels and geometric supports suspended in an ebon-black expanse.

Forever pointlessly warlike, the Warner Martian is nevertheless a creature who moves with gentleness. Accordingly, his mouthlessness posed some challenges to his animators. "We had to convey that he was speaking totally through his movements," Jones said. "It demanded a kind of expressive body mechanics." How the Martian eats, however, is anybody's guess.

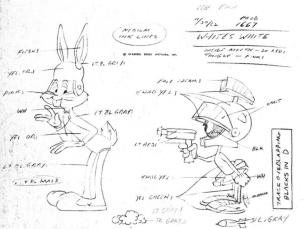

Mad as a Mars Hare, *1963.*

**Opposite**
*From* Duck Dodgers in the 24½th Century. Top: *Background painting by Philip De Guard of a typical Martian weapon. Layout by Maurice Noble.* Bottom: *Publicity frame.*

**Opposite**
*Animation drawings by Virgil Ross of Speedy's hip-hopping departure; used in* Speedy Gonzales *and other cartoons.*

# Speedy Gonzales

"**A**ndale, andale, ariba, ariba, eh-hah!"

The fastest mouse in all Mehico first made his whooshing getaways in Robert McKimson's *Cat-Tails for Two,* of 1953. Complete with a calling card, the mouse is discovered aboard a Mexican ship (the *Pancho Cucaracha*) by two nearly brain-dead cats—adapted from the doltish duo in John Steinbeck's *Of Mice and Men*—who are in the market for something to eat. Speedy continually outsmarts and outruns the cats, who are named Benny and George, and somehow the ship manages to stay afloat despite the many billowing explosions that accompany the pursuit. Yet in this film, Speedy looks little like his well-known self; he is browner, lankier, and rattier than his eventual incarnation, wears no hat and has lots of imperfect teeth—one of them gold. He is more directly a caricature of a Mexican street personality.

The character lay dormant for two years, until he was revived by Freleng for the 1955 cartoon *Speedy Gonzales.* Redesigned by Freleng and Hawley Pratt into his familiar form—bright-eyed, scrubbed up, and secure under his outsize sombrero—Speedy was here paired with Sylvester, as a kind of ever-elusive Road Runner–like antagonist to the hungry cat. The story is appealing: A group of Mexican mice plan to invade a cheese factory, and draw straws to see who will test the waters. But when the loser, Manuel, is easily nabbed by guard-cat Sylvester, the bunch sends for their heroic Mexican savior, Speedy. Highly spirited, charismatic, hopping with excesses of energy, Speedy easily gets past the dumbfounded Sylvester, who at one point gets caught in the dozens of mousetraps he had earlier set.

*Speedy Gonzales* went on to win an Academy Award, while the character went on to play in a series of cartoons directed by Freleng and McKimson. Usually pursued by Sylvester Gato, the burn-rubber rodent also had a few run-ins with a pair of hot-tempered crows. And often Speedy would keep company with a down-shifted sidekick called Slowpoke Rodriguez, the slowest mouse in all the world.

In 1957's *Tabasco Road,* Speedy plays the Good Samaritan, leading two extremely soused mouse-friends home from a celebration in honor of Speedy; the route goes past an "alley gato" whose attempts to get the mice in his mouth continually end with Speedy zipping into his maw and substituting a stick of dynamite. And in *West of the Pesos* (1960), Speedy is again the altruistic savior, when he is called in to rescue a group of mice who have been corralled in a laboratory for experiments. (However, the

*Background layout by Hawley Pratt from* Gonzales' Tamales, *1957.*

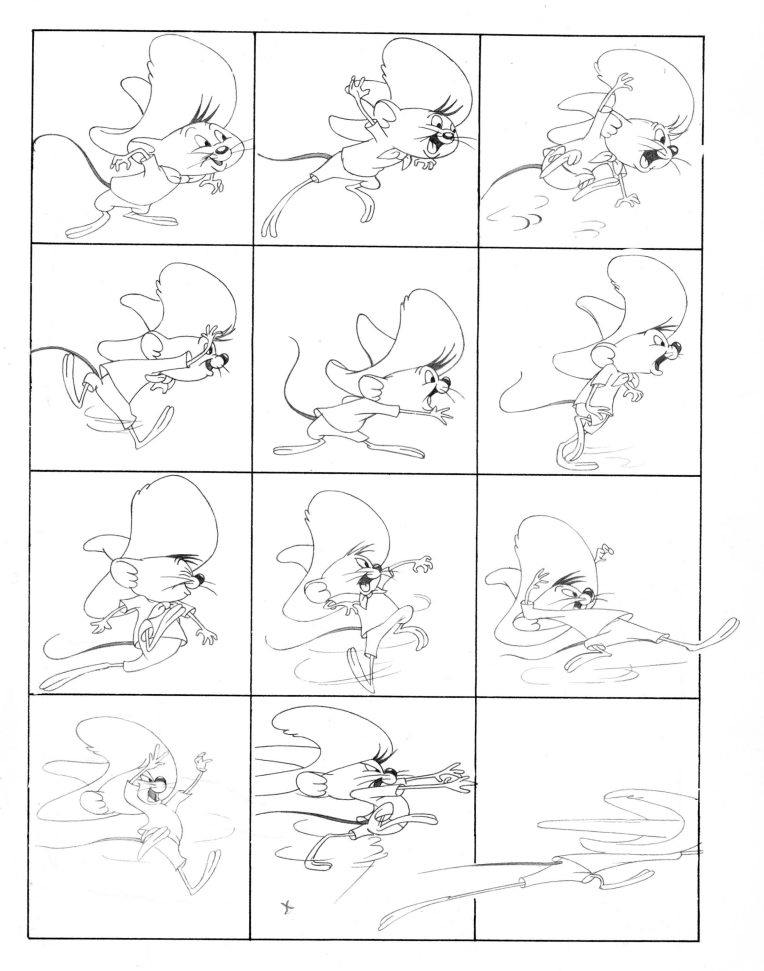

237

persecuted bunch is shrewd enough to send Camilla, one mouse's "seester," to get Speedy.) After Warner's had closed and reopened in the 1960s, Speedy became perhaps the studio's principal character; he scampered through nearly thirty cartoons, most often while escaping Daffy Duck.

Above: *Background painting by Richard H. Thomas from* Cat-Tails for Two, *1953.*
Right: *Color chart of the Two Crows, 1961.*

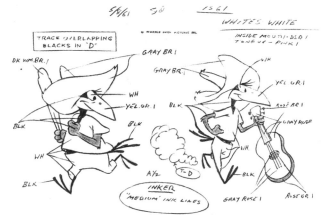

# The Tasmanian Devil

I f ever there was a creature that lived up to the description "omnivorous," it was the Tasmanian Devil. The Devil devoured boulders, trees, shrubbery, hillocks, and everything else in his path as he moved like a whirling, gyrating tornado through the jungle landscape. Accompanied by sounds that included clanging bells, pumping motors, and ever-more-intensely-racing engines, Tas sent all of the animals in sight stampeding for cover. When he stopped, his snorting, sputtering, spluttery effusions—as well as his waggling hands—indicated that his was an appetite that could never be slaked. Unfortunately, the meal he favored above all others was rabbit.

The Tasmanian Devil was introduced in Robert McKimson's 1954 *Devil May Hare* and was a kind of caricature of the rampaging animal hungers that serve as the basis for so many animated cartoons. In this film, he wrangles with Bugs Bunny, who, to rid himself of this stertorous nuisance, ends up phoning the "Tasmanian Post Dispatch" and placing a personals ad for a "lonely lady Devil, object: matrimony." The Devilette quickly arrives in an airplane, wearing a veil and carrying a bouquet, and drags the startled bridegroom away. Yet this film did not please Edward Selzer, executive producer of Warner's cartoon division, and he told McKimson to make no more Devil shorts. But some time thereafter, studio head Jack Warner asked Selzer what became of the character. When Selzer replied that Tas had been retired, Warner commanded Selzer to revive him. Apparently, a character that consumed everything it saw appealed to this Hollywood mogul.

McKimson brought Tas back in 1957's *Bedeviled Rabbit,* in which Bugs has hidden himself inside a crate of carrots, just before it is dropped in Tasmania. The female Devil also returns, but this time she has graduated to being Mrs. Tas—which gives her all the more reason for lacing into her spouse when Bugs impersonates a frilly she-Devil and hot-wires him. And in *Ducking the Devil,* from later in 1957, Tas steals the $1,000 that Daffy Duck has earned as a reward for capturing him after he has escaped from the zoo. Clearly, this Devil's appetite is not limited to food alone.

Above: *Layout drawing from* Devil May Hare. Left: *Color chart from* Bill of Hare, *1962.*

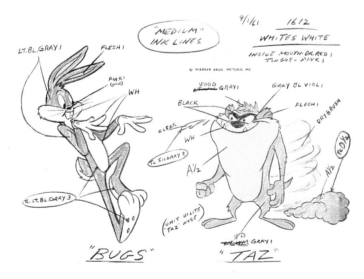

# FILMOGRAPHY

The following is a chronological list of all the "Looney Tunes" and "Merrie Melodies" theatrically released by Warner Bros. Titles are followed by release dates, as taken from Warner's original release sheets; "LT" for "Looney Tunes" or "MM" for "Merrie Melodies"; name character(s), if any; and directors. The more prolific Warner directors are represented by their last names only; they include Hugh Harman; Rudolph Ising (who usually spelled his first name "Rudolf" on screen because he preferred the way it looked); Jack King; Isadore "Friz" Freleng; J. B. "Bugs" Hardaway; Fred "Tex" Avery; Frank "Tash" or "Tish-Tash" Tashlin; Robert (Bob) Clampett; Cal Dalton; Charles M. (Chuck) Jones; Robert McKimson; and Arthur Davis.

Regrettably, for many years the Warner cartoon directors were denied their rightful status on screen. Leon Schlesinger insisted on giving them the meaningless credit of "Supervision," claiming that the functions they performed did not qualify as film direction; it has also been suggested that Schlesinger was trying to make it seem as if he was the creative force behind his cartoons. But after a lengthy outcry Schlesinger relented, and "Direction" credit began to be awarded with the 1944 title *Angel Puss.* Moreover, Schlesinger also implemented a system of "rotating credits," whereby only one animator and one writer would be given screen credit per cartoon. Under this arbitrary system, a writer's or an animator's strongest work might have been done on a film for which he received no mention on screen, while his name might decorate a cartoon on which he did almost nothing at all. Clearly inequitable, this procedure was terminated with help from the newly formed Cartoonists' Union; the first Warner cartoon to have a reasonably full slate of credits is 1945's *Hare Trigger.*

Another major change to the opening—and the closing—of the Warner cartoons came in 1936, when the familiar concentric circles began to be used. Later on, the color of these circles would change with every release season, although it is not known for how long this continued.

In addition to the cartoons listed below, Schlesinger and Warner's produced much additional animation. Some of the studio's wartime films are mentioned in the text. Beyond that, outside work included *Hitch in Time,* a production commissioned by the U.S. Air Force and released

in 1955; 1956's *90-Day Wonder,* commissioned by the U.S. Army; and 1957's *Drafty, Isn't it?,* also for the U.S. Army. In 1961, Warner Bros. released a 25-minute film entitled *The Adventures of the Road Runner,* which melded existing footage with new animation; the new work was later incorporated into two cartoons shown on television, *Zip, Zip Hurray* and *Road Runner a Go Go.* Also for television, the studio supplied animated sequences for a few Bell Telephone specials on NBC, including 1958's "Gateways to the Mind" and 1959's "The Alphabet Conspiracy"; a separate unit was established on the main Warner Bros. lot to work on layout, storyboards, and character designs for these hourlong programs. And Daffy, Porky, the Road Runner, and Sylvester and Tweety have had their own network series.

In 1961, Friz Freleng devised a concept for a half-hour television series called "Philbert," in which the animated title character would come to life and create havoc for his live-action cartoonist-creator. One episode was completed.

## 1930

**SINKIN' IN THE BATHTUB** May
LT *(Bosko, Honey) Harman/Ising*
**CONGO JAZZ** September
LT *(Bosko) Harman/Ising*
**HOLD ANYTHING** October
LT *(Bosko, Honey) Harman/Ising*
**THE BOOZE HANGS HIGH** November
LT *(Bosko) Harman/Ising*
**BOX CAR BLUES** December
LT *(Bosko) Harman/Ising*

## 1931

**BIG MAN FROM THE NORTH** January
LT *(Bosko, Honey) Harman/Ising*
**AIN'T NATURE GRAND** February
LT *(Bosko) Harman/Ising*
**UP'S N' DOWN'S** March
LT *(Bosko) Harman/Ising*
**THE DUMB PATROL** April
LT *(Bosko, Honey) Harman/Ising*

**YODELING YOKELS** May
LT *(Bosko, Honey) Harman/Ising*
**BOSKO'S HOLIDAY** June
LT *(Bosko, Honey) Harman/Ising*
**THE TREE'S KNEES** July
LT *(Bosko, Honey) Harman/Ising*
**LADY PLAY YOUR MANDOLIN** August
MM *(Foxy) Ising*
**SMILE, DARN YA, SMILE** September 5
MM *(Foxy) Ising*
**BOSKO SHIPWRECKED** September 19
LT *(Bosko) Harman*
**ONE MORE TIME** October 3
MM *(Foxy) Ising*
**BOSKO THE DOUGHBOY** October 17
LT *(Bosko) Harman*
**YOU DON'T KNOW WHAT YOU'RE DOIN'**
  October 31
MM *(Piggy) Ising*
**BOSKO'S SODA FOUNTAIN** November 14
LT *(Bosko, Honey) Harman*
**HITTIN' THE TRAIL TO HALLELUJAH LAND**
  November 28
MM *(Piggy) Ising*
**BOSKO'S FOX HUNT** December 12
LT *(Bosko) Harman*
**RED HEADED BABY** December 26
MM *Ising*

## 1932

**BOSKO AT THE ZOO** January 9
LT *(Bosko, Honey) Harman*
**PAGAN MOON** January 23
MM *Ising*
**BATTLING BOSKO** February 6
LT *(Bosko, Honey) Harman*
**FREDDIE THE FRESHMAN** February 20
MM *Ising*
**BIG HEARTED BOSKO** (working title: BOSKO'S
  ORPHANS) March 5
LT *(Bosko) Harman*
**CROSBY, COLUMBO AND VALLEE** March 19
MM *Ising*
**BOSKO'S PARTY** April 2
LT *(Bosko, Honey) Harman*
**GOOPY GEER** April 16
MM *Ising*
**BOSKO AND BRUNO** April 30
LT *(Bosko) Harman*
**IT'S GOT ME AGAIN** May 14
MM *Ising*
  Academy Award Nominee
**MOONLIGHT FOR TWO** June 11
MM *Ising*
**BOSKO'S DOG RACE** June 25
LT *(Bosko) Harman*

Promotional drawing for *Up's n' Down's,* 1931

**THE QUEEN WAS IN THE PARLOR** July 9
MM *Ising*

**BOSKO AT THE BEACH** July 23
LT *(Bosko, Honey) Harman*

**I LOVE A PARADE** August 6
MM *Ising*

**BOSKO'S STORE** August 13
LT *(Bosko, Honey) Harman*

**BOSKO THE LUMBERJACK** September 3
LT *(Bosko, Honey) Harman*

**YOU'RE TOO CARELESS WITH YOUR KISSES**
September 10
MM *Ising*

**RIDE HIM, BOSKO** September 17
LT *(Bosko, Honey) Harman*

**I WISH I HAD WINGS** October 15
MM *Ising*

**BOSKO THE DRAWBACK** October 22
LT *(Bosko) Harman*

**A GREAT BIG BUNCH OF YOU** November 12
MM *Ising*

**BOSKO'S DIZZY DATE** November 19
LT *(Bosko, Honey) Harman*

**THREE'S A CROWD** December 10
MM *Ising*

**BOSKO'S WOODLAND DAZE** December 17
LT *(Bosko) Harman*

## 1933

**THE SHANTY WHERE SANTA CLAUS LIVES**
January 7
MM *Ising*

**BOSKO IN DUTCH** January 14
LT *(Bosko, Honey) Harman*
*(Probably directed by Freleng, although uncredited)*

**ONE STEP AHEAD OF MY SHADOW** February 4
MM *Ising*

**BOSKO IN PERSON** February 11
LT *(Bosko, Honey) Harman*

**YOUNG AND HEALTHY** March 4
MM *Ising*

**BOSKO THE SPEED KING** March 11
LT *(Bosko, Honey) Harman*

**THE ORGAN GRINDER** April 8
MM *Ising*

**BOSKO'S KNIGHT-MARE** April 29
LT *(Bosko, Honey) Harman*

**WAKE UP THE GYPSY IN ME** May 13
MM *Ising*

**BOSKO THE SHEEP HERDER** June 3
LT *(Bosko) Harman*

**I LIKE MOUNTAIN MUSIC** June 10
MM *Ising*

**BEAU BOSKO** July 1
LT *(Bosko, Honey) Harman*

**SHUFFLE OFF TO BUFFALO** July 8
MM *Ising*
*(Probably directed by Freleng, although uncredited)*

**BOSKO'S MECHANICAL MAN** July 29
LT *(Bosko, Honey) Harman*

**THE DISH RAN AWAY WITH THE SPOON**
August 5
MM *Ising*

**BOSKO THE MUSKETEER** August 12
LT *(Bosko, Honey) Harman*

**WE'RE IN THE MONEY** August 26
MM *Ising*

**BOSKO'S PICTURE SHOW** August 26
LT *(Bosko, Honey) Harman*

**BUDDY'S DAY OUT** September 9
LT *(Buddy, Cookie) King*

**I'VE GOT TO SING A TORCH SONG**
September 30
MM *Tom Palmer*

**BUDDY'S BEER GARDEN** November 18
LT *(Buddy, Cookie) Earl Duvall*

**BUDDY'S SHOWBOAT** December 9
LT *(Buddy, Cookie) King*

**SITTIN' ON A BACKYARD FENCE** December 16
MM *Earl Duvall*

## 1934

**BUDDY THE GOB** January 13
LT *(Buddy) Freleng*

**PETTIN' IN THE PARK** January 27
MM *Bernard Brown*

**HONEYMOON HOTEL** February 17
MM *Earl Duvall*
First color cartoon released by Warner Bros.

**BUDDY AND TOWSER** February 24
LT *(Buddy) Freleng*

**BEAUTY AND THE BEAST** April 14
MM *Freleng*
In color

**BUDDY'S GARAGE** April 14
LT *(Buddy, Cookie) Earl Duvall*

**THOSE WERE WONDERFUL DAYS** April 28
MM *Bernard Brown*

**BUDDY'S TROLLEY TROUBLES** May 5
LT *(Buddy, Cookie) Freleng*

**GOIN' TO HEAVEN ON A MULE** May 19
MM *Freleng*

**BUDDY OF THE APES** May 19
LT *(Buddy) Hardaway*

**HOW DO I KNOW IT'S SUNDAY?** June 9
MM *Freleng*

**BUDDY'S BEARCATS** June 23
LT *(Buddy, Cookie) King*

**WHY DO I DREAM THOSE DREAMS?** June 30
MM *Freleng*

**BUDDY'S CIRCUS** August 25
LT *(Buddy) King*

**BUDDY THE WOODSMAN** August 27
LT *(Buddy, Cookie) King*

**THE MILLER'S DAUGHTER** September 8
MM *Freleng*

**BUDDY THE DETECTIVE** September 15
LT *(Buddy, Cookie) King*

**THE GIRL AT THE IRONING BOARD**
September 15
MM *Freleng*

**VIVA BUDDY** September 29
LT *(Buddy) King*

**SHAKE YOUR POWDER PUFF** September 29
MM *Freleng*

**RHYTHM IN THE BOW** October 20
MM *Hardaway*
Last black and white "Merrie Melodie"

**THOSE BEAUTIFUL DAMES** November 10
MM *Freleng*

**BUDDY'S ADVENTURES** November 17
LT *(Buddy, Cookie) Hardaway*

**POP GOES YOUR HEART** December 8
MM *Freleng*

**BUDDY THE DENTIST** December 15
LT *(Buddy, Cookie) Hardaway*

## 1935

**BUDDY OF THE LEGION** January 12
LT *(Buddy) Hardaway*

**MR. AND MRS. IS THE NAME** January 19
MM *Freleng*

**COUNTRY BOY** February 9
MM *Freleng*

**BUDDY'S THEATRE** February 16
LT *(Buddy, Cookie) Hardaway*

**I HAVEN'T GOT A HAT** March 2
MM *(Porky, Beans, Ham, Ex) Freleng*
First appearance of Porky Pig

**BUDDY'S PONY EXPRESS** March 9
LT *(Buddy) Hardaway*

**ALONG FLIRTATION WALK** April 6
MM *Freleng*

**BUDDY IN AFRICA** April 20
LT *(Buddy) Hardaway*

**MY GREEN FEDORA** May 4
MM *Freleng*

**BUDDY'S LOST WORLD** May 18
LT *(Buddy) King*

**INTO YOUR DANCE** June 8
MM *Freleng*

**BUDDY'S BUG HUNT** June 22
LT *(Buddy) King*

**COUNTRY MOUSE** July 13
MM *Freleng*

**BUDDY STEPS OUT** July 20
LT *(Buddy, Cookie) King*

**THE MERRY OLD SOUL** August 17
MM *Freleng*

**BUDDY THE GEE MAN** August 24
LT *(Buddy) King*

**THE LADY IN RED** September 7
MM *Freleng*

**A CARTOONIST'S NIGHTMARE** September 14
LT *(Beans) King*

**HOLLYWOOD CAPERS** October 19
LT *(Beans, Porky, Kitty, Oliver Owl) King*

**LITTLE DUTCH PLATE** October 19
MM *Freleng*

**GOLDDIGGERS OF '49** November 2
(Estimated)
LT *(Beans, Porky) Avery*

**BILLBOARD FROLICS** November 9
MM *Freleng*

**THE FIRE ALARM** November 23
LT *(Ham and Ex) King*

**FLOWERS FOR MADAME** November 30
MM *Freleng*
Warner's first cartoon in Three-Strip Technicolor

## 1936

**PLANE DIPPY** January 4
LT *(Porky) Avery*

**I WANNA PLAY HOUSE** January 11
MM *Freleng*

**ALPINE ANTICS** January 18
LT *(Beans, Porky, Kitty) King*

**THE PHANTOM SHIP** February 1
LT *(Beans, Ham, Ex) King*

**THE CAT CAME BACK** February 8
MM *Freleng*

**BOOM BOOM** February 29
LT *(Porky, Beans) King*

**PAGE MISS GLORY** March 7
MM *Avery*

**THE BLOW-OUT** April 4
LT *(Porky) Avery*

**I'M A BIG SHOT NOW** April 11
MM *Freleng*

**WESTWARD WHOA!** April 25
LT *(Porky, Beans, Ham, Ex, Kitty) King*

**LET IT BE ME** May 9
MM *Freleng*

**I'D LOVE TO TAKE ORDERS FROM YOU** May 16
MM *Avery*

**FISH TALES** May 23
LT *(Porky) King*

**BINGO CROSBYANA** May 30
MM *Freleng*

**SHANGHAIED SHIPMATES** June 20
LT *(Porky) King*

**WHEN I YOO HOO** June 27
MM *Freleng*

**PORKY'S PET** July 11
LT *(Porky) King*

**I LOVE TO SINGA** July 18
MM *Avery*

**PORKY THE RAINMAKER** August 1
LT *(Porky) Avery*

**SUNDAY GO TO MEETIN' TIME** August 8
MM *Freleng*

**PORKY'S POULTRY PLANT** August 22
LT *(Porky) Tashlin*

**AT YOUR SERVICE, MADAME** August 29
MM *Freleng*

**PORKY'S MOVING DAY** September 12
LT *(Porky) King*

**TOY TOWN HALL** September 19
MM *Freleng*

**MILK AND MONEY** October 3
LT *(Porky) Avery*

**BOULEVARDIER FROM THE BRONX** October 10
MM *Freleng*

**DON'T LOOK NOW** November 7
MM *Avery*

**LITTLE BEAU PORKY** November 14
LT *(Porky) Tashlin*

**COO-COO NUT GROVE** November 28
MM *Freleng*

**THE VILLAGE SMITHY** December 5
LT *(Porky) Avery*

**PORKY IN THE NORTHWOODS** December 19
LT *(Porky) Tashlin*

## 1937

**HE WAS HER MAN** January 2
MM *Freleng*

**PORKY THE WRESTLER** January 9
LT *(Porky) Avery*

**PIGS IS PIGS** January 30
MM *Freleng*

**PORKY'S ROAD RACE** February 6
LT *(Porky) Tashlin*

**PICADOR PORKY** February 27
LT *(Porky) Avery*

**I ONLY HAVE EYES FOR YOU** March 6
MM *Avery*

**THE FELLA WITH THE FIDDLE** March 27
MM *Freleng*

**PORKY'S ROMANCE** April 3
LT *(Porky, Petunia) Tashlin*
First appearance of Petunia Pig

**SHE WAS AN ACROBAT'S DAUGHTER** April 10
MM *Freleng*

**PORKY'S DUCK HUNT** April 17
LT *(Porky, Daffy) Avery*
First appearance of Daffy Duck

**AIN'T WE GOT FUN** May 1
MM *Avery*

**PORKY AND GABBY** May 15
LT *(Porky) Ub Iwerks*

**CLEAN PASTURES** May 22
MM *Freleng*

**UNCLE TOM'S BUNGALOW** June 5
MM *Avery*

**PORKY'S BUILDING** June 19
LT *(Porky) Tashlin*

**STREAMLINED GRETA GREEN** June 19
MM *Freleng*

**SWEET SIOUX** July 3
MM *Freleng*

**PORKY'S SUPER SERVICE** July 3
LT *(Porky) Ub Iwerks*

**EGGHEAD RIDES AGAIN** July 17
MM *(Egghead) Avery*
First appearance of Egghead

**PORKY'S BADTIME STORY** July 24
LT *(Porky) Clampett*

**PLENTY OF MONEY AND YOU** July 31
MM *Freleng*

**PORKY'S RAILROAD** August 7
LT *(Porky) Tashlin*

**A SUNBONNET BLUE** August 21
MM *Avery*

**GET RICH QUICK PORKY** August 28
LT *(Porky) Clampett*

**SPEAKING OF THE WEATHER** September 4
MM *Tashlin*

**PORKY'S GARDEN** September 11
LT *(Porky) Avery*

**DOG DAZE** September 18
MM *Freleng*

**I WANNA BE A SAILOR** September 25
MM *Avery*

**ROVER'S RIVAL** October 9
LT *(Porky) Clampett*

**THE LYIN' MOUSE** October 16
MM *Freleng*

**THE CASE OF THE STUTTERING PIG** October 30
LT *(Porky) Tashlin*

**LITTLE RED WALKING HOOD** November 6
MM *(Egghead) Avery*

**PORKY'S DOUBLE TROUBLE** November 13
LT *(Porky) Tashlin*

**THE WOODS ARE FULL OF CUCKOOS** December 4
MM *Tashlin*

**PORKY'S HERO AGENCY** December 4
LT *(Porky) Clampett*

**SEPTEMBER IN THE RAIN** December 18
MM *Freleng*

## 1938

**DAFFY DUCK AND EGGHEAD** January 1
MM *(Daffy, Egghead) Avery*

**PORKY'S POPPA** January 15
LT *(Porky) Clampett*

**MY LITTLE BUCKEROO** January 29
MM *Freleng*

**PORKY AT THE CROCADERO** February 5
LT *(Porky) Tashlin*

**JUNGLE JITTERS** February 19
MM *Freleng*

**WHAT PRICE PORKY** February 26
LT *(Porky) Clampett*

**THE SNEEZING WEASEL** March 12
MM *Avery*

**PORKY'S PHONEY EXPRESS** March 19
LT *(Porky) Dalton, Cal Howard*

**A STAR IS HATCHED** April 2
MM *Freleng*

**PORKY'S FIVE AND TEN** April 16
LT *(Porky) Clampett*

**THE PENGUIN PARADE** April 23
MM *Avery*

**PORKY'S HARE HUNT** April 30
LT *(Porky, early Bugs Bunny) Hardaway*
First appearance of the early Bugs Bunny

**NOW THAT SUMMER IS GONE** May 14
MM *Tashlin*

**INJUN TROUBLE** May 21
LT *(Porky) Clampett*

**THE ISLE OF PINGO PONGO** May 28
MM *(Egghead) Avery*

**PORKY THE FIREMAN** June 4
LT *(Porky) Tashlin*

**KATNIP KOLLEGE** June 11
MM *Hardaway, Dalton*

**PORKY'S PARTY** June 25
LT *(Porky) Clampett*

**HAVE YOU GOT ANY CASTLES?** June 25
MM *Tashlin*

**LOVE AND CURSES** July 9
MM *Hardaway, Dalton*

**PORKY'S SPRING PLANTING** July 16
LT *(Porky) Tashlin*

**CINDERELLA MEETS FELLA** July 23
MM *(Egghead) Avery*

**PORKY AND DAFFY** August 6
LT *(Porky, Daffy) Clampett*

**THE MAJOR LIED TILL DAWN** August 13
MM *Tashlin*

**WHOLLY SMOKE** August 27
LT *(Porky) Tashlin*

**A-LAD-IN BAGDAD** August 27
MM *(Egghead) Cal Howard, Dalton*

**CRACKED ICE** September 10
MM *Tashlin*

**A FEUD THERE WAS** September 24
MM *(Egghead, called Elmer Fudd) Avery*

**PORKY IN WACKYLAND** September 24
LT *(Porky) Clampett*

**LITTLE PANCHO VANILLA** October 8
MM *Tashlin*

**PORKY'S NAUGHTY NEPHEW** October 15
LT *(Porky) Clampett*

**JOHNNY SMITH AND POKER-HUNTAS** October 22
MM *(Egghead) Avery*

**PORKY IN EGYPT** November 5
LT *(Porky) Clampett*

**YOU'RE AN EDUCATION** November 5
MM *Tashlin*

**THE NIGHT WATCHMAN** November 19
MM *Jones*

**THE DAFFY DOC** November 26
LT *(Daffy, Porky) Clampett*

**DAFFY DUCK IN HOLLYWOOD** December 3
MM *(Daffy) Avery*

**PORKY THE GOB** December 17
LT *(Porky) Hardaway, Dalton*

**COUNT ME OUT** December 17
MM *(Egghead) Hardaway, Dalton*

**THE MICE WILL PLAY** December 31
MM *Avery*

## 1939

**THE LONE STRANGER AND PORKY** January 7
LT *(Porky) Clampett*

**DOG GONE MODERN** January 14
MM *Jones*

**IT'S AN ILL WIND** January 28
LT *(Porky) Hardaway, Dalton*

**HAMATEUR NIGHT** January 28
MM *(Egghead) Avery*

**ROBIN HOOD MAKES GOOD** February 11
MM *Jones*

**PORKY'S TIRE TROUBLE** February 18
LT *(Porky) Clampett*

**GOLD RUSH DAZE** February 25
MM *Hardaway, Dalton*

**PORKY'S MOVIE MYSTERY** March 11
LT *(Porky) Clampett*

**A DAY AT THE ZOO** March 11
MM *(Egghead) Avery*

**PREST-O CHANGE-O** March 25
MM *(early Bugs Bunny) Jones*

**CHICKEN JITTERS** April 1
LT *(Porky) Clampett*

**BARS AND STRIPES FOREVER** April 8
MM *Hardaway, Dalton*

**DAFFY DUCK AND THE DINOSAUR** April 22
MM *(Daffy) Jones*

**PORKY AND TEABISCUIT** April 22
LT *(Porky) Hardaway, Dalton*

**THUGS WITH DIRTY MUGS** May 6
MM *Avery*

**KRISTOPHER KOLUMBUS, JR.** May 13
LT *(Porky) Clampett*

**NAUGHTY BUT MICE** May 20
MM *(Sniffles) Jones*
First appearance of Sniffles

**HOBO GADGET BAND** May 27
MM *Hardaway, Dalton*

**POLAR PALS** June 3
LT *(Porky) Clampett*

**BELIEVE IT OR ELSE** June 3
MM *(Egghead) Avery*

**SCALP TROUBLE** June 24
LT *(Porky, Daffy) Clampett*

**OLD GLORY** July 1
MM *(Porky) Jones*

**PORKY'S PICNIC** July 15
LT *(Porky) Clampett*

**DANGEROUS DAN MCFOO** July 15
MM *Avery*

**SNOW MAN'S LAND** July 29
MM *Jones*

**WISE QUACKS** August 5
LT *(Daffy, Porky) Clampett*

**HARE-UM SCARE-UM** August 12
MM *(early Bugs Bunny) Hardaway, Dalton*
**DETOURING AMERICA** August 26
MM *Avery*
Academy Award Nominee
**PORKY'S HOTEL** September 2
LT *(Porky) Clampett*
**LITTLE BROTHER RAT** September 2
MM *(Sniffles) Jones*
**SIOUX ME** September 9
MM *Hardaway, Dalton*
**JEEPERS CREEPERS** September 23
LT *(Porky) Clampett*
**LAND OF THE MIDNIGHT FUN** September 23
MM *Avery*
**NAUGHTY NEIGHBORS** October 7
LT *(Porky) Clampett*
**LITTLE LION HUNTER** October 7
MM *(Inki) Jones*
First appearance of Inki
**THE GOOD EGG** October 21
MM *Jones*
**FRESH FISH** November 4
MM *Avery*
**PIED PIPER PORKY** November 4
LT *(Porky) Clampett*
**FAGIN'S FRESHMEN** November 18
MM *Hardaway, Dalton*
**PORKY THE GIANT KILLER** November 18
LT *(Porky) Hardaway, Dalton*
**SNIFFLES AND THE BOOKWORM** December 2
MM *(Sniffles, Bookworm) Jones*
**THE FILM FAN** December 16
LT *(Porky) Clampett*
**SCREWBALL FOOTBALL** December 16
MM *Avery*
**THE CURIOUS PUPPY** December 30
MM *Jones*

## 1940

**PORKY'S LAST STAND** January 6
LT *(Porky, Daffy) Clampett*
**THE EARLY WORM GETS THE BIRD** January 13
MM *Avery*
**AFRICA SQUEAKS** January 27
LT *(Porky) Clampett*
**MIGHTY HUNTERS** January 27
MM *(Canyon Kiddies) Jones*
**ALI BABA BOUND** February 10
LT *(Porky) Clampett*
**BUSY BAKERS** February 10
MM *Hardaway, Dalton*
**ELMER'S CANDID CAMERA** March 2
MM *(Elmer Fudd, early Bugs Bunny) Jones*
First appearance of Elmer Fudd
**PILGRIM PORKY** March 16
LT *(Porky) Clampett*
**CROSS COUNTRY DETOURS** March 16
MM *Avery*
**CONFEDERATE HONEY** March 30
MM *(Elmer) Freleng*
**SLAP HAPPY PAPPY** April 13
LT *(Porky) Clampett*
**THE BEAR'S TALE** April 13
MM *Avery*
**THE HARDSHIP OF MILES STANDISH** April 27
MM *(Elmer) Freleng*
**PORKY'S POOR FISH** April 27
LT *(Porky) Clampett*
**SNIFFLES TAKES A TRIP** May 11
MM *(Sniffles) Jones*
**YOU OUGHT TO BE IN PICTURES** May 18
LT *(Porky, Daffy) Freleng*
**A GANDER AT MOTHER GOOSE** May 25
MM *Avery*
**THE CHEWIN' BRUIN** June 8
LT *(Porky) Clampett*
**TOM THUMB IN TROUBLE** June 8
MM *Jones*

**CIRCUS TODAY** June 22
MM *Avery*
**PORKY'S BASEBALL BROADCAST** July 6
LT *(Porky) Freleng*
**LITTLE BLABBERMOUSE** July 6
MM *Freleng*
**THE EGG COLLECTOR** July 20
MM *(Sniffles, Bookworm) Jones*
**A WILD HARE** July 27
MM *(Bugs, Elmer) Avery*
First true Bugs Bunny
Academy Award Nominee
**GHOST WANTED** August 10
MM *Jones*
**PATIENT PORKY** August 24
LT *(Porky) Clampett*
**CEILING HERO** August 24
MM *Avery*
**MALIBU BEACH PARTY** September 14
MM *Freleng*
**CALLING DR. PORKY** September 21
LT *(Porky) Freleng*
**STAGE FRIGHT** September 28
MM *Jones*
**PREHISTORIC PORKY** October 12
LT *(Porky) Clampett*
**HOLIDAY HIGHLIGHTS** October 12
MM *Avery*
**GOOD NIGHT ELMER** October 26
MM *(Elmer) Jones*
**THE SOUR PUSS** November 2
LT *(Porky) Clampett*
**WACKY WILDLIFE** November 9
MM *Avery*
**BEDTIME FOR SNIFFLES** November 23
MM *(Sniffles) Jones*
**PORKY'S HIRED HAND** November 30
LT *(Porky) Freleng*
**OF FOX AND HOUNDS** December 7
MM *Avery*
**THE TIMID TOREADOR** December 21
LT *(Porky) Norm McCabe, Clampett*
**SHOP, LOOK AND LISTEN** December 21
MM *Freleng*

## 1941

**ELMER'S PET RABBIT** January 4
MM *(early Bugs, Elmer) Jones*
**PORKY'S SNOOZE REEL** January 11
LT *(Porky) Norm McCabe, Clampett*
**THE FIGHTING 69½TH** January 18
MM *Freleng*
**SNIFFLES BELLS THE CAT** February 1
MM *(Sniffles) Jones*
**THE HAUNTED MOUSE** February 15
LT *Avery*
**THE CRACKPOT QUAIL** February 15
MM *Avery*
**THE CAT'S TALE** March 1
MM *Freleng*
**JOE GLOW THE FIREFLY** March 8
LT *Jones*
**TORTOISE BEATS HARE** March 15
MM *(Bugs) Avery*
**PORKY'S BEAR FACTS** March 29
LT *(Porky) Freleng*
**GOOFY GROCERIES** March 29
MM *Clampett*
**TOY TROUBLE** April 12
MM *(Sniffles, Bookworm) Jones*
**PORKY'S PREVIEW** April 19
LT *(Porky) Avery*
**THE TRIAL OF MR. WOLF** April 26
MM *Freleng*
**PORKY'S ANT** May 10
LT *(Porky) Jones*
**FARM FROLICS** May 10
MM *Clampett*

**HOLLYWOOD STEPS OUT** May 24
MM *Avery*
**A COY DECOY** June 7
LT *(Porky, Daffy) Clampett*
**HIAWATHA'S RABBIT HUNT** June 7
MM *(Bugs) Freleng*
Academy Award Nominee
**PORKY'S PRIZE PONY** June 21
LT *(Porky) Jones*
**THE WACKY WORM** June 21
MM *Freleng*
**MEET JOHN DOUGHBOY** July 5
LT *(Porky) Clampett*
**THE HECKLING HARE** July 5
MM *(Bugs) Avery*
**INKI AND THE LION** July 19
MM *(Inki) Jones*
**AVIATION VACATION** August 2
MM *Avery*
**WE, THE ANIMALS, SQUEAK** August 9
LT *(Porky) Clampett*
**SPORT CHUMPIONS** August 16
MM *Freleng*
**THE HENPECKED DUCK** August 30
LT *(Porky, Daffy) Clampett*
**SNOW TIME FOR COMEDY** August 30
MM *Jones*
**ALL THIS AND RABBIT STEW** September 13
MM *(Bugs) Avery*
**NOTES TO YOU** September 20
LT *(Porky) Freleng*
**THE BRAVE LITTLE BAT** September 27
MM *(Sniffles) Jones*
**THE BUG PARADE** October 11
MM *Avery*
**ROBINSON CRUSOE, JR.** October 25
LT *(Porky) Norm McCabe*
**ROOKIE REVUE** October 25
MM *Freleng*
**SADDLE SILLY** November 8
MM *Jones*
**THE CAGEY CANARY** November 22
MM *Avery*
**PORKY'S MIDNIGHT MATINEE** November 22
LT *(Porky) Jones*
**RHAPSODY IN RIVETS** December 6
MM *Freleng*
Academy Award Nominee
**WABBIT TWOUBLE** December 20
MM *(Bugs, Elmer) Wobert Cwampett*
**PORKY'S POOCH** December 27
LT *(Porky) Clampett*

## 1942

**HOP, SKIP AND A CHUMP** January 3
MM *Freleng*
**PORKY'S PASTRY PIRATES** January 17
LT *(Porky) Freleng*
**THE BIRD CAME C.O.D.** January 17
MM *Jones*
**ALOHA HOOEY** January 31
MM *Avery*
**WHO'S WHO IN THE ZOO** February 14
LT *(Porky) Norm McCabe*
**PORKY'S CAFE** February 21
LT *(Porky) Jones*
**CONRAD THE SAILOR** February 28
MM *(Daffy) Jones*
**CRAZY CRUISE** March 14
MM *Avery*
**THE WABBIT WHO CAME TO SUPPER** March 28
MM *(Bugs, Elmer) Freleng*
**SAPS IN CHAPS** April 11
LT *Freleng*
**HORTON HATCHES THE EGG** April 11
MM *Clampett*
**DOG TIRED** April 25
MM *Jones*
**DAFFY'S SOUTHERN EXPOSURE** May 2
LT *(Daffy) Norm McCabe*

**THE WACKY WABBIT** May 2
MM *(Bugs, Elmer) Clampett*

**THE DRAFT HORSE** May 9
MM *Jones*

**NUTTY NEWS** May 23
LT *Clampett*

**LIGHTS FANTASTIC** May 23
MM *Freleng*

**HOBBY HORSE LAFFS** June 6
LT *Norm McCabe*

**HOLD THE LION, PLEASE** June 13
MM *(Bugs) Jones*

**GOPHER GOOFY** June 27
LT *Norm McCabe*

**DOUBLE CHASER** June 27
MM *Freleng*

**WACKY BLACKOUTS** July 11
LT *Clampett*

**BUGS BUNNY GETS THE BOID** July 11
MM *(Bugs, Beaky Buzzard) Clampett*
First appearance of Beaky Buzzard

**FONEY FABLES** August 1
MM *Freleng*

**THE DUCKTATORS** August 1
LT *Norm McCabe*

**THE SQUAWKIN' HAWK** August 8
MM *(Henery Hawk) Jones*
First appearance of Henery Hawk

**EATIN' ON THE CUFF** August 22
LT *Clampett*

**FRESH HARE** August 22
MM *(Bugs, Elmer) Freleng*

**THE IMPATIENT PATIENT** September 5
LT *(Daffy) Norm McCabe*

**FOX POP** September 5
MM *Jones*

**THE DOVER BOYS** September 19
MM *Jones*

**THE HEP CAT** October 3
LT *Clampett*
First "Looney Tune" in color

**THE SHEEPISH WOLF** October 17
MM *Freleng*

**THE DAFFY DUCKAROO** October 24
LT *(Daffy) Norm McCabe*

**THE HARE-BRAINED HYPNOTIST** October 31
MM *(Bugs, Elmer) Freleng*

**A TALE OF TWO KITTIES** November 21
MM *(Tweety) Clampett*
First appearance of Tweety

**MY FAVORITE DUCK** December 5
LT *(Daffy, Porky) Jones*

**DING DOG DADDY** December 5
MM *Freleng*

**CASE OF THE MISSING HARE** December 12
MM *(Bugs) Jones*

## 1943

**COAL BLACK AND DE SEBBEN DWARFS** January 16
MM *Clampett*

**CONFUSIONS OF A NUTZY SPY** January 23
LT *(Porky) Norm McCabe*

**PIGS IN A POLKA** February 6
MM *Freleng*
Academy Award Nominee

**TORTOISE WINS BY A HARE** February 20
MM *(Bugs) Clampett*

**FIFTH COLUMN MOUSE** March 6
MM *Freleng*

**TO DUCK OR NOT TO DUCK** March 6
LT *(Daffy, Elmer) Jones*

**FLOP GOES THE WEASEL** March 20
MM *Jones*

Background painting from *Rhapsody in Rivets*, 1941

**HOP AND GO** March 27
LT *Norm McCabe*

**SUPER RABBIT** April 3
MM *(Bugs) Jones*

**THE UNBEARABLE BEAR** April 17
MM *(Sniffles) Jones*

**THE WISE QUACKING DUCK** May 1
LT *(Daffy) Clampett*

**GREETINGS BAIT** May 15
MM *(Wacky Worm) Freleng*
Academy Award Nominee

**TOKIO JOKIO** May 15
LT *Norm McCabe*

**JACK-WABBIT AND THE BEANSTALK** June 12
MM *(Bugs) Freleng*

**THE ARISTO-CAT** June 19
MM *(Hubie and Bertie) Jones*

**YANKEE DOODLE DAFFY** July 3
LT *(Daffy, Porky) Freleng*

**WACKIKI WABBIT** July 3
MM *(Bugs) Jones*

**TIN PAN ALLEY CATS** July 17
MM *Clampett*

**PORKY PIG'S FEAT** July 17
LT *(Porky, Daffy) Tashlin*

**SCRAP HAPPY DAFFY** August 21
LT *(Daffy) Tashlin*

**HISS AND MAKE UP** September 11
MM *(early Granny) Freleng*

**A CORNY CONCERTO** September 25
MM *(Bugs, Porky, Elmer) Clampett*

**FIN' 'N CATTY** October 23
MM *Jones*

**FALLING HARE** October 30
MM *(Bugs) Clampett*

**INKI AND THE MINAH BIRD** November 13
MM *(Inki) Jones*

**DAFFY THE COMMANDO** November 20
LT *(Daffy) Freleng*

**AN ITCH IN TIME** December 4
MM *(Elmer) Clampett*

**PUSS 'N BOOTY** December 11
LT *Tashlin*
Last black and white "Looney Tune"

## 1944

**LITTLE RED RIDING RABBIT** January 1
MM *(Bugs) Freleng*

**WHAT'S COOKIN', DOC?** January 8
MM *(Bugs) Clampett*

**MEATLESS FLYDAY** January 29
MM *Freleng*

**TOM TURK AND DAFFY** February 12
LT *(Daffy, Porky) Jones*

**BUGS BUNNY AND THE THREE BEARS** February 26
MM *(Bugs) Jones*
First appearance of the Three Bears

**I GOT PLENTY OF MUTTON** March 11
LT *Tashlin*

**THE WEAKLY REPORTER** March 25
MM *Jones*

**TICK TOCK TUCKERED** April 8
LT *(Porky, Daffy) Clampett*
Remake of Porky's Badtime Story, 1937

**BUGS BUNNY NIPS THE NIPS** April 22
MM *(Bugs) Freleng*

**THE SWOONER CROONER** May 6
LT *(Porky) Tashlin*
Academy Award Nominee

**RUSSIAN RHAPSODY** May 20
MM *Clampett*

**DUCK SOUP TO NUTS** May 27
LT *(Daffy, Porky) Freleng*

**ANGEL PUSS** June 3
LT *Jones*

**SLIGHTLY DAFFY** June 17
MM *(Daffy, Porky) Freleng*
Remake of Scalp Trouble, 1939

**HARE RIBBIN'** June 24
MM *(Bugs) Clampett*

**BROTHER BRAT** July 15
LT *(Porky) Tashlin*

**HARE FORCE** July 22
MM *(Bugs, early Granny) Freleng*

**FROM HAND TO MOUSE** August 5
LT *Jones*

**BIRDY AND THE BEAST** August 19
MM *(Tweety) Clampett*

**BUCKAROO BUGS** August 26
LT *(Bugs) Clampett*

**GOLDILOCKS AND THE JIVIN' BEARS**
September 2
MM *Freleng*

**PLANE DAFFY** September 16
LT *(Daffy) Tashlin*

**LOST AND FOUNDLING** September 30
MM *(Sniffles) Jones*

**BOOBY HATCHED** October 14
LT *Tashlin*

**THE OLD GREY HARE** October 28
MM *(Bugs, Elmer) Clampett*

**THE STUPID CUPID** November 25
LT *(Elmer, Daffy) Tashlin*

**STAGE DOOR CARTOON** December 30
MM *(Bugs, Elmer) Freleng*

## 1945

**ODOR-ABLE KITTY** January 6
LT *(Pepé Le Pew) Jones*
First appearance of Pepé Le Pew

**HERR MEETS HARE** January 13
MM *(Bugs) Freleng*

**DRAFTEE DAFFY** January 27
LT *(Daffy) Clampett*

**THE UNRULY HARE** February 10
MM *(Bugs, Elmer) Tashlin*

**TRAP HAPPY PORKY** February 24
LT *(Porky) Jones*

**LIFE WITH FEATHERS** March 24
MM *(Sylvester) Freleng*
First appearance of Sylvester
Academy Award Nominee

**BEHIND THE MEAT BALL** April 7
LT *Tashlin*

**HARE TRIGGER** May 5
MM *(Bugs, Yosemite Sam) Freleng*
First appearance of Yosemite Sam

**AIN'T THAT DUCKY** May 19
LT *(Daffy) Freleng*

**A GRUESOME TWOSOME** June 9
MM *(Tweety) Clampett*

**A TALE OF TWO MICE** June 30
LT *Tashlin*

**WAGON HEELS** July 28
MM *(Porky) Clampett*
Remake of Injun Trouble, 1938

**HARE CONDITIONED** August 11
LT *(Bugs) Jones*

**FRESH AIREDALE** August 25
MM *Jones*

**THE BASHFUL BUZZARD** September 15
LT *(Beaky Buzzard) Clampett*

**PECK UP YOUR TROUBLES** October 20
MM *(Sylvester) Freleng*

**HARE TONIC** November 10
LT *(Bugs, Elmer) Jones*

**NASTY QUACKS** December 1
MM *(Daffy) Tashlin*

## 1946

**BOOK REVUE**
January 5
LT *(Daffy) Clampett*

**BASEBALL BUGS** February 2
LT *(Bugs) Freleng*

**HOLIDAY FOR SHOESTRINGS** February 23
MM *Freleng*

**QUENTIN QUAIL** March 2
MM *Jones*

**BABY BOTTLENECK** March 16
LT *(Porky, Daffy) Clampett*

**HARE REMOVER** March 23
MM *(Bugs, Elmer) Tashlin*

**DAFFY DOODLES** April 6
LT *(Daffy, Porky) McKimson*

**HOLLYWOOD CANINE CANTEEN** April 20
MM *McKimson*

**HUSH MY MOUSE** May 4
LT *(Sniffles) Jones*

**HAIR-RAISING HARE** May 25
MM *(Bugs) Jones*

**KITTY KORNERED** June 8
LT *(Porky, Sylvester) Clampett*

**HOLLYWOOD DAFFY** June 22
MM *(Daffy) Freleng*

**ACROBATTY BUNNY** June 29
LT *(Bugs) McKimson*

**THE EAGER BEAVER** July 13
MM *Jones*

**THE GREAT PIGGY BANK ROBBERY** July 20
LT *(Daffy) Clampett*

**BACALL TO ARMS** August 3
MM *Clampett*

**OF THEE I STING** August 17
LT *Freleng*

**WALKY TALKY HAWKY** August 31
MM *(Foghorn Leghorn, Henery Hawk) McKimson*
First appearance of Foghorn Leghorn
Academy Award Nominee

**RACKETEER RABBIT** September 14
LT *(Bugs) Freleng*

**FAIR AND WORM-ER** September 28
MM *Jones*

**THE BIG SNOOZE** October 5
LT *(Bugs, Elmer) Clampett*

**THE MOUSE-MERIZED CAT** October 19
MM *McKimson*

**MOUSE MENACE** November 2
LT *(Porky) Davis*

**RHAPSODY RABBIT** November 9
MM *(Bugs) Freleng*

**ROUGHLY SQUEAKING** November 23
LT *(Hubie and Bertie) Jones*

## 1947

**ONE MEAT BRAWL** January 18
MM *(Porky, Grover Groundhog) McKimson*

**THE GOOFY GOPHERS** January 25
LT *Davis*
First appearance of the Goofy Gophers

**THE GAY ANTIES** February 15
MM *Freleng*

**SCENT-IMENTAL OVER YOU** March 8
LT *(Pepé Le Pew) Jones*

**A HARE GROWS IN MANHATTAN** March 22
MM *(Bugs) Freleng*

**THE BIRTH OF A NOTION** April 12
LT *(Daffy) McKimson*

**TWEETIE PIE** May 3
MM *(Tweety and Sylvester) Freleng*
Warner Cartoons' first Academy Award
Winner

**RABBIT TRANSIT** May 10
LT *(Bugs) Freleng*

**HOBO BOBO** May 17
MM *(Bobo) McKimson*

**ALONG CAME DAFFY** June 14
LT *(Daffy) Freleng*

**INKI AT THE CIRCUS** June 21
MM *(Inki) Jones*

**EASTER YEGGS** June 28
LT *(Bugs, Elmer) McKimson*

**CROWING PAINS** July 12
LT *(Foghorn Leghorn, Henery Hawk, Sylvester)*
*McKimson*

**HOBO BOBO** May 17
MM *(Bobo) McKimson*

**ALONG CAME DAFFY** June 14
LT *(Daffy) Freleng*

**INKI AT THE CIRCUS** June 21
MM *(Inki) Jones*

**A PEST IN THE HOUSE** August 2
MM *(Daffy, Elmer) Jones*

**THE FOXY DUCKLING** August 23
MM *Davis*

**HOUSE HUNTING MICE** September 6
LT *(Hubie and Bertie) Jones*

**LITTLE ORPHAN AIREDALE** October 4
LT *(Charlie Dog, Porky) Jones*
First appearance of Charlie Dog

**DOGGONE CATS** October 25
MM *Davis*

**SLICK HARE** November 1
MM *(Bugs, Elmer) Freleng*

**MEXICAN JOYRIDE** November 29
LT *(Daffy) Davis*

**CATCH AS CATS CAN** December 6
MM *(quasi Sylvester) Davis*

**A HORSEFLY FLEAS** December 13
LT *McKimson*

## 1948

**GORILLA MY DREAMS** January 3
LT *(Bugs) McKimson*

Background painting from *Hare Splitter*, 1948

**BEWITCHED BUNNY** July 24
LT *(Bugs, Witch Hazel) Jones*

**SATAN'S WAITIN'** August 7
LT *(Tweety and Sylvester) Freleng*

**STOP, LOOK AND HASTEN** August 14
MM *(Road Runner) Jones*

**YANKEE DOODLE BUGS** August 28
LT *(Bugs) Freleng*

**GONE BATTY** September 4
LT *(Bobo) McKimson*

**GOO GOO GOLIATH** September 18
MM *Freleng*

**BY WORD OF MOUSE** October 2
LT *(Sylvester) Freleng*

**FROM A TO Z-Z-Z-Z** October 16
LT *(Ralph Phillips) Jones*
Academy Award Nominee

**QUACK SHOT** October 30
MM *(Daffy, Elmer) McKimson*

**LUMBER JACK RABBIT** November 13
LT *(Bugs) Jones*
Made in 3-D

**MY LITTLE DUCKAROO** November 27
MM *(Daffy, Porky) Jones*

**SHEEP AHOY** December 11
MM *(Wolf and Sheepdog) Jones*

**BABY BUGGY BUNNY** December 18
MM *(Bugs) Jones*

## 1955

**PIZZICATO PUSSYCAT** January 1
MM *Freleng*

**FEATHER DUSTER** January 15
MM *(Foghorn Leghorn) McKimson*

**PESTS FOR GUESTS** January 29
MM *(Elmer, Goofy Gophers) Freleng*

**BEANSTALK BUNNY** February 12
MM *(Bugs, Daffy, Elmer) Jones*

**ALL FOWLED UP** February 19
LT *(Foghorn Leghorn, Henery Hawk) McKimson*

**STORK NAKED** February 26
MM *(Daffy) Freleng*

**LIGHTHOUSE MOUSE** March 12
MM *(Sylvester, Hippety Hopper) McKimson*

**SAHARA HARE** March 26
LT *(Bugs, Yosemite Sam) Freleng*

**SANDY CLAWS** April 2
LT *(Tweety and Sylvester, Granny) Freleng*
Academy Award Nominee

**THE HOLE IDEA** April 16
LT *McKimson*

**READY, SET, ZOOM!** April 30
LT *(Road Runner) Jones*

**HARE BRUSH** May 7
MM *(Bugs, Elmer) Freleng*

**PAST PERFUMANCE** May 21
MM *(Pepé Le Pew) Jones*

**TWEETY'S CIRCUS** June 4
MM *(Tweety and Sylvester) Freleng*

**RABBIT RAMPAGE** June 11
LT *(Bugs) Jones*

**LUMBER JERKS** June 25
LT *(Goofy Gophers) Freleng*

**THIS IS A LIFE?** July 9
MM *(Bugs, Daffy, Elmer, Yosemite Sam) Freleng*

**DOUBLE OR MUTTON** July 23
LT *(Wolf and Sheepdog) Jones*

**JUMPIN' JUPITER** August 6
MM *(Porky, Sylvester) Jones*

**A KIDDIE'S KITTY** August 20
MM *(Sylvester) Freleng*

**HYDE AND HARE** August 27
LT *(Bugs) Freleng*

**DIME TO RETIRE** September 3
LT *(Porky, Daffy) McKimson*

**SPEEDY GONZALES** September 17
MM *(Speedy, Sylvester) Freleng*
Academy Award Winner

**KNIGHT-MARE HARE** October 1
MM *(Bugs) Jones*

**TWO SCENTS WORTH** October 15
MM *(Pepé Le Pew) Jones*

**RED RIDING HOODWINKED** October 29
LT *(Tweety and Sylvester, Granny) Freleng*

**ROMAN LEGION HARE** November 12
LT *(Bugs, Yosemite Sam) Freleng*

**HEIR CONDITIONED** November 26
LT *(Sylvester, Elmer) Freleng*

**GUIDED MUSCLE** December 10
LT *(Road Runner) Jones*

**PAPPY'S PUPPY** December 17
MM *(Sylvester) Freleng*

**ONE FROGGY EVENING** December 31
MM *Jones*

## 1956

**BUGS BONNETS** January 14
MM *(Bugs, Elmer) Jones*

**TOO HOP TO HANDLE** January 28
LT *(Sylvester, Junior, Hippety Hopper) McKimson*

**WEASEL STOP** February 11
LT *(Foghorn Leghorn) McKimson*

**THE HIGH AND THE FLIGHTY** February 18
MM *(Foghorn Leghorn, Daffy) McKimson*

**BROOM-STICK BUNNY** February 25
LT *(Bugs, Witch Hazel) Jones*

**ROCKET SQUAD** March 10
MM *(Daffy, Porky) Jones*

**TWEET AND SOUR** March 24
LT *(Tweety and Sylvester, Granny) Freleng*

**HEAVEN SCENT** March 31
MM *(Pepé Le Pew) Jones*

**MIXED MASTER** April 14
LT *McKimson*

**RABBITSON CRUSOE** April 28
LT *(Bugs, Yosemite Sam) Freleng*

**GEE WHIZ-Z-Z-Z** May 5
LT *(Road Runner) Jones*

**TREE CORNERED TWEETY** May 19
MM *(Tweety and Sylvester) Freleng*

**THE UNEXPECTED PEST** June 2
MM *(Sylvester) McKimson*

**NAPOLEON BUNNY-PART** June 16
MM *(Bugs) Freleng*

**TUGBOAT GRANNY** June 23
MM *(Tweety and Sylvester, Granny) Freleng*

**STUPOR DUCK** July 7
LT *(Daffy) McKimson*

**BARBARY COAST BUNNY** July 21
LT *(Bugs) Jones*

**ROCKET BYE BABY** August 4
MM *Jones*

**HALF-FARE HARE** August 18
MM *(Bugs) McKimson*

**RAW! RAW! ROOSTER** August 25
LT *(Foghorn Leghorn) McKimson*

**SLAP-HOPPY MOUSE** September 1
MM *(Sylvester, Junior, Hippety Hopper) McKimson*

**A STAR IS BORED** September 15
LT *(Bugs, Daffy) Freleng*

**DEDUCE, YOU SAY** September 29
LT *(Daffy, Porky) Jones*

**YANKEE DOOD IT** October 13
MM *(Sylvester) Freleng*

**WIDEO WABBIT** October 27
MM *(Bugs, Elmer) McKimson*

**THERE THEY GO-GO-GO** November 10
LT *(Road Runner) Jones*

**TWO CROWS FROM TACOS** November 24
MM *Freleng*

**THE HONEY-MOUSERS** December 8
LT *McKimson*

**TO HARE IS HUMAN** December 15
MM *(Bugs, Wile E. Coyote) Jones*

## 1957

**THE THREE LITTLE BOPS** January 5
LT *Freleng*

**TWEET ZOO** January 12
MM *(Tweety and Sylvester) Freleng*

**SCRAMBLED ACHES** January 26
LT *(Road Runner) Jones*

**ALI BABA BUNNY** February 9
MM *(Bugs, Daffy) Jones*

**GO FLY A KIT** February 23
LT *Jones*

**TWEETY AND THE BEANSTALK** March 16
MM *(Tweety and Sylvester) Freleng*

**BEDEVILLED RABBIT** April 13
MM *(Bugs, Tasmanian Devil) McKimson*

**BOYHOOD DAZE** April 20
MM *(Ralph Phillips) Jones*

**CHEESE IT, THE CAT** May 4
LT *(Honey-Mousers) McKimson*

**FOX TERROR** May 11
MM *(Foghorn Leghorn) McKimson*

**PIKER'S PEAK** May 25
LT *(Bugs, Yosemite Sam) Freleng*

**STEAL WOOL** June 8
LT *(Wolf and Sheepdog) Jones*

**BOSTON QUACKIE** June 22
LT *(Daffy, Porky) McKimson*

**WHAT'S OPERA, DOC?** July 6
MM *(Bugs, Elmer) Jones*

**TABASCO ROAD** July 20
LT *(Speedy) McKimson*
Academy Award Nominee

**BIRDS ANONYMOUS** August 10
MM *(Sylvester and Tweety) Freleng*
Academy Award Winner

Layout drawing from *Pizzicato Pussycat*, 1955

249

**DUCKING THE DEVIL** August 17
MM *(Daffy, Tasmanian Devil) McKimson*

**BUGSY AND MUGSY** August 31
LT *(Bugs, Rocky and Mugsy) Freleng*

**ZOOM AND BORED** September 14
LT *(Road Runner) Jones*

**GREEDY FOR TWEETY** September 28
LT *(Tweety and Sylvester, Granny) Freleng*

**TOUCHÉ AND GO** October 12
MM *(Pepé Le Pew) Jones*

**SHOW BIZ BUGS** November 2
LT *(Bugs, Daffy) Freleng*

**MOUSE-TAKEN IDENTITY** November 16
MM *(Sylvester, Junior, Hippety Hopper) Freleng*

**GONZALES' TAMALES** November 30
LT *(Speedy, Sylvester) Freleng*

**RABBIT ROMEO** December 14
MM *(Bugs, Elmer) McKimson*

## 1958

**DON'T AXE ME** January 4
MM *(Daffy, Elmer) McKimson*

**TORTILLA FLAPS** January 18
LT *(Speedy, the Two Crows) Freleng*

**HARE-LESS Wolf** February 1
MM *(Bugs) Freleng*

**A PIZZA TWEETY PIE** February 22
LT *(Tweety and Sylvester, Granny) Freleng*

**ROBIN HOOD DAFFY** March 8
MM *(Daffy, Porky) Jones*

**HARE-WAY TO THE STARS** March 29
LT *(Bugs, Martian) Jones*

**WHOA, BE GONE** April 12
MM *(Road Runner) Jones*

**A WAGGILY TALE** April 26
LT *Freleng*

**FEATHER BLUSTER** May 10
MM *(Foghorn Leghorn) McKimson*

**NOW HARE THIS** May 31
LT *(Bugs) McKimson*

**TO ITCH HIS OWN** June 28
MM *Jones*

**DOG TALES** July 26
LT *McKimson*

**KNIGHTY KNIGHT BUGS** August 23
LT *(Bugs, Yosemite Sam) Freleng*
Academy Award Winner

**WEASEL WHILE YOU WORK** September 6
MM *(Foghorn Leghorn) McKimson*

**A BIRD IN A BONNET** September 27
MM *(Tweety and Sylvester, Granny) Freleng*

**HOOK, LINE AND STINKER** October 11
LT *(Road Runner) Jones*

**PRE-HYSTERICAL HARE** November 1
LT *(Bugs, Elmer) McKimson*

**GOPHER BROKE** November 15
LT *(Goofy Gophers) McKimson*

**HIP, HIP—HURRY!** December 6
MM *(Road Runner) Jones*

**CAT FEUD** December 20
MM *(Marc Antony) Jones*

## 1959

**BATON BUNNY** January 10
LT *(Bugs) Jones*

**MOUSE PLACED KITTEN** January 24
MM *McKimson*

**CHINA JONES** February 14
LT *(Daffy, Porky) McKimson*

**HARE-ABIAN NIGHTS** February 28
MM *(Bugs, Yosemite Sam) Ken Harris*

**TRICK OR TWEET** March 21
MM *(Tweety and Sylvester) Freleng*

**THE MOUSE THAT JACK BUILT** April 4
MM *McKimson*

**APES OF WRATH** April 18
MM *(Bugs) Freleng*

**HOT ROD AND REEL** May 9
LT *(Road Runner) Jones*

**A MUTT IN A RUT** May 23
LT *(Elmer) McKimson*

**BACKWOODS BUNNY** June 13
MM *(Bugs) McKimson*

**REALLY SCENT** June 27
MM *(Pepé Le Pew) Abe Levitow*

**MEXICALI SHMOES** July 4
LT *(Speedy) Freleng*
Academy Award Nominee

**TWEET AND LOVELY** July 18
MM *(Tweety and Sylvester) Freleng*

**WILD AND WOOLY HARE** August 1
LT *(Bugs, Yosemite Sam) Freleng*

**THE CAT'S PAW** August 15
LT *(Sylvester, Junior) McKimson*

**HERE TODAY, GONE TAMALE** August 29
LT *(Speedy, the Two Crows) Freleng*

**BONANZA BUNNY** September 5
MM *(Bugs) McKimson*

**A BROKEN LEGHORN** September 26
LT *(Foghorn Leghorn) McKimson*

**WILD ABOUT HURRY** October 10
MM *(Road Runner) Jones*

**A WITCH'S TANGLED HARE** October 31
LT *(Bugs, Witch Hazel) Abe Levitow*

**UNNATURAL HISTORY** November 14
MM *Abe Levitow*

**TWEET DREAMS** December 5
LT *(Tweety and Sylvester) Freleng*

**PEOPLE ARE BUNNY** December 19
MM *(Bugs, Daffy) McKimson*

## 1960

**FASTEST WITH THE MOSTEST** January 9
LT *(Road Runner) Jones*

**WEST OF THE PESOS** January 23
MM *(Speedy, Sylvester) Freleng*

**HORSE HARE** February 13
LT *(Bugs, Yosemite Sam) Freleng*

**WILD WILD WORLD** Feburary 27
MM *McKimson*

**GOLDIMOUSE AND THE THREE CATS** March 19
LT *(Sylvester, Junior) Freleng*

**PERSON TO BUNNY** April 2
MM *(Bugs, Daffy, Elmer) Freleng*

**WHO SCENT YOU?** April 23
LT *(Pepé Le Pew) Jones*

**HYDE AND GO TWEET** May 14
MM *(Tweety and Sylvester) Freleng*

**RABBIT'S FEAT** June 4
LT *(Bugs, Wile E. Coyote) Jones*

**CROCKETT-DOODLE-DO** June 25
MM *(Foghorn Leghorn) McKimson*

**MOUSE AND GARDEN** July 16
LT *(Sylvester) Freleng*
Academy Award Nominee

**READY, WOOLEN AND ABLE** July 30
MM *(Wolf and Sheepdog) Jones*

**MICE FOLLIES** August 20
LT *(Honey-Mousers) McKimson*

**FROM HARE TO HEIR** September 3
MM *(Bugs, Yosemite Sam) Freleng*

**THE DIXIE FRYER** September 24
MM *(Foghorn Leghorn) McKimson*

**HOPALONG CASUALTY** October 8
MM *(Road Runner) Jones*

**TRIP FOR TAT** October 29
MM *(Tweety and Sylvester) Freleng*

**DOGGONE PEOPLE** November 12
MM *(Elmer) McKimson*

**HIGH NOTE** December 3
LT *Jones*
Academy Award Nominee

**LIGHTER THAN HARE** December 17
MM *(Bugs, Yosemite Sam) Freleng*

## 1961

**CANNERY WOE** January 7
LT *(Speedy, Sylvester) Freleng*

**ZIP 'N SNORT** January 21
MM *(Road Runner) Jones*

**HOPPY DAZE** February 11
LT *(Sylvester, Hippety Hopper) McKimson*

**THE MOUSE ON 57TH STREET** February 25
MM *Jones*

**STRANGLED EGGS** March 18
MM *(Foghorn Leghorn, Henery Hawk, Miss Prissy) McKimson*

**BIRDS OF A FATHER** April 1
MM *(Sylvester and Junior) McKimson*

**D' FIGHTIN' ONES** April 22
MM *(Sylvester) Freleng*

**THE ABOMINABLE SNOW RABBIT** May 20
LT *(Bugs, Daffy) Jones*

**LICKETY SPLAT** June 3
LT *(Road Runner) Jones*

**A SCENT OF THE MATTERHORN** June 24
LT *(Pepé Le Pew) Jones*

**THE REBEL WITHOUT CLAWS** July 15
LT *(Tweety and Sylvester) Freleng*

**COMPRESSED HARE** July 29
MM *(Bugs, Wile E. Coyote) Jones*

**THE PIED PIPER OF GUADALUPE** August 19
LT *(Speedy, Sylvester) Freleng*
Academy Award Nominee

**PRINCE VIOLENT** September 2
LT *(Bugs, Yosemite Sam) Freleng*
Renamed Prince Varmint for Television

**DAFFY'S INN TROUBLE** September 23
LT *(Daffy, Porky) McKimson*

**WHAT'S MY LION?** October 21
LT *(Elmer) McKimson*

**BEEP PREPARED** November 11
MM *(Road Runner) Jones*
Academy Award Nominee

**THE LAST HUNGRY CAT** December 2
MM *(Tweety and Sylvester) Freleng*

**NELLY'S FOLLY** December 30
MM *Jones*
Academy Award Nominee

## 1962

**WET HARE** January 20
LT *(Bugs) McKimson*

**A SHEEP IN THE DEEP** February 10
MM *(Wolf and Sheepdog) Jones*

**FISH AND SLIPS** March 10
LT *(Sylvester, Junior) McKimson*

**QUACKODILE TEARS** March 31
MM *(Daffy) Freleng*

**CROW'S FEAT** April 21
MM *(The Two Crows) Freleng*

**MEXICAN BOARDERS** May 12
LT *(Speedy, Sylvester) Freleng*

**BILL OF HARE** June 9
MM *(Bugs, Tasmanian Devil) McKimson*

**ZOOM AT THE TOP** June 30
MM *(Road Runner) Jones*

**THE SLICK CHICK** July 21
LT *(Foghorn Leghorn) McKimson*

**LOUVRE COME BACK TO ME** August 18
LT *(Pepé Le Pew) Jones*

**HONEY'S MONEY** September 1
MM *(Yosemite Sam) Freleng*

**THE JET CAGE** September 22
LT *(Tweety and Sylvester, Granny) Freleng*

**MOTHER WAS A ROOSTER** October 20
MM *(Foghorn Leghorn) McKimson*

**GOOD NOOSE** November 10
LT *(Daffy) McKimson*

**SHISHKABUGS** December 8
LT *(Bugs, Yosemite Sam) Freleng*

**MARTIAN THROUGH GEORGIA** December 29
LT *Jones*

## 1963

**I WAS A TEENAGE THUMB** January 19
MM *Jones*

Color chart from *Nelly's Folly*, 1961

**DEVIL'S FEUD CAKE** February 9
MM *(Bugs, Yosemite Sam) Freleng*

**FAST BUCK DUCK** March 9
MM *(Daffy) McKimson, Ted Bonnicksen*

**THE MILLION-HARE** April 6
LT *(Bugs, Daffy) McKimson*

**MEXICAN CAT DANCE** April 20
LT *(Speedy, Sylvester) Freleng*

**NOW HEAR THIS** April 27
LT *Jones*
Academy Award Nominee

**WOOLEN UNDER WHERE** May 11
MM *(Wolf and Sheepdog) Jones*

**HARE-BREADTH HURRY** June 8
LT *(Bugs, Wile E. Coyote) Jones*

**BANTY RAIDS** June 29
MM *(Foghorn Leghorn) McKimson*

**CHILI WEATHER** August 17
MM *(Speedy, Sylvester) Freleng*

**THE UNMENTIONABLES** September 7
MM *(Bugs, Rocky and Mugsy) Freleng*

**AQUA DUCK** September 28
MM *(Daffy) McKimson*

**MAD AS A MARS HARE** October 19
MM *(Bugs, Martian) Jones*

**CLAWS IN THE LEASE** November 9
MM *(Sylvester, Junior) McKimson*

**TRANSYLVANIA 6–5000** November 30
MM *(Bugs) Jones*

**TO BEEP OR NOT TO BEEP** December 28
MM *(Road Runner) Jones*

## 1964

**DUMB PATROL** January 18
LT *(Bugs, Yosemite Sam) Gerry Chiniquy*

**A MESSAGE TO GRACIAS** February 8
LT *(Speedy, Sylvester) McKimson*

**BARTHOLOMEW VERSUS THE WHEEL** February 29
MM *McKimson*

**FREUDY CAT** March 14
LT *(Sylvester, Juntor, Hippety Hopper) McKimson*

**DR. DEVIL AND MR. HARE** March 28
MM *(Bugs, Tasmanian Devil) McKimson*

**NUTS AND VOLTS** April 25
LT *(Speedy, Sylvester) Freleng*

**THE ICEMAN DUCKETH** May 16
LT *(Daffy, Bugs) Phil Monroe*

**WAR AND PIECES** June 6
LT *(Road Runner) Jones*

**HAWAIIAN AYE AYE** June 27
MM *(Tweety and Sylvester) Gerry Chiniquy*

**FALSE HARE** July 18
LT *(Bugs) McKimson*

**SENORELLA AND THE GLASS HUARACHE** August 1
LT *Hawley Pratt*

**PANCHO'S HIDEAWAY** October 24
LT *(Speedy, Yosemite Sam) Freleng*

**ROAD TO ANDALAY** (working title: TEQUILA MOCKING BIRD) December 26
MM *(Speedy, Sylvester) Freleng*

## 1965

**IT'S NICE TO HAVE A MOUSE AROUND THE HOUSE** January 16
LT *(Speedy, Daffy, Granny, Sylvester) Freleng*

**CATS AND BRUISES** January 30
MM *(Speedy, Sylvester) Freleng*

**THE WILD CHASE** February 27
MM *(Road Runner, Coyote, Speedy, Sylvester) Hawley Pratt*

**MOBY DUCK** March 27
MM *(Daffy, Speedy) McKimson*

**ASSAULT AND PEPPERED** April 24
MM *(Daffy, Speedy) McKimson*

**WELL WORN DAFFY** May 22
LT *(Daffy, Speedy) McKimson*

**SUPPRESSED DUCK** June 26
MM *(Daffy) McKimson*

**CORN ON THE COP** July 24
MM *(Porky, Daffy) Irv Spector*

**RUSHING ROULETTE** July 31
MM *(Road Runner) McKimson*

**RUN, RUN SWEET ROAD RUNNER** August 21
MM *(Road Runner) Rudy Larriva*

**TEASE FOR TWO** August 28
LT *(Daffy, Goofy Gophers) McKimson*

**TIRED AND FEATHERED** September 18
MM *(Road Runner) Rudy Larriva*

**BOULDER WHAM** October 9
MM *(Road Runner) Rudy Larriva*

**CHILI CON CORNY** October 23
LT *(Speedy, Daffy) McKimson*

**JUST PLANE BEEP** October 30
MM *(Road Runner) Rudy Larriva*

**HARRIED AND HURRIED** November 13
MM *(Road Runner) Rudy Larriva*

**GO GO AMIGO** November 20
MM *(Speedy, Daffy) McKimson*

**HIGHWAY RUNNERY** December 11
LT *(Road Runner) Rudy Larriva*

**CHASER ON THE ROCKS** December 25
MM *(Road Runner) Rudy Larriva*

## 1966

**ASTRODUCK** January 1
LT *(Daffy, Speedy) McKimson*

**SHOT AND BOTHERED** January 8
LT *(Road Runner) Rudy Larriva*

**MUCHO LOCOS** January 29
MM *(Speedy, Daffy)* McKimson

**MEXICAN MOUSEPIECE** February 12
MM *(Speedy, Daffy)* McKimson

**THE SOLID TIN COYOTE** February 19
LT *(Road Runner)* Rudy Larriva

**OUT AND OUT ROUT** March 12
MM *(Road Runner)* Rudy Larriva

**DAFFY RENTS** March 19
LT *(Daffy, Speedy)* McKimson

**CLIPPETY CLOBBERED** March 26
LT *(Road Runner)* Rudy Larriva

**A HAUNTING WE WILL GO** April 16
LT *(Speedy, Daffy)* McKimson

**SNOW EXCUSE** May 21
MM *(Speedy, Daffy)* McKimson

**A SQUEAK IN THE DEEP** July 9
LT *(Daffy, Speedy)* McKimson

**FEATHER FINGER** August 20
MM *(Speedy, Daffy)* McKimson

**SWING DING AMIGO** September 17
LT *(Speedy, Daffy)* McKimson

**SUGAR AND SPIES** November 5
LT *(Road Runner)* McKimson

**A TASTE OF CATNIP** December 3
MM *(Speedy, Daffy)* McKimson

## 1967

**DAFFY'S DINER** January 28
MM *(Speedy, Daffy)* McKimson

**THE QUACKER TRACKER** April 29
LT *(Speedy, Daffy)* Rudy Larriva

**THE MUSIC MICE-TRO** May 27
MM *(Speedy, Daffy)* Rudy Larriva

**THE SPY SWATTER** June 24
LT *(Speedy, Daffy)* Rudy Larriva

**SPEEDY GHOST TO TOWN** July 29
MM *(Speedy, Daffy)* Alex Lovy

**RODENT TO STARDOM** September 23
LT *(Speedy, Daffy)* Alex Lovy

**GO AWAY STOWAWAY** September 30
MM *(Speedy, Daffy)* Alex Lovy

**COOL CAT** October 14
LT *(Cool Cat)* Alex Lovy

**MERLIN THE MAGIC MOUSE** November 18
MM *(Merlin the Magic Mouse)* Alex Lovy

**FIESTA FIASCO** December 9
LT *(Speedy, Daffy)* Alex Lovy

## 1968

**HOCUS POCUS POWWOW** January 13
LT *(Merlin the Magic Mouse)* Alex Lovy

**NORMAN NORMAL** February 3
MM *Alex Lovy*

**BIG GAME HAUNT** February 10
MM *(Cool Cat)* Alex Lovy

**SKYSCRAPER CAPER** March 9
MM *(Speedy, Daffy)* Alex Lovy

**HIPPYDROME TIGER** March 30
MM *(Cool Cat)* Alex Lovy

**A FEUD WITH A DUDE** May 25
MM *(Merlin the Magic Mouse)* Alex Lovy

**THE DOOR** June 1
MM *Ken Mundie*

**SEE YA LATER GLADIATOR** June 29
LT *(Daffy, Speedy)* Alex Lovy

**3-RING WING-DING** August 24
LT *(Cool Cat)* Alex Lovy

**FLYING CIRCUS** October 12
LT *Alex Lovy*

**BUNNY AND CLAUDE** November 23
MM *(Bunny and Claude)* McKimson .

**CHIMP AND ZEE** November 30
MM *Alex Lovy*

## 1969

**THE GREAT CARROT TRAIN ROBBERY** January 25
MM *(Bunny and Claude)* McKimson

**FISTIC MYSTIC** February 22
LT *(Merlin and the Magic Mouse)* McKimson

**RABBIT STEW AND RABBITS TOO** June 7
MM *(Rapid Rabbit)* McKimson

**SHAMROCK AND ROLL** June 28
MM *(Merlin the Magic Mouse)* McKimson

**BUGGED BY A BEE** August 9
MM *(Cool Cat)* McKimson

**INJUN TROUBLE** September 20
MM *(Cool Cat)* McKimson

## 1987

**THE DUXORCIST** November 20
LT *(Daffy)* Greg Ford, Terry Lennon

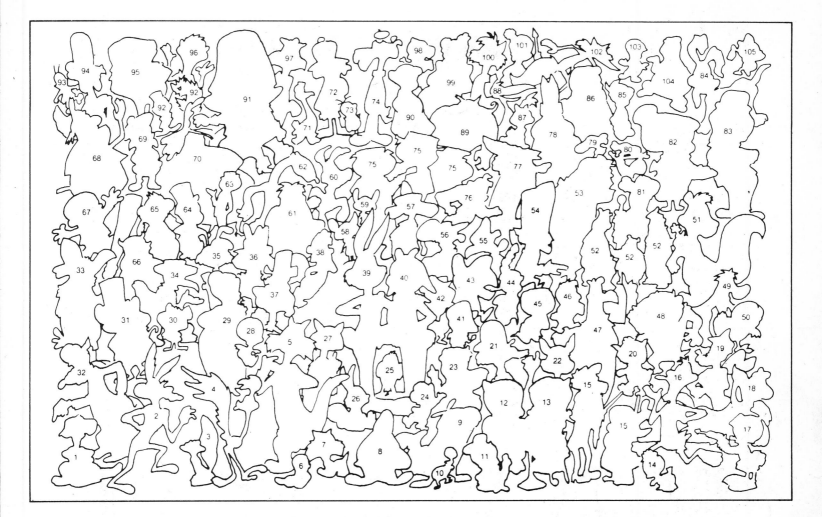

1. Hippety Hopper
2. Wile E. Coyote
3. Squirrel
4. Road Runner
5. Sylvester
6. The Bookworm
7. Sylvester, Jr.
8. A Flea
9. Abomb
10. Ant
11. Cicero
12. Porky Pig
13. Petunia Pig
14. Baby Owl
15. Feudin' Mountain Boys
16. Daffy Duck
17. Martian
18. Wellington
19. Grogan
20. Ollie Owl
21. B.B. Wolf
22. Nephew of
    B.B. Wolf
23. Mary Jane
24. Sniffles
25. Minah Bird
26. Clyde
27. Clarence
28. Tweety
29. Granny
30. Second Banana
31. Merlin the Magic
    Mouse

32. Mr. Wolff
33. El Vulturo
34. Beaky Buzzard
35. Bunny
36. Claude
37. The Sheriff
38. Eager Beaver
39. Bugs Bunny
40. Honey Bunny
41. Speedy Gonzales
42. Minniesoda Fats
43. Hoppy
44. Hiawatha
45. Ralph Phillips
46. Henery Hawk
47. Foghorn Leghorn
48. Tasmanian Devil
49. Robert
50. Banty the Cock
51. Pepé Le Pew
52. Three Bears
53. Mugsy
54. Rocky
55. Cro-Crow
56. Hysterical Hyram
57. Slowpoke Rodriguez
58. Boy Mouse
59. Girl Mouse
60. Charlie Dog
61. Fistic Mystic
62. Weasel
63. Philbert
64. Playboy Penguin

65. Goofy Gopher
66. Eric the Viking
67. Buddy
68. The Poor Indian
69. MacRory
70. Miss Witch Hazel
71. Sammy Sea Gull
72. Colonel Rimfire
73. Bee
74. Cool Cat
75. The Three Little Bops
76. Marc Antony
77. Wolf
78. Millie
79. Bertie
80. Hubie
81. Rover
82. Mrs. Fudd
83. Elmer Fudd
84. Puppy
85. Tom Thumb
86. Tom Thumb's Father
87. Pussyfoot
88. Stork
89. The Mighty Angelo
90. Red
91. Yosemite Sam
92. The Moth & His
    Flame
93. Gambling Bug
94. Prissy
95. Napoleon
96. Willie Weasel

97. Claude
98. Little Blabbermouse
99. Gra'ma
100. Sam
101. Inki
102. Quick Brown Fox
103. Little Ghost
104. Big Ghost
105. Joe Glow